"The most comprehensive under national politics from a biblical, theological, and historical perspective to date. A classic for generations. Research in *Faithful Politics* is extensive yet reads with ease. This is an essential book for leaders in all walks of life to have depth of understanding in public morals and social concerns impacting decision-making of the same."

Jo Anne Lyon, general superintendent emerita of The Wesleyan Church

"Do we really need another book on Christianity and politics? After reading Dr. Cruz's *Faithful Politics*, my answer is a resounding yes! Drawing from theology, history, and political science, she has written a fresh, nuanced, and engaging guide to Christian political engagement for our polarized times. I particularly appreciate her clear and winsome voice as she helpfully analyzes and synthesizes various existing approaches. This is a book I wish I had written. I can't wait to read it with my students and hear what they say about it."

Chan Woong Shin, associate professor of political science and international affairs at Gordon College

"Dr. Cruz asks the timely question, How do we live faithfully as citizens in the kingdom of God while being engaged influencers in the political systems we also inhabit? Cruz describes several approaches and provides the historical context, theological implications, and main tenets of each, along with how that approach is practically lived into, the challenges of it, and the benefits. The emphasis of the book is to encourage thoughtful reflection and to offer practical ways we can engage with and in our political systems while being faithful to Christ's calling. A must-read for all of us today!"

Colleen Derr, president of Eastern Nazarene College

"In an era dominated by clickbait headlines and disingenuous proof texts, Cruz's *Faithful Politics* is a breath of fresh air. This book is a trusty guide for any and all believers who are struggling to faithfully navigate the oft-bewildering and sometimes downright distressing landscape of American public life."

Heath W. Carter, associate professor of American Christianity and director of PhD studies at Princeton Theological Seminary

FAITHFUL POLITICS

TEN APPROACHES TO CHRISTIAN CITIZENSHIP AND WHY IT MATTERS

MIRANDA
ZAPOR
CRUZ

Stay salty!
Miranda Zapor Cruz

ivp
Academic
An imprint of InterVarsity Press
Downers Grove, Illinois

InterVarsity Press
P.O. Box 1400 | Downers Grove, IL 60515-1426
ivpress.com | email@ivpress.com

InterVarsity Press® is the publishing division of InterVarsity Christian Fellowship/USA®. For more information, visit intervarsity.org.

Scripture quotations, unless otherwise noted, are from the New Revised Standard Version, Updated Edition. Copyright © 2021 National Council of Churches of Christ in the United States of America. Used by permission. All rights reserved worldwide.

While any stories in this book are true, some names and identifying information may have been changed to protect the privacy of individuals.

The publisher cannot verify the accuracy or functionality of website URLs used in this book beyond the date of publication.

Cover design: David Fassett
Interior design: Daniel van Loon

ISBN 978-1-5140-0749-5 (print) | ISBN 978-1-5140-0750-1 (digital)

Printed in the United States of America ♾

Library of Congress Cataloging-in-Publication Data
Names: Cruz, Miranda Zapor, 1982- author.
Title: Faithful politics : ten approaches to Christian citizenship and why
  it matters / Miranda Zapor Cruz.
Description: Downers Grove, IL : IVP Academic, [2024] | Includes
  bibliographical references and index.
Identifiers: LCCN 2024008237 (print) | LCCN 2024008238 (ebook) | ISBN
  9781514007495 (paperback) | ISBN 9781514007501 (ebook)
Subjects: LCSH: Christianity and politics. | Citizenship–Religious
  aspects–Christianity. | BISAC: RELIGION / Religion, Politics & State |
  POLITICAL SCIENCE / Civics & Citizenship
Classification: LCC BR115.P7 C758 2024 (print) | LCC BR115.P7 (ebook) |
  DDC 261.7–dc23/eng/20240317
LC record available at https://lccn.loc.gov/2024008237
LC ebook record available at https://lccn.loc.gov/2024008238

31   30   29   28   27   26   25   24 | 13   12   11   10   9   8   7   6   5   4   3   2   1

For Jonathan and our Renata,

"If we lay a strong enough foundation

We'll pass it on to you, we'll give the world to you

And you'll blow us all away."

Leslie Odom Jr. and Lin Manuel Miranda,

"Dear Theodosia," *Hamilton*

CONTENTS

ACKNOWLEDGMENTS

THIS BOOK REPRESENTS THE CUMULATIVE impact of the many teachers, friends, pastors, students, and colleagues who have influenced and encouraged me.

Jonathan has been my unwavering supporter and meticulous editor. This book is better because of him. There's no one I'd rather talk theology or politics with. Renata has shared her early years with this project. It is for her, in hope that she can grow up in a more faithful church and less acrimonious public square. My parents raised me to read, think, and write. I am thankful for their example and love.

The faculty of the School of Theology and Ministry at Indiana Wesleyan University have supported me with their encouragement, coffee breaks, and friendship. It is a gift to love what I do and the people I get to serve alongside. I am especially grateful to my former dean, Chris Bounds, for urging me to write the book now instead of someday.

My students have come of age in a rancorous political world that resists the kind of critical thinking that is essential to Christian faithfulness. They have sought to know and love Christ, even as they wrestle with politics. I have written with their questions and frustrations in mind. I am particularly thankful for the students who discussed the manuscript as I was writing it.

My interest in faith and politics started at Whitworth College in Jerry Sittser's and Jim Edwards's church history classes. They taught me to "live in the tension" and introduced me to Augustine, Bonhoeffer, and so many other saints of the church. My best friend Claire and I were together for many of those classes and the experiences I share in these pages, and through everything important in our lives since. I would not be who I am without her friendship. Josiah, here is my book. I know it took a long time. I hope I get to read one of yours someday.

I also thank Jon Boyd and Rebecca Carhart at IVP Academic, as well as the designers, copyeditors, and reviewers who have worked to bring this book to the public.

Finally, I wrote this book as an act of faithfulness to God's calling and a means of loving God with mind and heart. While writing this book, the Lord kept me focused through long days, woke me up early, protected me from stress, surrounded me with support, and gave me courage to enter fraught conversations. It is an unnerving time to be writing about faith and politics. I believe I have been faithful to write truth that honors God and serves the Kingdom, and I trust God with the outcome.

CHRISTIAN CITIZENSHIP IN THE KINGDOM AND THE COUNTRY

"HE'S A PASTOR, so people should vote for him because he'll do what God wants him to do," I confidently told my mother in response to the news broadcast playing on the car radio.

It was the 1980s, and several clergymen were competing in the presidential primaries. Why should their party matter as long as the candidate had the direct clergy-only line to God? I thought. I had the relationship between faith and politics all figured out before I was ten years old: elect the person who would follow God. It was that easy, right? I think my mother had the wherewithal to say something like, "It's not quite that simple." We arrived at our destination before she had to answer my "Why not?" follow-up question.

I turned eighteen and registered to vote during my senior year of high school, and I approached that voting decision with little knowledge and even less nuance. My high school government teacher had made it very clear that one party was aligned with evil, and the other party was the only one that could rescue the country from its current state of decline. The decision of whom to vote for was handed to me, and I believed I was doing the Christian thing when I voted the way I did.

Four years later, as a college senior majoring in religion, the interplay of faith and politics had become so complicated to me that I was paralyzed by indecision and didn't vote in the presidential election. Of my three roommates, one voted Republican, one voted Democratic, and one wasn't a US citizen, so we all canceled each other out and avoided conflict over the outcome. By the time I graduated from college, questions about the relationship between faith and politics had a hold of me. Through seminary, graduate school, and now as a historical theology professor, these questions have not let me go.

"Our citizenship is in heaven," the apostle Paul writes (Philippians 3:20). "I pledge allegiance to the flag," we recite at the beginning of the school day. What is the proper relationship between these statements of identity and commitment? What does it mean to be a faithful citizen of the Kingdom of God, while also being a citizen of a country? What are the practical implications of our answers to these questions for voting, for holding public office, for our policy positions, and for partisan alignment?

These should be difficult questions. These questions should cause tension, even internal dissonance. In asking these questions, we recognize the potential for incongruity between our faith convictions and our political behavior. We force ourselves to consider whether Christ is truly Lord of our whole lives, including our civic lives. Discerning how and whether to use our influence as citizens in a representative government should raise serious questions about our ethics, values, convictions, and rights. Some Christian organizations will try to make the decision easier with voter information cards or candidate position checklists. Some pastors and Christian writers will make passionate arguments for their candidate or political party of choice. In response, many of us resolve the tension by either adopting a party line or bifurcating our faith and politics.

The truth is, we do not need a simplified rubric for the "right" way to vote. A solution to the faith-and-politics dilemma that excuses us from the work of discernment and reflection cannot be a faithful Christian solution. Rather, we need a nuanced framework for determining what faithful Christian political participation looks like *for us*. We need to excavate the foundations of our political engagement to unearth the core principles that inform our understanding of the relationship between citizenship in the Kingdom of God and citizenship in the United States.

In this book, I will not offer easy answers, checklists, rubrics, or partisan talking points. Instead, I will provide tools to help us navigate the complexities of Christian faithfulness in an increasingly polarized and diverse society. These tools include biblical, theological, and historical insights into the relationship between Kingdom of God and country, which will help us become more comfortable with tension. As we live in the faith-and-politics tension, we will be better equipped to live as faithful witnesses to the lordship of Jesus Christ, even in our political lives.

The way we engage with or disengage from the political processes of the United States has implications for our personal faith and public witness.

And yet for many Christians, our politics are disconnected from our faith convictions or our faith only influences our position on specific issues. When we have this piecemeal approach to faith and politics, we are ill-equipped to critique our own positions and to faithfully evaluate new issues. We need a robust framework for bringing our faith convictions to bear on our political participation. Such a framework will enable us to be more faithful to Christ in our political lives and to respect fellow Christians who arrive at different political conclusions.

BEING FAITHFUL IN POLITICS

What does it mean for us to be faithful in our political engagement? That's a question we will explore throughout the book, but we can put several characteristics of faithful politics in place at the outset. First, and most importantly, faithfulness depends on our understanding of God's salvation narrative. From creation, to fall, to redemption, to restoration, God is at work reconciling the world, and we have a part in that work. That means we must see our political behaviors and positions as part of the way we contribute to or hinder God's mission. Political parties do not see the world through the lens of the biblical narrative, so it is our job as Christians to faithfully discern how political narratives conflict or coincide with a Christian way of seeing the world. Christians are challenged when we discover that we do not all agree about the political implications of the Scriptures.

Second, faithfulness requires us to be well informed. We should not make decisions about policies, parties, or candidates from a place of ignorance, nor should we simply assume that we agree with a policy or candidate because they sound appealing. We have a great deal of information, misinformation, and disinformation available to us, and we need to learn how to differentiate facts from opinions and truth from lies so we can make decisions based on accurate information. Faithfulness also requires us to be responsible citizens who steward our political engagement as one aspect of our stewardship of the world. The way we vote, the candidates we support, the issues we promote all have real effects on people's lives and livelihoods. We need to be informed about this impact and take responsibility for the influence with which we are entrusted.

Third, faithfulness also means being realistic. We need to function according to the reality of the systems and laws and structures in place, even as we sometimes attempt to change the laws and systems. One important reality is that the necessity of compromise is built into the two-party system. The Constitution presupposes disagreement and lays out means by which people who disagree can collaborate for the sake of the common good. Compromises are required for government to function, while refusing to compromise contributes to political dysfunction. At the same time, Christian faithfulness requires uncompromising submission to Christ's lordship. How can we be uncompromising in our allegiance to Christ, and yet compromise in policymaking? Too often, Christians resolve this tension by bending our faith to align with our politics, or by adopting an ideological rigidity that prevents necessary government action.

We also need to be realistic about the influence and witness of the church in society. The reality is, adherence to Christianity is declining in the United States, though Christianity is still the majority religion by a large margin. We do not live in a society in which the whole population shares a Christian foundation, and even Christians are not united in our beliefs and values. We need to bear in mind that our political behavior is part of our Christian witness to an increasingly secular country. We must consider how non-Christians perceive Christ based on the political positions and behaviors of Christians.

BIBLICAL, THEOLOGICAL, HISTORICAL, AND POLITICAL FOUNDATIONS

Engaging the complex relationship between faith and politics requires us to integrate many fields of knowledge. We need a rebar grid to securely stand on, not barred windows to gaze through. Theology influences politics. History shapes theology. Biblical interpretation informs political science and theology. Theology affects history and biblical interpretation. This book removes silos that isolate political science, history, theology, and hermeneutics and carefully examines the ways they inform each other and shape the framework of our political engagement. My goal is not to bring you into agreement with my theological or political perspectives, but rather to equip you to engage faith and politics with wisdom and understanding.

I hope to earn your trust as we explore a range of approaches to the relationship between faith and politics. To that end, allow me to share some of the presuppositions that inform this book so you can read with an open-yet-critical mind. First, I am a Christian, and this book is born out of my desire to equip Christians to engage with politics in a way that contributes positively to the mission and witness of Christ's church. As a Christian, I affirm the authority and sufficiency of Scripture. I believe the Bible can be trusted to communicate God's purposes for our faith and life, and therefore no area of life is exempt from being informed by God's written word.

I also recognize there are many issues of contemporary political concern that the Bible does not explicitly address, and also that Scripture was written in a geopolitical context that bears little resemblance to the twenty-first-century United States. Therefore, our interpretation and application of Scripture must be contextually informed and hermeneutically nuanced. The Bible is not a bullet-pointed list of position statements; rather, it is a unified narrative revealing the character of God and his work of creation and redemption. I will primarily employ Scripture to help us understand the principles that inform our political engagement, rather than argue for positions on specific issues.

Our theology shapes how we live, and our theological backgrounds inform our approaches to politics, sometimes without our realizing it. My own theological and church background is Methodist/Wesleyan, and I have inhabited both mainline Protestant and evangelical spaces of worship, education, and friendship throughout my adult life. My experience and education have formed in me an appreciation for ecumenism, so I see the various Christian theological traditions as branches of a family tree. Each branch of the Christian family tree has its own theology of the relationship between church and society, and locating these theological differences is helpful for forming our own theological positions and considering how they apply to our political engagement. I focus on Western Christian theologies in this book due to their influence in historical and contemporary American politics, but that limit is not intended to devalue the global contributions of the Eastern Orthodox, Oriental Orthodox, or the Church of the East.

As a historian, I understand the present through the past. Contemporary approaches to Christian political engagement have developed out of historical events and ideas, so we will examine those historical roots to make sense of the ways we can engage with politics today. In addition to providing context, history shows us examples of how Christians in the past faced challenges similar to those we encounter today. As the author of

Ecclesiastes wrote, "there is nothing new under the sun" (Ecclesiastes 1:9). Therefore, history will be our companion in exploring frameworks for Christian political engagement. We will learn from the great cloud of witnesses who have preceded us into the tensions of faith and politics, and come to a greater understanding of the historical roots of the various approaches to political engagement.

This book brings Scripture, theology, and history into conversation with politics. What do we talk about when we talk about politics? In the broadest sense, politics refers to anything that affects the *polis*, which is simply Greek for "city." Anything that affects the way people function as a society is "politics." For the purposes of this book, we will think of politics in terms of governing structures, public policy, political parties, elected and appointed officials—the kinds of things we can influence through voting, advocacy, running for office, and so on.

For Aristotle, politics was about achieving the good life, or *eudaimonia*. He recognized the interdependence of humans, and defined politics in terms of "our ability to cooperate in groups, to differentiate our roles and coordinate our activities in pursuit of a common goal, not just of surviving but of living well, thus realizing our humanity."[1] Christians will differ from Aristotle about how to cooperate and what exactly constitutes "living well," but we can agree on the premise that we are members of communities and we have opportunities and responsibilities to contribute to the common good. Another key idea about government comes from seventeenth-century philosopher John Locke, who advanced the notion that humans are by nature free and equal, which is a philosophical basis for the Declaration of Independence and the Constitution and is largely compatible with Christian teaching about humanity.[2] Drawing on Aristotle, Locke, and others, I presuppose that government has a positive function and that participation in government can serve the common good.

In this book, I am committed to nonpartisanship, but not necessarily to neutrality. I argue that partisan platforms are inevitably out of step with the Kingdom of God; therefore no single political party should capture the full allegiance of a Christian. While I will not present any political party or church-state framework as inherently more Christian than

---

[1] Lenn E. Goodman and Robert B. Talisse, *Aristotle's Politics Today* (Albany, NY: SUNY Press, 2007), 7.

[2] John Locke, "Of Civil Government," in *Two Treatises of Government and a Letter Concerning Toleration*, ed. Ian Shapiro (New Haven, CT: Yale University Press, 2003), 101-6.

others, I do not believe Christians should be neutral regarding the ways faith interacts with politics. There are multiple modes of political engagement that can be consistent with Christian convictions, but there are also modes that I will argue are incompatible with Christian faith. I focus on approaches to faithful political engagement, not positions on specific policy issues; therefore, I will not be arguing that Christians ought to hold specific policy positions.

This is not a book about which party Christians should agree with or what a Christian ought to think about controversial issues. Rather, I will argue that Christians can come to different conclusions about policies because we have different approaches to political engagement, and that such differences can and must coexist among citizens of the Kingdom of God.

Finally, I write as a Christian in the United States with fellow Christians and Americans as my primary audience. Much of the history I examine will take us overseas; however, I do not attempt the complicated task of applying the ten approaches expounded here to international political systems and challenges. That said, my interest in faith and politics began with studying Christianity under Communism in Eastern Europe and I follow current events in religion and politics around the world. Thus, I can say with confidence that the approaches examined here can also inform Christians in other geopolitical contexts.

My international readers can find connections to their own circumstances, whether they are in Albania, where religion was banned in 1967 and has slowly rebounded since, or in Lebanon, the Middle Eastern country with the largest Christian population, or in Zambia, which declared itself a Christian nation in 1990.[3] In particular, the rise of far-right nativism and religious nationalism in the United States has strong parallels around the world, from Brazil to Hungary to Japan. Even as I write with American Christians at the forefront of my mind, I hope my sisters and brothers in Nicaragua, Ghana, and Lithuania will likewise find these chapters instructive.

OVERVIEW OF CHAPTERS

The purpose of *Faithful Politics* is to equip Christians to engage with politics as faithful servants of Jesus Christ. To that end, I argue that the United

---

[3]Gina A. Zurlo, *Global Christianity: A Guide to the World's Largest Religion from Afghanistan to Zimbabwe* (Grand Rapids, MI: Zondervan, 2022), 36, 178, 316.

States and the Kingdom of God are distinct; therefore, Christians live as dual citizens in a country that is not our true home. As dual citizens, we look for biblical models of political engagement, which lead us to participate in politics in a way that adds salt—much-needed flavor—to civic life. Christians can approach politics in a variety of faithful ways. When we understand and respect that Christians can approach politics differently, yet faithfully, we can contribute to the common good and advance the mission and witness of the church.

Chapter one, "Citizens of the Kingdom," contrasts the Kingdom of God with the United States. The United States is not, has never been, and will never become the Kingdom of God; the Kingdom of God is not, has never been, and will never become the United States. When we conflate the Kingdom and the country, we submit to the powers and principalities of this world instead of submitting to the lordship of Jesus Christ. An understanding of the contrasts between the Kingdom of God and the United States helps us recognize when our political loyalties threaten to overtake our Christian convictions. The approaches presented in the subsequent chapters will build on this foundational Kingdom/country contrast.

Chapter two, "Biblical Dual Citizenship," examines biblical narratives that inform our understanding of citizenship in the Kingdom of God and in a country. The ancient Near East, first-century Palestine, and the contemporary United States occupy very different geopolitical contexts, so we should be cautious about drawing one-to-one correspondence between them. Despite the differences, we can glean principles from Scripture to guide our political engagement. We will look closely at how people like Moses and Jeremiah navigated government and what Jesus and Paul taught the first Christians about their dual citizenship.

Chapter three, "Salty Citizenship," provides background on the US political systems, and examines Christians' recent political behavior. Political partisanship influences Christian mission and witness in the world, so we will consider "salty" versus "bland" approaches to party politics. Salty citizens have a clear vision for the Kingdom of God that allows us to discern where our convictions are and are not compatible with partisan platforms. Salty citizens bring our convictions into public discourse in a way that adds much-needed flavor, consistent with Jesus' instruction to be like salt in the world. Salty citizens are able to articulate substantive commitments in a way that contributes positively to civil discourse. On the other hand, bland citizens lay aside their identity as the "salt of the earth" in favor of a politically defined identity, sometimes without realizing they've done so. We will examine the forces that pull us toward blandness and how to resist them to stay salty.

The next six chapters introduce ten approaches to the relationship between faith and politics. The approaches are arranged from the strictest isolation of Kingdom from country on one end, to complete conflation of Kingdom with country on the other. I will explain the historical and theological roots of each approach and how they show up in American politics today, and I'll highlight the benefits and shortfalls of each. The approaches are not necessarily mutually exclusive, so we may find ourselves drawing on different approaches for different aspects of political engagement, like electing a candidate versus voting for a policy. Consistent with my commitment to nonpartisanship, I argue that each of the approaches in chapters four through seven is a viable option for faithful Christian political engagement; then, since neutrality is not one of my goals, I argue that the approaches in chapters eight and nine are incompatible with Christian faithfulness in the political sphere.

Chapter four, "Keeping the Kingdom out of the Country," examines the first three approaches to Christian citizenship: the separatist models. Isolationist separatism is committed to preserving the purity of the Christian community by being isolated from the wider society and not participating in politics. Prophetic separatism maintains a critical distance from politics while also speaking truth to the political reality. Both of these approaches are rooted in the Anabaptist tradition. Evangelical separatism calls on Christians to form communities that are untainted by and protected from the world to the degree possible. Each of these approaches has theological and practical benefits and drawbacks.

Chapter five, "Keeping the Country out of the Kingdom," presents the next two approaches to Christian citizenship: the separationist options. Historic Baptist separation is rooted in the Baptist theological commitment to separation of church and state, which has been very influential in the United States. Two Kingdoms separation, based in the political theology of Martin Luther, delineates separate spheres of influence for the church and the government. Both models are helpful for understanding the American approach to separation of church and state, and each can guide us and warn us as we follow Christ in the United States.

Chapter six, "Bringing the Kingdom into the Country," introduces the sixth approach to Christian citizenship: the social gospel. In the nineteenth century, proponents of the social gospel labored to transform the United States into a Christian country through social and moral reform. The social gospel's reform emphasis continues through the civil rights movement, through some mainline Protestant denominations, and through the so-called evangelical left. Contemporary iterations of the social gospel share a commitment to social and political transformation, and each has its benefits and pitfalls.

Chapter seven, "Keeping the Country Under the Kingdom," examines the seventh and eighth approaches to Christian citizenship: two Calvinist options. Both approaches begin with the political theology of John Calvin but diverge in their application of his ideas. The principled pluralist approach emphasizes God's sovereignty and teaches that the different spheres of society are ordained by God for different functions, while each exists under God's power and judgment. The direct Christian influence approach also emphasizes God's sovereignty, but sees Christians as charged with bringing the country into alignment with certain Christian values and convictions. Again, both of these Calvinist approaches have their unique strengths and weaknesses.

In chapters eight and nine, "Invading the Country to Establish the Kingdom" and "Eroding the Distinction Between Kingdom and Country," I examine two approaches that I argue are incompatible with Christian faithfulness: dominionism and Christian nationalism. Dominionism is a theological movement that claims Christians ought to gain power over every sphere of society to establish God's Kingdom on earth, and its influential contemporary iterations are Christian Reconstructionism and the New Apostolic Reformation (NAR). Christian nationalism is a political movement that employs Christian language and symbols, but it is fundamentally at odds with Christian orthodoxy. These approaches are grounded in theological errors and have damaged Christian mission and witness, thus they are not compatible with Christian faithfulness.

In the conclusion, I will make the case that Kingdom citizens ought to be salty, prophetic, separationist, social, and pluralist, drawing together the most faithful elements of the approaches to Christian citizenship. This constellation of characteristics keeps our faithfulness to Christ at the center, while considering the ways our political engagement affects the mission and witness of the church. This framework eschews easy answers and "correct" policy positions, and instead requires us to be comfortable with tension and nuance. This will make political engagement more complicated, but also more faithful to our Christian convictions.

I hope you will proceed with an open mind and a discerning spirit, ready to be challenged, to think carefully, to rethink critically, and to act faithfully.

1

CITIZENS OF THE KINGDOM

In the weeks leading up to my first Fourth of July weekend as a Texas resident, I started to notice signs that I wasn't in New Jersey anymore. I had moved to Waco, also known as "Jerusalem on the Brazos," after living in New Jersey for five years. Rounding the corner on my church, I was surprised to discover that the sidewalk surrounding the building was lined with American flags. I soon learned my church celebrated Independence Day by meeting for only one weekend service, instead of the usual five, with music led by a patriotic band. I realized this wasn't unusual for the region, as I noticed billboards and radio ads promoting various "God and Country" services.

For some, this may be a familiar and unremarkable element of celebrating the Fourth of July. For others, it may be confusing or even off-putting, seemingly conflating worship of God with worship of the United States. The different reactions to a church lined with American flags illustrates the range of positions on the relationship between the Kingdom of God and the country. Are Kingdom and country mutually exclusive, or do they complement each other? Do they merely coexist, or are they mutually supporting? What does it mean to celebrate and participate in both citizenships?

Understanding what it means for Christians to be citizens of the Kingdom of God and of the United States requires us to recognize crucial distinctions between the two. I say "crucial," a word whose root is *crux* or cross, because the distinction is, indeed, the cross of Jesus Christ. The life, death, and resurrection of Jesus Christ is the core reality that defines the Kingdom of God, and it is not the core reality that defines the United States—at least not constitutionally or legally. The Kingdom of God is not the United States, and the United States is not the Kingdom of God. What is the difference? And why does the difference matter?

THE CITY OF GOD

Questions about the relationship between Kingdom and country are not new. The earliest Christians wrestled with what it meant for them to live in a pagan society as Christians. Christians faced sporadic waves of persecution from the first to early fourth centuries because the government perceived them as anti-Roman, among other reasons. Minucius Felix (d. 260) accused Christians by saying, "[you] do not go to our shows, you take no part in our processions, you are not present at our public banquets, you shrink in horror from our social games."[1] Christians wrestled with whether and how much to isolate themselves from society. Could they work for the government? Could they attend games or festivals that included pagan sacrifices? Early Christians were pacifist, but what of soldiers who became believers? Christian separation from society caused suspicion and confusion, and it marked them as something other than *real* Romans.

The writings of early Christians show them working through the complex dynamics of being in the empire, but not of it. The late-second-century "Epistle to Diognetus" describes the situation this way:[2]

> For Christians are no different from other people in terms of their country, language, or customs. Nowhere do they inhabit cities of their own, use a strange dialect, or live life out of the ordinary. . . . And they show forth the character of their own citizenship in a marvelous and admittedly paradoxical way by following local customs in what they wear and what they eat and in the rest of their lives. They live in their respective countries, but only as resident aliens; they participate in all things as citizens, and they endure all things as foreigners. Every foreign territory is a homeland for them, every homeland foreign territory.[3]

---

[1] Robert L. Wilken, *The Christians as the Romans Saw Them*, 2nd ed. (New Haven, CT: Yale University Press, 2003), 66. All dates are CE unless otherwise designated.

[2] Diognetus was a tutor to emperor Marcus Aurelius. Robert M. Grant, *The Anchor Bible Dictionary*, vol. 2, ed. David Noel Freedman (New York: Doubleday, 1992), 201.

[3] "Epistle to Diognetus," in *The Apostolic Fathers*, vol. 2, trans. Bart D. Ehrman, Loeb Classical Library (Cambridge, MA: Harvard University Press, 2003), 139-41.

Similarly, Justin Martyr (ca. 100–165) wrote his "First Apology" to defend Christians who were being accused and unjustly punished on the basis of rumors about Christian beliefs and practices. Justin reassured Roman officials, and especially the emperor, that Christians were a benefit to the empire, because, "more than all other men are we your helpers and allies in promoting peace" and "to God alone we render worship, but in other things we gladly serve you, acknowledging you as kings and rulers of men, and praying that with your kingly power you be found to possess also sound judgment."[4] Thus, early Christians endeavored to balance their citizenship in heaven with their citizenship in the Roman Empire by contributing to peace and the common good, while refusing to participate in idolatry.

Everything changed in the year 312, when Emperor Constantine saw a vision of a cross as he led his troops into battle and shifted his allegiance from the Roman deities to the God of the Christians, according to the fourth-century historian Eusebius.[5] In 313, Constantine declared Christianity to be legally tolerated. Emperor Theodosius then made Christianity the official religion of the Roman Empire in 380. Christians hailed this as God's triumph over powers and principalities and a sign that the end times were rapidly approaching. The Roman Empire had become Christian. The tension between citizenship in heaven and citizenship in the empire seemed to dissolve. The city of Rome was already significant for Christians as the site of Peter's and Paul's martyrdoms and the seat of the bishop of Rome, who had primacy among all bishops of the Western church. Now that the cultural capital of the Western world was also the ecclesial capital of a Christian empire, Christians granted it even greater theological importance.[6]

Until it all came crashing down. The Visigoths sacked the city of Rome in 410, laying siege to what Christians had come to see as the Holy City. This was more than a military defeat; it was an existential and theological crisis for which Christians were completely unprepared. Having conflated

---

[4]Justin Martyr, "First Apology," Ante-Nicene Fathers, vol. I, trans. Philip Schaff (1885), ch. XII, CCEL.org, https://ccel.org/ccel/justin_martyr/first_apology/anf01.viii.ii.html.

[5]Eusebius, *Church History of Eusebius*, Nicene and Post-Nicene Fathers, vol. I, ed. Philip Schaff (Grand Rapids, MI: Eerdmans, 1890), Book IX, Ch. IX, https://ccel.org/ccel/schaff/npnf201/npnf201.iii.xv.ix.html.

[6]Rome had long ceased to be the seat of the imperial government, but it retained cultural and political significance in the west even as Rome's capital moved east to Constantinople. Peter Brown, *Augustine of Hippo* (Los Angeles: University of California Press, 2000), 287.

the Kingdom of God with the Roman Empire for several generations, Christians hardly knew how to separate the collapse of the imperial capital from the collapse of God's Kingdom itself.

Augustine (354–430), bishop of Hippo, witnessed the panic and dread in his congregants as the Eternal City, as the poet Virgil had called it in his *Aeneid*, was laid waste and refugees flooded across the Mediterranean to North Africa. He wrote to his shaken congregation:

> What are you scared about, just because earthly kingdoms perish? That's the reason that a heavenly one's been promised you, that you won't perish with the earthly. . . . Earthly kingdoms go through changes, but there will be One coming of whom it is said: "And of His kingdom there will be no end" (Luke 1:33). . . . Why do we place our heart on earth when we can see earth is getting turned upside down?[7]

Amid this political and theological crisis, Augustine wrote his famous tome *City of God*. In it, he differentiated "the earthly city" from the "City of God," recognizing that a failure to make such a distinction had devastating consequences for the church. Augustine wrote that God created the earthly city, and it was originally good and glorified its Creator. But when sin entered the world, it infected everything humanity did, including forming societies and governments, and twisted humanity toward self-glorification. Therefore, Augustine characterized the earthly city as sinful, violent, and temporal, in contrast to the holy, peaceable, and eternal City of God. The earthly city's inhabitants "live according to man," while the inhabitants of the City of God "live according to God."[8]

Perhaps the most fundamental difference between the inhabitants of each city is the orientation of their love. Augustine wrote, "Love of self, even to the point of contempt for God, made the earthly city, and love of God, even to the point of contempt for self, made the heavenly city . . . The former loves its own strength, displayed in its men of power; the latter says to its God, *I love you, O Lord, my Strength*."[9] Because of the sharp contrast between the city of man and City of God, Christians needed guidance for how to live in the present age as citizens of both cities.

[7] Augustine of Hippo, "Sermon 105," in *Augustine in His Own Words*, ed. William Harmless, SJ (Washington, DC: Catholic University of America Press, 2010), 322.
[8] Augustine of Hippo, *The City of God* XV.I, vol. 7 of *The Works of Saint Augustine: A Translation for the 21st Century*, trans. William Babcock (Hyde Park, NY: New City Press, 2013), 139.
[9] Augustine, *City of God* XIV.28, vol. 7 of *Works of Saint Augustine*, 136-37. Italics in original.

Augustine described Christians as dual citizens of the City of God and the city of man, and provided instruction for how to live as citizens of the earthly city without forsaking citizenship in the heavenly city. For dual citizens, the highest law was the love of God and neighbor. Christians should obey the laws of the land as model citizens contributing to the common good, do no harm, and help whenever possible. They should not become utopian, believing they will bring about the City of God through their good works; but neither should they be cynical, seeing all earthly effort as meaningless.

Augustine also explained there is no such thing as a Christian empire, because the temporal and militant nature of empire is at odds with the eternal and peaceable nature of the heavenly city. The city of man was not and would not become the City of God; therefore, people must not consider the city of man to be an end in itself or an object of worship. Since earthly kingdoms are temporary and infected with sin, there are limits to the earthly dominion and authority of any earthly kingdom, in contrast with the universal dominion and authority of God. Despite these sharp distinctions, Christians ought to seek earthly peace and follow the laws and customs of the earthly city, as long as they do not interfere with worship of the one true God.[10]

These distinctions between the City of God and the earthly city have been foundational for Western Christianity since the fifth century. Despite a sixteen-century gap between Augustine's time and ours, the distinction between the City of God and the city of man can be adapted to the circumstances of twenty-first-century Christians living in the United States.

Opposing Foundations of the Kingdom and the Country

A building's foundation determines how it functions. Whether it is the house built on the rock versus the sand (Matthew 7:24-27), or on concrete slab versus cinder blocks, the foundation determines the permanence, purpose, and stability of the structure. The Kingdom of God and the United States are built on different foundations; therefore, the two function very differently. Where the Kingdom of God is eternal, the United States is temporal; where the Kingdom is universal, the country has boundaries; while the Kingdom has abundant resources, the country has limited resources. These opposing foundations demonstrate the differences between

---

[10]Augustine, *City of God* XIX.17, vol. 7 of *Works of Saint Augustine*, 375.

Kingdom and country and should raise questions about the character of Christian citizenship in the country.

Eternal vs. temporal. Those of us who watched in horror as the Twin Towers collapsed on September 11, 2001, felt something similar to what the Romans felt in 410. The attack on the Twin Towers and the Pentagon shook to the core many American Christians who had assumed America was unshakable, or even uniquely ordained to stand as a symbol of God's providential favor. Americans have trouble conceiving of the United States as inherently temporal. We learn the history and mythology of the country's origins in grade school, but in learning about how the country began we do not also consider how it might end. We learn about the collapse of empires around the world and throughout history, but as a country we prefer not to imagine a similar fate might one day befall the United States. We think our military or our economic dominance will secure our future, or our system of government will prevent collapse. Other countries may disintegrate, but the United States will endure until, well, forever.

Augustine gives us a stark reminder that "earthly kingdoms perish." Only God and his Kingdom are imperishable, and we cannot ascribe imperishability to anyone or anything other than God. Even as we work to preserve and protect the stability of the United States, we must not pretend it is eternal. Whether its demise is geopolitical or eschatological, the United States will come to an end. It is temporary, perishable, impermanent, by its very nature. This temporality of the United States stands in stark contrast to the eternal Kingdom of God. As unsettling as the collapse of earthly kingdoms might be, the permanence of God's Kingdom has been and should continue to be a source of profound comfort to the people of God.

The Hebrew people invoked God's eternal reign repeatedly in circumstances of temporal threat. The prophetess Miriam declared, "the LORD will reign forever and ever" as she watched the destruction of Pharoah's army (Exodus 15:18). The author of Lamentations, writing in the midst of devastating exile, cried out, "But you, O LORD, reign forever; your throne endures to all generations" (Lamentations 5:19). And John of Patmos wrote of a choir of angels proclaiming, "he will reign forever and ever" (Revelation 11:15). In times of earthly upheaval, the eternal Kingdom is a source of hope for Christians.

At the time of the September 11 attacks, I was taking a sociology course with a professor who was a Christian from Bethlehem and had grown up as a refugee in Gaza. In the wake of the tragedy, even as he urged his family to remain at home for fear of anti-Middle Eastern violence and prejudice, he taught us about the temporality of earthly kingdoms. He had grown up in the liminal space that was created when one earthly kingdom supplanted another. While the attack on the Twin Towers and the Pentagon was shocking to him, it did not cause existential fear the way it did for many of his students and colleagues. He knew that earthly kingdoms pass away, and that we are only secure when our identity and hope are firmly settled in the Kingdom of God. He handled our shock and fear gently, while also urging us to reconsider our perceptions of American strength and permanence.

Earthly kingdoms are temporal, and we await the establishment of the eternal kingdom of God. While we wait, we work for the stability and well-being of the earthly cities we inhabit, even as we recognize that we are sojourners awaiting the return of our King.

Universal vs. boundaried. To say that the Kingdom of God is universal is to say that there is no realm of heaven or earth that is beyond God's sovereign jurisdiction. As Creator of all things, seen and unseen, all powers and principalities exist within and beneath God's authority, not in an autonomous realm beyond God's reach. The manner and degree to which God exercises authority in the world is a point of doctrine about which Christians differ; but Christians of all theological persuasions affirm that God's eternal Kingdom is a world without temporal or geographic limits.

In Revelation 21:25, John describes the new Jerusalem as having gates that are never shut, a powerful image of God's Kingdom as open and unthreatened. Fortified cities, including ancient Jerusalem, were surrounded by walls with gates that were shut to ward off attack. When John describes the gates that will "never be shut by day" (Revelation 21:25), he is describing a Kingdom whose boundaries are permeable, not fortified. The new Jerusalem never ends because there is no existential threat to God's eternal Kingdom.

The United States and all other countries, kingdoms, or empires sharply differ from the Kingdom of God in that they have geographical borders that demarcate the limits of governing authorities. Borders are abstract concepts that are codified in maps and treaties, and they are as permeable or impermeable as the geopolitical or economic or cultural conditions dictate. These often-arbitrary borders play a powerful role in the ways we define ourselves and our communities, connecting and dividing people based on invisible lines. If a government attempts to extend its authority beyond those boundaries, it is an act of war or colonization. Boundaries shift—empires expand and contract, countries are created and divided— but the boundaries exist, even when they are contested. In the United States, "The Border" has strong political resonance in recent years, evoking anger, fear, compassion, resentment, welcome, and a whole range of partisan talking points. Securing the border is a common goal across the political spectrum today, though people mean different things by it. How do we live as dual citizens of countries with borders and the Kingdom of God that transcends geography?

Living with primary citizenship in the Kingdom of God and secondary citizenship in the United States has implications for the way we think about the people across our geopolitical borders. For Christians, our understanding of God's universal Kingdom, and the way we regard humans who inhabit it, begins with the images of humanity in Genesis 2:23 and Revelation 7:9. Genesis 2 tells the story of God creating the man and the woman. The key point for conceptualizing human-made borders is the man's reaction to the woman: "This at last is bone of my bones and flesh of my flesh; this one shall be called Woman, for out of Man this one was taken" (Genesis 2:23). The man has two reactions: first, he regards the woman as the same as he is, then he recognizes her as different. Critically, the man reacts positively to both the sameness and the difference. The difference (woman) complements, rather than negates, the sameness (bones and flesh).

When sin enters the world, humans become alienated from one another. The recognition of sameness is diminished and difference is weaponized. In short, humans now notice difference first, view difference negatively, and elevate difference above sameness. This alienation contributes to everything from lunch table segregation to xenophobic violence. For citizens of the Kingdom of God, part of the sanctifying work of the Holy Spirit is to reorder the way we recognize people: as same first, as different second, and both sameness and difference as good. Human difference should evoke the same "Ah!" Adam experienced when he welcomed Eve's difference rather than feeling threatened by it. The difference drew them together instead of driving them apart, illustrating God's design for human community.

Borders and the policies governing them can be complicated, but our recognition of our fellow humans as "bone of my bone" should define the way we talk about and treat people of all nationalities and creeds. A biblical vision of humanity leaves no room for dehumanizing the "bone of our bones" across borders.

Our fraternal ties to sisters and brothers in the body of Christ also inform our understanding of borders. Revelation 7:9 presents an image of the eternal Kingdom of God in which "a great multitude that no one could count, from every nation, from all tribes and peoples and languages" worship God as one body. It may surprise some Christians in the United States to learn that of the ten countries with the highest number of Christians, seven of them are in Latin America, Asia, or Africa. In the Kingdom of God, Christians from the United States will be worshiping alongside Christians from Mexico, Nigeria, China, and Italy — all countries that have fraught histories with the US border and immigration policies. Immigration policy is complicated, but it is not complicated to recognize Christians from other countries and cultures as people with whom we will worship in the Kingdom of God.

Perhaps you've had a taste of the eternal Kingdom when traveling or worshiping in a very diverse church context. This is one benefit of international short-term missions or domestic crosscultural partnerships. When they are done well, these crosscultural encounters can expand people's vision of the Kingdom of God and reorder the way Christians think about and treat people from across borders. When we worship as one body with believers of different nationalities and cultures, the Spirit can work to reorder the way we see other people, sanctifying our eyes to recognize sameness first, then to welcome difference. This does not necessarily lead to an "open borders" policy for nation-states, but it must factor into the way we think about the reasons for and means of enforcing geopolitical boundaries.

Abundance vs. scarcity. The economies of the Kingdom of God and the United States operate on fundamentally different bases. The Kingdom of God distributes resources based on abundance, confident there is plenty for all. The biblical narrative is teeming with examples of this abundance principle. Humanity's story begins in a garden where God has provided humanity everything they need (Genesis 2:8-9). Scarcity and selfishness result from sin's entry into the world. God taught the Israelites the abundance principle by providing manna and quail in the desert. Moses assured the wandering Israelites that God would provide sufficient food for each day's needs, but he warned them not to store any excess for the next day. When some attempted to hold back extra manna, it rotted (Exodus 16).

Similarly, the so-called gleaning laws illustrate the expectation that the people of God should operate according to Kingdom economics of abundance in order to care for the poor and oppressed (Leviticus 19 and 23). The Israelites were to trust there would be plenty to feed their own tribes, even when they left 10 percent of the crop unharvested. The widow of Zarephath miraculously had enough grain and oil to feed herself and her son for many days, a reminder of God's abundant provision (1 Kings 17:8-16). The Hebrew prophets reserved some of their harshest words of judgment for those who amassed great wealth while neglecting the needs of the poor. Jesus also provided an object lesson in abundance when he fed thousands by multiplying a few loaves and fishes (Matthew 14:13-21). Those who were fed experienced a foretaste of the Kingdom of God, which John of Patmos described as a restoration of Eden, with its river and tree of life that feeds the restored humanity without any fear of scarcity (Revelation 22:1-2). Where there is no concern about lack, there is no selfishness, hoarding, or regarding of fellow human beings as mere competition.

In contrast, the United States and all other countries distribute resources on the basis of scarcity, concerned there is not enough to go around. While people in many parts of the world are well-acquainted with scarce resources, people in the United States generally assume that when we go to the store we will find what we need, although the ability to afford basic necessities varies greatly. Many Americans were alarmed to discover in the early months of the COVID-19 pandemic that our local grocery stores were out of toilet paper, and a baby formula shortage frightened parents in the spring of 2022. In some cases, these shortages brought people together through sharing information and resources. But they also illustrated a fundamental selfishness of humanity, as many hoarded resources or even tried to sell necessities online at inflated prices.[11]

---

[11]Jumaane D. Williams, "Price Gouging and the COVID-19 Pandemic: Policy Brief," Office of the New York City Public Advocate, March 25, 2020, www.pubadvocate.nyc.gov/reports/price -gouging-amid-covid-19-pandemic/.

The reasons resources become scarce vary and can be complicated, but whatever the root causes of scarcity, the economic principal at work is the relationship between supply, demand, and price. Basic macroeconomics dictates that when supply is low and demand is high, prices are high. Prices are set based on real or perceived scarcity of a product or service. Demand is also influenced by real or perceived scarcity. Scarcity can influence the way people treat one another. It brings out the best and the worst in us. Some people find ingenious ways to meet their needs and band together in mutual support, while others attain things through violence or corruption. Scarcity can be devastating and deadly, whether it is real or only perceived.[12] And the scarcity principle forms the foundation for how the United States and other global economies function.

We cannot expect the United States to run its economy according to principles of abundance. Since the world is fallen, resources are indeed limited, and those limits have real human and financial consequences that Christians cannot ignore or pretend away. This reality demonstrates just how radically different the United States or any other country is from the Kingdom of God. God does not subscribe to the economic theories of Friedrich Hayek, John Maynard Keynes, or Karl Marx, but Christians live in countries that do. Citizens of the Kingdom of God can live according to the abundance principle as much as possible through extravagant generosity and a level of trust in God's provision that may seem to defy logic.

OPPOSING VALUES OF THE KINGDOM AND THE COUNTRY

The Kingdom of God and the United States are built on different foundations, and they also advance different values. Values that animate both the Kingdom of God and the United States include loyalty, freedom, power, and justice. However, these values have different meanings in the Kingdom of God than they do in the country. Christians damage our mission and witness in the world when we confuse Kingdom of God values with the values of the United States.

Loyalty. The Kingdom of God and the country vie for our loyalty, sometimes resulting in confusion about the connection between God and country. In the classic film *National Lampoon's Christmas Vacation*, elderly

---

[12]Maysa DeSousa and Kaitlyn Rego, "Perceived Scarcity Across Sociodemographic Backgrounds Predicts Self-Reported Health," *European Journal of Health Psychology* 30, no. 2 (2023): 74-86, https://doi.org/10.1027/2512-8442/a000122.

Aunt Bethany folds her hands to say grace over Christmas dinner, then begins to recite the Pledge of Allegiance, prompting the whole family to reflexively recite along, Cousin Eddie standing with his hand over his heart. In the equally classic film *Sister Act*, the lounge-singer-turned-fake-nun Sister Deloris Van Cartier concludes her first mealtime prayer with "and to the republic for which it stands . . ." before declaring the gathered sisters "ready to eat, Amen." These amusing moments illustrate how engrained the recitation of the Pledge of Allegiance is: if we're reciting, it must be the Pledge. They also illustrate how complicated loyalty can be for Christians, when prayer and pledge can be conflated.

While a faithful Christian would not likely confuse the Pledge of Allegiance with a mealtime prayer, it is not at all unusual for loyalty to country to be confused or conflated with loyalty to God's Kingdom. Since the United States is not and will not become the Kingdom of God, loyalty to the two must also be clearly differentiated. For Christians in the United States, both Kingdom and country demand loyalty. The difference is that loyalty to the Kingdom must be unconditional, while loyalty to the country must be conditional. Loyalty to the Kingdom must be absolute, relativizing all other loyalties. Loyalty to the country must be subordinated to the Kingdom and generously seasoned with critique.

If you grew up in the United States, you likely recited the Pledge of Allegiance in school and sang the national anthem at sporting events. You may have taken an oath of enlistment for military service or participated in an oath ceremony to become a naturalized citizen. Citizenship requires some degree of loyalty to country, at least enough to motivate a citizen to obey the law and contribute to her community. Loyalty to country may take the form of working in public service, standing for the national anthem, displaying the American flag, serving in the armed forces, or observing national holidays. Some people also express loyalty to country through protesting the country's failures, while others express loyalty through celebrating its accomplishments, and many citizens do both. It can be difficult for American Christians to be simultaneously loyal and critical, because critique of the country's failures can be perceived as unpatriotic or disloyal. But absolute loyalty to the country, loyalty that is unconditional and refuses to recognize ways in which the country falls short of its own ideals and of the Kingdom, is not an option for Christians. Our loyalty to the country must have limits, and if it doesn't, then it trespasses into the loyalty reserved for God alone.

Loyalty to the Kingdom of God, on the other hand, is absolute and has no limit. Shadrach, Meshach, and Abednego demonstrate the limited loyalty to a king in contrast to unlimited loyalty to God (Daniel 3). King Nebuchadnezzar of Babylon conscripted these exiled Judahite men to serve in his palace, which they did willingly and skillfully. But their service to the king had strict limits: they would not eat unclean food or worship the golden statue Nebuchadnezzar constructed. Loyalty to God placed limits on their royal service, and Shadrach, Meshach, and Abednego were prepared to die rather than violate their commitment to God. When our country or its leaders make demands on our loyalty that contradict our obedience to God, then our loyalty must find its limit.

If we find ourselves making excuses to remain loyal to a country or its leaders where that loyalty should have found a limit, we transgress the allegiance appropriate for a temporal kingdom. Americans in the armed services or government employees may find themselves in circumstances that directly test the limits of loyalty, but any of us may be called upon to live out our loyalty in costly ways in a country that is not the Kingdom of God. If we find ourselves making excuses to disobey commands to love God and neighbor, we are likely sacrificing our loyalty to the Kingdom for the sake of obedience to the lesser authority.

Freedom. "For freedom Christ has set us free," and "where the Spirit of the Lord is, there is freedom," Paul wrote to the fledgling Christian communities (Galatians 5:1, 2 Corinthians 3:17). Scanning the wares at a local Christian book and gift store, I see these verses emblazoned on T-shirts, bumper stickers, and home decor, frequently combined with American flags or other patriotic symbols. The message of the patriotic images is that the freedom to which Paul was referring is the same freedom about which Americans sing, "from every mountainside, let freedom ring." But in fact, it is not the same freedom at all.

I remember learning the phrase "it's a free country" in elementary school. I promptly started to tell my parents and teacher that it meant I could do whatever I wanted, as they struggled in vain to explain my misinterpretation. In the United States and many other countries, freedom primarily refers to personal autonomy and individual rights. We are legally free to worship, to assemble, to speak, to pursue happiness without undue interference from neighbors or government. The adage, "your liberty to swing your fist ends where my nose begins," attributed to Justice Oliver

Wendell Holmes (1841–1935), is a tidy summary of the American political definition of freedom. I am free to do as I please, as long as it does not cause harm to another person or violate their freedom to do as they please. The government's role is often described as preserving individual freedoms, even as political parties disagree about how the government should fulfill that function.

The fear of restricted liberty is so deeply rooted in the US collective consciousness that any perceived threat to individual freedom is often equated with tyranny, harkening back to the Revolutionary War. In recent years, the rhetoric of tyranny has been applied frequently to government efforts to address societal problems, from the mask mandates of the COVID-19 pandemic to attempts at gun regulations in the wake of thousands of mass shootings. The resistance to limitations on personal freedom illustrates the way Americans conceptualize freedom as individual autonomy. Any real or perceived threat to autonomy is vigorously, even violently, opposed.

Contrast this American meaning of freedom or liberty with the freedom for which Christ sets us free. One is hard-pressed to find Scripture passages emphasizing or promising to protect individual autonomy. In the Old Testament, freedom most often refers to setting captives free, such as in the Year of Jubilee or during the Babylonian exile. Jesus connected this freedom to his own ministry when he read from Isaiah, "he has sent me to proclaim release to the captives, and recovery of sight to the blind, to set free those who are oppressed" (Luke 4:18 quoting Isaiah 61:1).

While the New Testament continues the emphasis on freedom for the oppressed, it also emphasizes spiritual freedom from the oppression of sin. When one is free, as Christian Scripture defines freedom, that means one is set free from sin and therefore at liberty to follow Christ. Indeed, this was how Paul explained freedom to the church in Galatia (Galatians 5:1-15). The way of Christ is not the way of individual autonomy. It is quite the opposite, as Paul explained to the church at Philippi. Christians are to have the mind of Christ, who "did not regard equality with God as something to be grasped, but emptied himself, taking the form of a slave . . . and became obedient to the point of death" (Philippians 2:6-8). Freedom enables Christians to "do nothing from selfish ambition or empty conceit, but in humility regard others as better than yourselves. Let each of you look not to your own interests, but to the interests of others" (Philippians 2:3-4).

Freedom from sin turns the heart outward toward God and neighbor, instead of inward toward the self.

We see a stark contrast here between American and Christian definitions of freedom. America conceptualizes freedom as *for self*; the Kingdom conceptualizes freedom *for others*. Dietrich Bonhoeffer (1906–1945), German theologian and resister of the Nazi regime, explained freedom this way: "The creature is free in that one creature exists in relation to another creature, in that one human being is *free for another* human being."[13] Christian freedom liberates us from American freedom. This contrast highlights the reality that the Kingdom of God and the United States are fundamentally different entities.

When Christian and American definitions of freedom come into conflict, citizens of the Kingdom of God are called to live according to the Christian vision of freedom as *for others*, even when being for others requires us to limit our individual autonomy and set aside our own rights and preferences. Common phrases like "God-given freedom" can conflate Christian and American concepts of freedom so thoroughly that we can delude ourselves into believing that we are being faithful to God's call even when we are causing harm to others by elevating personal autonomy above love of neighbor. When Christians baptize the American definition of freedom, we compromise our witness to the world. When Christians are perceived as being more concerned about our individual autonomy than we are about the needs of others, the gospel message becomes nothing more than a spiritualization of selfishness.

Power. Along a similar vein, a Christian concept of power radically differs from the American political concept of power. A Christian concept of power is correlated to sovereignty and, paradoxically, weakness. An American, or more broadly human, conception of power is based on the ability to coerce or bend people or institutions to one's will. The power of any government is limited and potentially threatened, whereas the power of God is limitless and secure. The way political leaders exercise their power is conditioned by the way they understand their own limits and threats, resulting in various applications of positive and negative coercion. Suzanne Collins's *The Hunger Games* trilogy provides a fictional dystopian example: President Snow positively coerces the people

---

[13]Dietrich Bonhoeffer, *Creation and Fall*, vol. 3 in *Dietrich Bonhoeffer Works*, ed. John W. de Gruchy, trans. Douglas Stephen Bax (Minneapolis: Fortress Press, 2004), 64. Emphasis added.

of the Capital with food and games (based on the "bread and circuses" model of the Roman Empire), while he negatively coerces the Districts by drafting their children into the arena to kill each other. The way God exercises power over his Kingdom is not conditioned upon anything other than God's own being. Therefore, it has no limits, except those that God imposes upon himself, and no threats, except temporary ones over which God's triumph is certain.

The US government has self-imposed limitations on its power, as well as internal and external threats to its power. Geography limits the range of its authority, as does the Constitution, and the consent of the governed. Geographic sovereignty is foundational for much of international law, and protecting that sovereignty "against all enemies, foreign and domestic" is one of the primary roles of the federal government and the military in the United States. The potential threat of a foreign power exerting its authority over the United States or its allies is the basis of most military and diplomatic policies. Foreign adversaries threaten the safety and stability of the United States, especially in a world that is increasingly global and susceptible to cyberwarfare. The US Constitution places internal limits on power, as the executive, judicial, and legislative branches of government provide checks and balances to prevent any branch of government from becoming tyrannical. In short, the structure of the government itself intentionally limits political power.

In the United States, the "consent of the governed" is perhaps the most significant and unique limit and threat to the government's power. According to the Declaration of Independence, governments derive "their just powers from the consent of the governed," or at least they ought to. While Americans take for granted the idea that citizens have a say in how we are governed, it was a radical, indeed a revolutionary, concept in the eighteenth century. While England had a Parliament with elected regional representatives, the system by which members of Parliament were elected was notoriously corrupt and not all regions were represented.[14] Philosophically, England's monarchy was rooted in the Divine Right of Kings, under which "kings are . . . God's lieutenants upon earth" and "their power . . . is

---

[14]"The Origins of Parliament," UK Parliament, accessed September 14, 2023, www.parliament .uk/about/living-heritage/transformingsociety/electionsvoting/chartists/overview/originsof parliament/.

compared to divine power."[15] The monarch received his or her power to govern from God and exercised that power as God's representative on earth. The American Revolution turned this notion of government on its head, declaring that the government's power derived from the people, not from God. Thus, the citizens place limits upon and can even threaten the government's power. People disagree about God's role in the government, as we will see throughout this book, but as a starting point we need to recognize that limits and threats condition political power in the United States. Because America's power is inherently limited and threatened, it is different from the power the triune God exercises over God's Kingdom.

In sharp contrast to the power of the American government, God's power is limitless and unthreatened. Because the power of God is essential to God's very being, and its legitimacy is not subject to any external validation, God is free to exercise power in ways that sharply contrast with governments. There are no internal or external threats to God's omnipotence. Nothing is beyond God's power or outside of God's jurisdiction. The Kingdom of God has no need for checks and balances or internal limitations, because it is governed by a perfect, just, merciful King. Because God's power is absolute and unrivaled, God is free to demonstrate power through weakness, sacrifice, death, and resurrection.

Governments and God exercise power in the modes that are proper to their natures. Governments do not have absolute or unlimited power, and when they attempt to gain power beyond their due, people call them tyrannical, resulting in popular rebellion or economic sanctions, or a host of other internal and external attempts to impose limits on power. When God exercises absolute and unlimited authority, God is simply being God. Humans and our governments cannot, and must not, attempt to exercise the authority that is proper to God alone. The power of the US government is fundamentally different from the power of God.

Justice. The United States and the Kingdom of God also differ in their norms of justice. The Kingdom of God has a single standard and source for justice, which is God's own just nature. The United States has many competing definitions of justice that yield different methods and goals in civil society. In a diverse country like the United States, we should not be

---

[15]King James VI and I, "Speech to Parliament of 21 March 1610," in *King James VI and I: Political Writings*, ed. Johann P. Sommerville, Cambridge Texts in the History of Political Thought (Cambridge: Cambridge University Press, 1994), 181.

surprised when different religions, philosophies, social movements, or individuals offer different visions of a just society. Any justice-oriented movement can be inspired by Dr. Martin Luther King Jr.'s vision of a "beloved community," for example, while fundamentally differing about what that community should look like and how to work toward it.

What is justice? Is justice the result of citizens agreeing upon "the same political conception of justice, for example, a particular natural rights doctrine, or a form of utilitarianism, or justice as fairness," as American political philosopher John Rawls (1921–2002) suggested?[16] Because the American people do not share the same vision or definition of justice, what one person or movement advocates as just another might reject as unjust. Moreover, different means of working toward justice are informed by different ideas about the role of government in the pursuit of a more just society. There is no reason to think that the people of the United States will ever adopt a single definition of justice or the same methods for pursuing it. Indeed, John Rawls claims such agreement is impossible, "given the fact of reasonable pluralism."[17] Thus, the pursuit of justice is inherently limited and will always involve conflict, as ideologies compete for power and influence. In a diverse society, we often seek justice through trial and error, recognizing the lack of justice when we acknowledge the victims of injustice.

The Kingdom of God, on the other hand, has a single source and norm for justice, which is God's own being. While Christians may disagree about what constitutes God's justice, God is not confused or internally conflicted. In the eschatological Kingdom, justice simply will be reality, not something that must be strived for against the countervailing force of sin. Jesus' instruction to pray for God's Kingdom to come and will to be done on earth as in heaven (Matthew 6:10) is a directive for Christians to discern the justice of God, and to bring it into reality here and now, even as we recognize that it cannot be fully realized through the actions of any single person or government. Inasmuch as other religious or secular groups share a similar vision for justice, Christians can partner with them. However, Christians cannot abandon the justice of the Kingdom of God to settle for a secular definition of justice and/or adopt means of attaining justice that violate love of God and love of neighbor.

---

[16]John Rawls, *Justice as Fairness: A Restatement*, ed. Erin Kelly (Cambridge, MA: Belknap Press, 2001), 9.

[17]Rawls, *Justice as Fairness*, 9.

Citizens of the Kingdom (and of the Country)

It is common for Christians to take mission trips to parts of the country or the globe that get us out of our "comfort zone." These kinds of experiences can help us think through our citizenship in the Kingdom and country. One of the reasons crosscultural life can be exhausting is our brains and bodies are constantly calculating what is appropriate and evaluating our own behaviors through the eyes of a culture that may find our mannerisms strange, incomprehensible, or even insulting. But crosscultural tension creates opportunities for deeper levels of self-examination and mutual understanding. The apostle Peter described Christians as "aliens and exiles" in the world (1 Peter 2:11), because we follow a Savior who "has nowhere to lay his head" (Matthew 8:20). Or, as Stanley Hauerwas and Will Willimon put it, "Christianity is an invitation to be part of an alien people who make a difference because they see something that cannot otherwise be seen without Christ."[18]

We should become comfortable with the idea that living as Christians may sometimes place us at odds with the culture of the United States. We should embrace a crosscultural mindset that holds tight to our Kingdom citizenship, with its values and demands, while thoughtfully navigating the culture, values, systems, and laws of the earthly country in which we hold secondary citizenship.

The contrasts outlined in this chapter should make it clear that the Kingdom of God and the United States differ in foundational and radical ways. As such, they cannot and should not be treated as one and the same. While the demands of each may be compatible at times, their origin and direction diverge from each other significantly. These differences do not mean that the United States, or any other earthly country, is bad for failing to be the Kingdom of God, any more than a window is bad for failing to be a door. They are simply different in origin and aim. The United States is not, and will not become, the Kingdom of God, any more than a kiwi can grow into a cantaloupe. And yet, Christians live in both simultaneously, and must therefore learn how to live in the tension between the eternal Kingdom of God and the temporal United States.

How do we live according to the Kingdom truth of abundance and also the economic reality of scarcity? How do we live according to the

---

[18]Stanley Hauerwas and William H. Willimon, *Resident Aliens*, 25th anniversary ed. (Nashville: Abingdon Press, 2014), 24.

Kingdom's justice, while being subject to flawed legal systems and laws that cannot make God's justice a reality? How do we recite the Pledge of Allegiance, run for political office, vote, protest, advocate, or engage in other civic activities while also keeping our political loyalty subordinate to our citizenship in the Kingdom of God? These questions should rattle around in our minds and hearts, refusing to let us settle for simple answers. The next step in our exploration of faithful approaches to citizenship in the Kingdom and the country is an examination of what guidance Scripture offers as we navigate our dual citizenship.

2

BIBLICAL DUAL CITIZENSHIP

"Do you believe in aliens?" I typed out the question to my fellow seventh grader and hit send. I waited for my computer to chime, signaling his reply. This was instant messaging in the mid-1990s. "I'd have to see what the Bible says about it," he emailed in response. I had not read very much of the Bible yet, but I was pretty sure it did not mention aliens. Why would he go to the Bible with a question the Bible doesn't answer? I wondered.

Contemporary American politics may not be extraterrestrials, but, like life on other planets, it is not something the Holy Spirit inspired the biblical writers to address. The Bible lacks any mention of Democrats, Republicans, elections, presidents, Congress, or voting. We cannot simply hunt for verses that tell us which political position is right, nor can we tally the number of references to a topic then declare a policy position biblical—not if we want to be faithful interpreters of God's Word. Rather than seeking political injunctions, the Bible calls us to seek the Kingdom of God, which has direct implications for the ways we live as citizens of a country that does not legally or culturally endorse Christianity. We must approach Scripture with nuance if we are to discern God's will for our political lives.

Living faithfully as a dual citizen in the Kingdom of God and the United States demands more of us than an internet search for Bible verses about the controversial policy du jour. The biblical authors inhabited fundamentally different contexts than their twenty-first-century interpreters, and the

Bible's primary purpose is not to serve as a template for contemporary politics. But that does not mean the Bible has nothing to offer as we navigate the murky waters of civic engagement. We cannot usually draw direct correspondence between the Bible and contemporary American politics, but neither can we dismiss Scripture as irrelevant to our geopolitical reality. While the biblical writers were not trying to decide whom to vote for or which political party to register with, many of them were wrestling with how to live faithfully within a political order that did not align with their religious convictions. Whether in exile in Babylon or under Roman occupation in Palestine, the communities whose stories are included in the Christian Scriptures can guide our approach to living as Kingdom citizens in our country of residence. Understanding what Scripture says about politics can lead us to principles to guide Christian political engagement: we are allowed to engage with government, we must differentiate the United States from biblical Israel, we should seek the common good, we ought to do Kingdom work on earth, and we must discern when to submit versus when to resist governing authorities.

ENGAGING WITH GOVERNMENT

Christians might ask whether it is appropriate for us to participate in party politics at all, given the divisiveness of the two-party system, the pervasive corruption and moral compromise among elected officials, and the overall tendency toward secularism. The biblical witness shows us that engaging with government is permissible, even when that government is oppositional to Christianity. The biblical stories of Daniel, Esther, and Paul provide examples of engaging with the government without compromising convictions.

Daniel was among the Israelites who were taken into exile when Babylon conquered Judah in 586 BCE.[1] King Nebuchadnezzar of Babylon summoned him along with Shadrach, Meshach, and Abednego, and had them educated for service in his government. Daniel did not object to this role, but he did place firm boundaries around it. He would continue to worship only his God. He applied his intellect to his job and served the king, up to the point that it violated his religious convictions. King Darius outlawed

---

[1]For the sake of clarity, I will use *Israel* and *Israelites* throughout this chapter to refer to the ethnoreligious nation at the center of the Old Testament, though at points it would be more accurate to refer to Hebrews, Judahites, or Jews.

prayer to any gods except the king himself, but Daniel continued to pray to God alone (Daniel 6:6-10).

Daniel's example demonstrates that it is possible to serve in government, even a government whose religious foundations differ from ours, without violating religious convictions. It also demonstrates that boundaries must be firmly in place, and we must be willing to suffer the consequences if our faithfulness leads us to violate the law. In Daniel's case, the consequence was being cast into a den of lions (Daniel 6:10-28). God rescued Daniel, but we are not guaranteed safety or survival when we defy the government. In a country with a representative government, we have the option to participate and make positive contributions to society through political participation, but there will be times when our faith is in tension with our participation in government.

Queen Esther is another example of someone influencing government while in exile, this time in Persia. Esther was taken into King Ahasuerus's harem, along with other young women, when the king needed a new queen (Esther 2). The king chose Esther, which placed her in close proximity to power, a position she neither sought nor shunned. When Mordecai, Esther's uncle, learned that the king's adviser, Haman, was plotting to kill all the Jews in Persia, Mordecai urged Esther to intervene. Esther pulled the levers of power to which she had unique access to avert genocide (Esther 4–5). From Esther we learn that proximity to power, when used in a godly way, can have godly results. Proximity to power can, however, also lead to corruption and violence, as with Haman, and therefore power must be handled cautiously and selflessly.

The apostle Paul offers a third example of engaging with government. When Paul became a Christian and gave his wholehearted loyalty to Christ alone, he did not disavow his Roman citizenship or the rights it afforded him. To the contrary, Paul leveraged his citizenship when he was arrested and about to be flogged in Jerusalem. He asserted his status as one "born a citizen," which caused his jailer to be fearful when he "realized that Paul was a Roman [citizen] and that he had bound him" (Acts 22:29). Paul's citizenship was a get-out-of-jail card in this case, and he did not hesitate to play it. This shows us that we can benefit from the rights and privileges that come with citizenship, without concern that simply exercising those rights is an intolerable compromise of loyalty. In the United States, the rights and privileges of citizenship include things like due process, voting, or running for office.

So, it appears Scripture supports—or at least does not rule out—some kind of political participation, although it does not translate directly to representative democracy. We might want to isolate ourselves from government, as we will see in chapter four, but we are not obligated to do so. A more specific question remains: is it appropriate for Christians to participate in *party* politics? Can a Christian be a member of a political party, or should Christians be "Independent" by default? Can a Christian donate to a campaign or sport a candidate's swag without automatically compromising his loyalty to Jesus Christ? We will return to these questions in chapter three.

DIFFERENTIATING THE UNITED STATES FROM BIBLICAL ISRAEL

Another biblical principle for Christian political engagement is the need to make clear distinctions between the United States—or any other country—and biblical Israel. Failure to recognize the basic differences between the United States and biblical Israel has led to problematic interpretations and conflations. Just as the United States is not and will not become the eternal Kingdom of God, so also the United States is not and never was identical with the Old Testament nation of Israel. A typological reading of the Old Testament, in which biblical Israel was read as an archetype for the United States, led some political leaders in American history to overlay the Promised Land of the Pentateuch onto America's founding. As sociologist Philip Gorski explains, "The Puritans—and the English in general—often read events in the same [typological] way and gave themselves the starring role: as the Pentateuch described the Old Israel, so would the English become the New Israel."[2]

One of the most famous examples of reading biblical Israel onto the New World comes from John Winthrop (1588–1649), the first governor of the Massachusetts Bay Colony. His "Model of Christian Charity" speech, delivered in 1630 upon departure for Massachusetts Bay, was replete with Old Testament references. He concluded the speech by reciting Moses' parting words to the Israelites before they entered the Promised Land (Deuteronomy 30:15-18):

> Beloved there is now set before us life and good, Death and evil, in that we
> are commanded this day to love the Lord our God, and to love one another,

---

[2]Philip Gorski, *American Covenant: A History of Civil Religion from the Puritans to the Present* (Princeton, NJ: Princeton University Press), 39.

to walk in his ways and to keep his Commandments and his Ordinance and his laws, and the articles of our Covenant with him, that we may live and be multiplied, and that the Lord our God may bless us in the land whither we go to possess it. But if our hearts shall turn away, so that we will not obey, but shall be seduced, and worship and serve other Gods, our pleasure and profits, and serve them; it is propounded unto us this day, we shall surely perish out of the good land whither we pass over this vast sea to possess it.[3]

Winthrop's linking of the New World with biblical Israel prefigures interpretations of the United States' identity and purpose that persist to the present day.

Government officials have employed similar covenant language frequently throughout America's history and into the present. In 1788, Rev. Samuel Langdon promoted the Israelite's political systems as a template for republicanism in the newly independent United States. He exhorted his New Hampshire congregation,

If I am not mistaken, instead of the twelve tribes of Israel, we may substitute the thirteen states of the American union, and see this application plainly offering itself, viz.—That as God in the course of his kind providence hath given you an excellent constitution of government, founded on the most rational, equitable, and liberal principles, by which all that liberty is secured which a people can reasonably claim, and you are impowered to make righteous laws for promoting public order and good morals; . . . it will be your wisdom in the eyes of the nations, and your true interest and happiness, to conform your practice in the strictest manner to the excellent principles of your government, adhere faithfully to the doctrines and commands of the gospel, and practice every public and private virtue.[4]

Here Langdon used biblical language to describe the new United States and closely intertwined the Constitution with biblical law. He and Winthrop, along with others, read the United States as God's second chance for a chosen people to hold up their end of the covenant by succeeding in faithfulness where the Israelites had failed.

Equating the United States or Americans with ancient Israel and the chosen people has persisted in various forms. In his 1850 novel *White*

---

[3]John Winthrop, "A Modell of Christian Charity (1630)," *Hanover Historical Texts Collection*, accessed May 30, 2023, https://history.hanover.edu/texts/winthmod.html. Spelling updated.
[4]Samuel Langdon, "The Republic of the Israelites an Example to the American States" (June 5, 1788), www.consource.org/document/the-republic-of-the-israelites-an-example-to-the-american-states-by-samuel-langdon-1788-6-5/.

Jacket, Herman Melville wrote, "We Americans are the peculiar, chosen people—the Israel of our time; we bear the ark of the liberties of the world. God has predestined, mankind expects, great things from our race; and great things we feel in our souls."[5] During the First World War, President Woodrow Wilson "believed that God had chosen America to complete John Winthrop's 1630 mission—to establish a model Christian state that would be an example to the rest of the world."[6] As recently as January 2021, some of the participants in the riots at the US Capitol understood themselves to be following in the footsteps of the Israelites: "Just as Joshua was instructed to march around the walls of Jericho, Jericho Marchers march around at a specific place and time until that darkness is exposed and the walls of corruption fall down."[7] Identifying the United States with Israel is problematic as a political orientation and as a biblical hermeneutic.

Lamentably, the idea of America as a new chosen people can contribute to antisemitism. While George Washington promised the Hebrew congregation of Newport, Rhode Island in 1790 that the United States "gives to bigotry no sanction, to persecution no acceptance," antisemitism is nevertheless deeply rooted in our religious and political history.[8] Historian Leonard Dinnerstein notes in *Antisemitism in America,* "antisemitism is a real and ignoble part of America's cultural heritage. It was brought to the New World by the first settlers, instilled by Christian teachings, and continually reinforced by successive waves of Protestants and Catholics who populated American shores."[9] This is not to say that all Christians or all Americans are antisemitic, of course. But we should be wary of expressing America's status with God in a way that can enliven or justify antisemitic attitudes. While the theological relationship between Jews and Christians is a matter of genuine debate, we must be cautious about portraying the Jewish people as rejected by God in favor of America or Christians. The potential for antisemitism

---

[5] Herman Melville, *White-Jacket* (Auckland, NZ: The Floating Press, 2011), 202.
[6] John D. Wilsey, *American Exceptionalism and Civil Religion: Reassessing the History of an Idea* (Downers Grove, IL: IVP Academic, 2015), 125.
[7] Quoted in Miranda Zapor Cruz, "The United States Is Not the Israelites; Washington Is Not Jericho," https://mirandazaporcruz.com/the-united-states-is-not-the-israelites-washington-is-not-jericho/ (blog), January 6, 2021. The original Jericho March website is no longer active.
[8] "From George Washington to the Hebrew Congregation in Newport, Rhode Island, 18 August 1790," Founders Online, National Archives, https://founders.archives.gov/documents/Washington/05-06-02-0135.
[9] Leonard Dinnerstein, *Antisemitism in America* (New York: Oxford University Press, 1995), xix.

makes it all the more important to differentiate the United States from biblical Israel.

Biblical Israel differs from the United States in many ways, one of the most politically relevant being national identity. The Israelites were Israelites because they were the descendants of Abraham, Isaac, and Jacob, who worshiped the God of their fathers. Shared ethnicity and religion constituted their national identity. Americans are Americans because we are born or naturalized citizens of the United States, which is an ethnically and religiously diverse country. American national identity is neither ethnic nor religious, although these identities do affect American culture. The distinction between biblical Israelites and the United States means we should not assume that descriptions of, commands to, or promises for the Israelites apply to the United States. Does that mean the Old Testament is irrelevant to our efforts to live in the country as Kingdom citizens? Not at all! It simply means we cannot always read God's Words to the Israelites as if they are God's Words for the United States.

Not only is biblical Israelite national identity fundamentally different from American national identity, the forms of government are completely different. In Israelite society, the government's primary purpose was to ensure proper worship of Yahweh. The Israelites functioned under several forms of government during the historical periods recounted in the Old Testament.[10] The first form of government was theocratic. Prophets and judges mediated between God and the Israelites, who were organized as a loose confederacy of tribes. From Moses to Deborah to Samuel, the theocratic mediators focused on upholding and enforcing the Mosaic law, in which civil regulations and religious rituals were inseparable. The Israelites eventually rejected this system.

The second form of government was monarchy, instituted when the Israelites demanded "a king to govern us, like other nations" (1 Samuel 8:5). Their political structure changed, but their identity continued to be based on shared ethnicity and worship. The Israelites remembered their kings as righteous or wicked based on how faithfully they upheld the Mosaic law, especially the first commandment, "you shall have no other gods before me" (Exodus 20:3). The greatest of these kings was David, who ensured proper worship by bringing the Ark of the Covenant to Jerusalem. David's

---

[10]Daniel J. Elazar, "Government in Biblical Israel," *Tradition: A Journal of Orthodox Jewish Thought* 13, no. 4 (1973).

son and successor, Solomon, continued this monarchic oversight of religion by building the temple. King Hezekiah was praised for restoring temple worship, and Josiah was celebrated for reinstituting the Passover festival. In short, the king's primary role was the oversight of proper worship.[11]

The third period of government began when Babylon conquered the southern kingdom in 586 BCE. The monarchy crumbled, the temple was destroyed, and the period of exile began. Babylon removed the most educated, influential, and wealthy Israelites and relocated them in an effort to prevent organized revolt. While in exile, the Israelites preserved their ethnoreligious identity, but not their government. After Persia conquered Babylon in 538 BCE, King Cyrus permitted Ezra and Nehemiah to lead the exiled Israelites back to Jerusalem to rebuild the city walls and the temple. Worship and priestly leadership continued under Persian (538–332 BCE), then Greek (332–63 BCE), then Roman (63 BCE–313 CE) occupation until the temple was destroyed in 70; thus, worship of God, not political sovereignty, set apart the Israelites.

Biblical Israel's government structures and political circumstances do not correspond directly to the United States. Therefore, we cannot necessarily apply to the US biblical instructions addressed to the Israelites. For example, after King Solomon dedicated the temple, God appeared to him and said, "if my people who are called by my name humble themselves, pray, seek my face, and turn from their wicked ways, then I will hear from heaven and will forgive their sin and heal their land" (2 Chronicles 7:14). Russell Moore, director of the *Christianity Today* public theology project, writes of this verse, "Often, the way this verse will be preached in many evangelical pulpits is as a rallying cry. In so many sermons, the 'people' referred to in the passage are the American people, and the 'land' is the American land. The meaning of the text is understood as an invitation to 21st century America to 'return to God' and then enjoy God's blessing once again."[12]

The logical corollary is that the tragedies America suffers are the result of people's unfaithfulness. If only the country turned to God, the logic goes,

---

[11]Bruce C. Birch et al., *A Theological Introduction to the Old Testament*, 2nd ed. (Nashville: Abingdon Press, 2005), 265.

[12]Russell Moore, "2 Chronicles 7:14 Isn't About American Politics," January 14, 2016, *Russell Moore* (blog), www.russellmoore.com/2016/01/14/2-chronicles-714-isnt-about-american-politics/.

we would not have natural disasters or mass shootings.[13] The problem is, not all people in the United States are "my people who are called by my name." In the biblical context, that identifier belonged to the Israelites, but it cannot transfer to the United States. Christians can possibly identify ourselves with this verse; however, the body of Christ does not have a "land" to be healed. The context in which the biblical instructions were written determines how the original audience interpreted them and should condition Christian interpretations today. Christians in the United States can be tempted to read any biblical reference to a nation or a people as a word from God to America; we need to resist that temptation, lest we reduce the Kingdom of God to the United States.

SEEK THE COMMON GOOD

When Christians engage with politics, it should be for the purpose of seeking the common good. Because Christians live as foreigners wherever we are, we can look to the Israelites and the first Christians for guidance about how to conduct ourselves. The prophet Jeremiah and the apostle Peter each urged God's people to live honorably as exiles, doing good for the sake of their neighbors' well-being and as a positive witness to the world.

When the Babylonians destroyed the temple and carried the Israelites into exile, God's people did not know how to live in a foreign land. Their ethnic and religious identity was connected to the physical land that God had promised to their patriarch Abraham, where their ancestors had worshiped God in the tabernacle then the temple for generations.

Prior to the Babylonian invasion, the prophet Jeremiah faithfully warned the people about the consequences of abandoning worship of God, including losing their land and temple. Jeremiah exhorted the king and the Israelites, "amend your ways and your doings, and obey the voice of the LORD your God, and the LORD will change his mind about the disaster that he has pronounced against you" (Jeremiah 26:13). He gave these warnings even though Uriah, his fellow prophet, had been executed for making similar pronouncements (Jeremiah 26:23). But King Zedekiah and the Israelites persisted in disobedience, so King Nebuchadnezzar of Babylon invaded and carried a contingency of the Israelites into exile.

---

[13]Laura Gish, "Urgent Prayer Alert: U.S. Mass Shootings," American Bible Society, May 16, 2022, https://news.americanbible.org/blog/entry/prayer-blog/urgent-prayer-alert-u-s-mass-shootings.

Jeremiah prophesied the exile would last seventy years. And so the Israelites had to learn what it meant to worship Yahweh without a temple or a
Promised Land while living as exiles under a foreign government.

In a letter to Israelites in Babylon, Jeremiah explained how they should
live as God's people in exile. He told the Israelites,

> Build houses and live in them; plant gardens and eat what they produce.
> Take wives and have sons and daughters; take wives for your sons, and give
> your daughters in marriage, that they may bear sons and daughters; mul-
> tiply there, and do not decrease. But seek the welfare of the city where I have
> sent you into exile, and pray to the LORD on its behalf, for in its welfare you
> will find your welfare. (Jeremiah 29:5-7)

When in a land whose people do not worship God, under the power of
rulers who do not acknowledge God's sovereignty, the people of God
should seek the city's welfare. The word translated "welfare" in Jeremiah's
letter is the Hebrew word *shalom,* also often translated "peace." Christian
philosopher Cornelius Plantinga explains, "in the Bible, shalom means
universal flourishing, wholeness, and delight. . . . Shalom, in other words, is
the way things ought to be."[14] Thus, the Israelites were not merely to seek
survival. They had to promote the shalom of the Babylonians, as their own
shalom depended upon the shalom of their land of exile.

The Israelites had options in Babylon: deny, resist, assimilate, or something in between. Hananiah, who was called a false prophet, encouraged
denial by insisting that their exile would be brief. They could have resisted
their captors and made their own lives miserable and violent in the process.
They could also have assimilated to Babylonian society and religion, as the
Babylonian government incentivized them to do. Instead, Jeremiah urged
a different approach: settle in for the long haul and work for the well-being
of your captors, because you will only be as secure and whole as the place
of your exile. The Israelites' shalom was tied to their captors' shalom. After
giving these instructions and reiterating that the exile would last seventy
years, Jeremiah wrote the words that many Christians memorize and paint
on home decor: "For surely I know the plans I have for you, says the LORD,
plans for your welfare and not for harm, to give you a future with hope"
(Jeremiah 29:11). Given the exilic context, the vision of a hopeful future is

---

[14]Cornelius Plantinga Jr., *Not the Way It's Supposed to Be: A Breviary of Sin* (Grand Rapids, MI:
Eerdmans, 1995), 10. Italics in original.

that much more significant. Jeremiah's guidance provides all Christians in exile with a framework for relating to our countries and communities. Work for their shalom, because our well-being is inextricably tied to the well-being of our neighbors, our political leaders, and our civic institutions.

A New Testament example tells us more about how to seek the shalom of our cities. The first Christians struggled to navigate the relationship between their new Christian identity and their life in the Roman Empire, in which government and religion were interwoven. Daily life in the empire involved animal sacrifice, pouring libations, and festivals honoring the gods. Christians risked violating the exclusivity of their faith if they participated in or attended these rituals. Or Romans might interpret Jesus simply as a new addition to the pantheon of Roman gods, just another option in the imperial cult.[15] Christ's claims to loyalty and worship were exclusive, but Roman paganism was not. Some of the first generation of Christians also questioned whether they were obligated to follow any civil or religious law at all, since they were free in Christ. New Testament scholar Judith Diehl explains, these new Christians had "one foot in God's world, as 'a chosen people, a royal priesthood, a holy nation, a people belonging to God' (1 Peter 2:9)," but had "the other foot in the Roman Empire, as 'aliens and strangers' in the world (1 Peter 2:11)."[16] How were Christians to live in this world?

The apostle Peter drew on the collective memory of exile when he wrote to Jewish Christ-followers to instruct them about the Christian life. He wrote,

> Conduct yourselves honorably among the gentiles, so that, though they malign you as evildoers, they may see your honorable deeds and glorify God when he comes to judge. For the Lord's sake be subject to every human authority, whether to the emperor as supreme or to governors as sent by him to punish those who do wrong and to praise those who do right. For it is God's will that by doing right you should silence the ignorance of the foolish. As servants of God, live as free people, yet do not use your freedom as a pretext for evil. Honor everyone. Love the family of believers. Fear God. Honor the emperor. (1 Peter 2:12-17)

---

[15]David Nystrom, "We Have No King but Caesar," in *Jesus Is Lord, Caesar Is Not*, ed. Scott McKnight and Joseph B. Modica (Downers Grove, IL: IVP Academic, 2013), 29.
[16]Judith A. Diehl, "Anti-Imperial Rhetoric in the New Testament," in *Jesus Is Lord*, 67.

Peter emphasized the potential for their holy conduct to have a positive influence on their communities, and he urged them to honor governing authorities, because when they did so they presented a positive witness to society. By living as upstanding neighbors, they glorified God. As their exiled ancestors did in Babylon, so Christians are to live as exiles, not in revolution or assimilation, but as positive contributors to the societies in which we are foreigners.

Exile is an apt metaphor for the circumstances of Christians in the United States, as Christians can find ourselves isolated from the culture and institutions that shape the world we inhabit. In 2020, around 64 percent of American adults self-identified as Christian, a remarkable decline from 90 percent in 1972 and 70 percent in 2014. Sociologists project ongoing decline to below 50 percent within fifty years.[17] As the percentage of Christians declines, so does the degree to which American society reinforces Christian culture and convictions. We may not be geographically displaced like the Israelites, but like them we experience what Old Testament scholar Walter Brueggemann describes as "a loss of the structured, reliable world which gave them meaning and coherence."[18] Like the Israelites, we may find ourselves in a "context where [our] most treasured and trusted symbols of faith were mocked, trivialized, or dismissed."[19] As citizens of heaven, we are in a place that is not our true home, discerning what it means to follow God while in exile.

The people of God have a responsibility to seek the good of the places where we live, rather than to seek their destruction or to pretend they do not exist. It is not only appropriate, but imperative, that we contribute to the wholeness and flourishing of the country in ways that are consistent with faithfulness to Jesus Christ. Christians will disagree about what seeking the shalom of the city means for political engagement in the United States, but political participation is one possible means of seeking the common good, albeit through very flawed systems led by sinful people.

---

[17]Pew Research Center, "Modeling the Future of Religion in America," September 13, 2022, www .pewresearch.org/religion/2022/09/13/modeling-the-future-of-religion-in-america/; Pew Research Center, "America's Changing Religious Landscape," May 12, 2015, www.pewresearch.org /religion/2015/05/12/americas-changing-religious-landscape/.

[18]Walter Brueggemann, *Cadences of Home: Preaching Among Exiles* (Louisville, KY: Westminster John Knox, 1997), 2.

[19]Brueggemann, *Cadences of Home*, 2.

DO KINGDOM WORK ON EARTH

During Jesus' earthly ministry, the Jews were exiles in their own land, and some were seeking a revolutionary leader to set them free from Roman oppression and reclaim their political autonomy. Jesus instead redefined freedom and invited gentiles into the household of God. The Christians would not be defined by ancestry or land, as the Jews were, but would include people "from every nation, from all tribes and peoples and languages" (Revelation 7:9). The shift from ethnonational identity to confessional identity could have led Jesus' followers to retreat from the world. After all, if Jesus' Kingdom was not of this world (John 18:36), then was it appropriate for Jesus' followers to engage with the empire at all?

Jesus taught his followers that, although his Kingdom is heavenly, citizenship in the Kingdom has implications for the material world. When Jesus instructed his followers, "This, then, is how you should pray: 'Our Father in heaven, hallowed be your name, your kingdom come, your will be done, on earth as it is in heaven,'" he inextricably connected his followers' eternal lives in heaven with their temporal lives on earth (Matthew 6:9-10 NIV). Indeed, Jesus himself embodied the union of heaven and earth through his incarnation. Therefore, the material reality of earthly life, and not only the spiritual realm, is the context in which Christians do God's will. Similar to Jeremiah's instruction to seek shalom, Jesus' teaching makes it clear that God does not expect Christians to abandon the world while waiting for the Kingdom of God to be realized.

Jesus elaborated on his followers' relationship with the government when religious leaders targeted him for his radical teaching. They asked Jesus, "Is it lawful to pay taxes to Caesar or not?" (Matthew 22:17). Jews in the province of Judea disagreed about whether paying taxes was permissible under Mosaic Law, but these religious leaders were not asking in earnest.[20] They were either trying to catch Jesus openly defying the emperor so they would have cause to turn him over to the civil authorities, or trying to catch him accepting the emperor's occupation so they could reject him as a sympathizer with their oppressors. Would Jesus' response put him in league with Judas the Galilean, a Jew who had led a failed revolt against Caesar two decades earlier, or in league with Caesar himself? Jesus, aware of their motives, responded, "Give therefore to Caesar the things that are Caesar's and to God the things that are God's" (Matthew 22:21). At first glance, we could

---

[20]F. F. Bruce, *Hard Sayings of Jesus* (Downers Grove, IL: IVP Academic, 1983), 215.

interpret this verse as an endorsement of isolating the Kingdom of God from human empires. Pay Caesar with the left hand and God with the right hand. But to read the text in that way presupposes a division of the world into sacred and secular that was foreign to Jesus' audience. Jesus was not setting up church and state as two opposing forces, with Christians rendering fealty to the one, then the other, depending on the circumstances. Neither did Jesus give his followers license to abandon their societal obligations. Rather, Jesus was illustrating the limit of Caesar's authority.

Roman coins like the one Jesus used in this teaching were inscribed with Emperor Tiberius's image and the words, "Tiberius Caesar, son of the divine Augustus and high priest." This inscription claimed the emperor had divine status, which implied a demand of unconditional loyalty from the people using the coins. When Jesus instructed the people to give Caesar what is Caesar's, he was not teaching a bifurcation of loyalties; he was placing limits on obedience to civil authorities. Give Caesar what is Caesar's: mere taxes. Do not give Caesar what is God's: your heart and soul.[21] Coins are merely coins. If that is all Caesar wants, he can have them. What are coins compared to the riches of God's Kingdom and the treasures stored up in heaven? This instruction reinforced God's sovereignty over the emperor and called Christians to be clear about the limits of Caesar's claim to their obedience. Caesar had the right to demand taxes, but he had no right to demand worship or uncritical obeisance. God alone demands and deserves our unconditional loyalty, our worship, our hearts, minds, and souls.

If Jesus had responded to the religious leaders by urging them not to pay taxes, that would have opened the door to political revolution or political retreat. If he had simply told them to pay taxes, without subordinating Caesar to God, it would have opened the door to assimilation. Thus, Jesus' followers had the same options as the Israelites in exile, and, like Jeremiah, Jesus showed them another way. Do the work of God here and now, including by giving the empire what is appropriate. Neither relegate the work of the Kingdom to spiritual or eschatological realms, nor set up the Kingdom and the empire as equal competitors; instead, reinterpret the empire through the lens of the Kingdom so Kingdom citizenship informs the ways we do Kingdom work in the world.

---

[21]David Garland, *Reading Matthew: A Literary and Theological Commentary* (Macon, GA: Smyth and Helwys, 2001), 227.

DISCERN BETWEEN SUBMISSION AND RESISTANCE

A final principle for Christian political participation is we must discern when it is appropriate to submit to the government, versus when submission compromises our citizenship in the Kingdom. Jesus' earliest followers continued to build on and interpret his instructions about engagement with political powers. Romans 13 and Revelation 13 illustrate two views of Christian dual citizenship. Paul of Tarsus wrote in Romans 13, "Let every person be subject to the governing authorities, for there is no authority except from God, and those authorities that exist have been instituted by God" (Romans 13:1). He explained that Christians should not resist authority, and that Christians have nothing to fear from the authorities as long as they live upright and law-abiding lives.

John of Patmos wrote in Revelation 13 of Christians encountering the frightening image of "a beast rising out of the sea, with ten horns and seven heads," who "was allowed to wage war on the saints and to conquer them" (Revelation 13:1, 7). This beast had been "given authority over every tribe and people and language and nation" (Revelation 13:7). Are Christians to be subject to such an authority? Depending on who wins an election, Christians might interpret political victory through the lens of Romans or Revelation. When our preferred candidate wins, Romans 13 assures us that they were put in their position by God and people are obligated to obey their authority. When our political opponent wins, we may describe them as a Revelation 13 antichrist, obligating Christians to resist.

To discern how Christians should apply these chapters today, we must understand the differences between Paul and John's political contexts and our own. Christians and Jews in first-century Palestine lived under a military occupation that was primarily extractive. As long as taxes were paid, the imperial government was generally content to let regional governors manage the affairs of their localities. Local governors ended organized resistance to the empire swiftly and harshly. There was no place in this system for conquered peoples to influence government, whether through legislation or protest. In contrast, the United States is founded on the proposition that people ought to influence their government. Therefore, biblical instructions regarding obedience to governing authorities should be read in the context of the options available to the original audience: obey or be punished. Given these options, Paul and John are circumspect in their guidance about submission and resistance, not wishing to bring persecution upon the Christian community if it could be avoided. Paul encouraged submission to the government, while John placed limits on that submission.

Paul's guidance presupposed a government operating within the proper limits of its authority. He did not propose a strategy for resistance if the government made demands that were incompatible with Christian faith. He did not acknowledge that the government can, in reality, be a terror even to people who have not violated civil law and seek only to live peaceably. Paul seems to be saying subjection to authorities is absolute, that all authorities are the direct result of God's active appointment and are therefore beyond questioning; however, he was presuming a government that was functioning justly and not requiring Christians to violate their beliefs. For Paul, a Christian's default position was to be a law-abiding citizen, showing respect to governing authorities and conducting oneself peaceably. This default position was a general principle to which there might be occasional exceptions. Paul's Roman audience did not, apparently, need instructions about the expectation to submit; instead, they needed encouragement not to make their allegiance to God a reason for political revolt.

Romans 13 indirectly states expectations for ruling authorities. Rulers are under God's sovereign authority, "for there is no authority except from God," whether they acknowledge it or not (Romans 13:1). They are not to be a "terror to good conduct, but to bad" (Romans 13:3). Rulers should serve the common good, including by punishing wrongdoers (Romans 13:4). God's appointment of governing authorities does not necessarily mean that rulers *will* act in accordance with God's intentions, only that they *should* do so. In the gap between *will* and *should*, Christians discern our response to government. New Testament scholar Esau McCaulley explains, Romans 13 "does not place limits on our ability as Christians to call evil by its name . . . The state has duties, and we can hold them accountable even if it means that we suffer for doing so peacefully."[22] Thus, Christians should not interpret Romans 13 as an excuse for authorities to govern in any way they choose, nor as a requirement to submit to rulers who fail to govern justly.

Romans 13 sets up Revelation 13 and the need to discern between a ruler who is God's agent for good and one who is "waging war on the saints"

---

[22]Esau McCaulley, *Reading While Black: African American Biblical Interpretation as an Exercise in Hope* (Downers Grove, IL: IVP Academic, 2020), 33-34.

(Revelation 13:7). The heart of Revelation is "a call for the endurance and faith of the saints," while rulers are "arrogant and blasphemous" and even when everyone else bows down to worship the unjust ruler (Revelation 13:10, 5, 8). Revelation 13 is a call to resist the government when it demands worship and unconditional loyalty, and to endure the consequences of resistance, up to and including death.

How is a Christian to discern whether to submit to or resist a governing authority? When does our posture toward government shift from Romans 13 submission to Revelation 13 endurance? Not on the basis of party or personal preference, but on the basis of the government's just and righteous use of power and appropriate demands for loyalty. Christians should have a default posture of submission to and respect for governing authorities—even those for whom we did not vote or whose policies we disagree with. At the same time, we should have a posture of discernment to recognize when our political loyalties or the government's demands move us toward idolatry. We must discern when agreeing with a president or party becomes loyalty that should be reserved for God alone. We must discern when a legal demand for action or inaction is incompatible with love of God and neighbor. We must be willing to endure the consequences when obedience to God alone becomes incompatible with submission to government.

LIFE AS DUAL CITIZENS

The political circumstances of Christians in the United States are radically different from biblical Israel or Jesus' first followers. If there were simple one-to-one correspondence between the biblical context and the twenty-first-century United States, then we would not need the Holy Spirit to illuminate the implications of Scripture for our own faithful citizenship. Scripture is not a collection of demands and promises that apply directly to the United States. Instead, Scripture is God's gracious revelation of what it means to live as resurrection people in a fallen world, which includes our lives within political systems.

Scripture should guide our political engagement. On the basis of biblical examples, we can say we are permitted to participate in politics, and we can do so with integrity. We must differentiate biblical Israel from the United States, noting the differences of government structure and national identities, and thus not assume that texts directed toward Israel apply to the United States. Christians are to promote the shalom of our communities and our country, while living as exiles whose primary citizenship is in heaven. Jesus instructs us to pray for the Father's will to be done on earth; therefore we can participate in society in ways that are consistent with that prayer. Finally, Christians ought to obey the laws and respect the authorities that govern the societies in which we live, even as we discern when obedience to God demands disobedience of earthly rulers.

Christians can and do disagree about the details of living out these principles in the real circumstances of the twenty-first-century United States. We do not always see eye-to-eye on whether a law is just or whether an authority is to be respected or reviled. We will not resolve these disagreements by locating the right Bible verse and convincing ourselves that our favorite politician or party is biblical. Faithful citizenship requires more of us than proof texting and sloppy hermeneutics. Faithful citizenship requires thoughtful discernment that will often lead to tension. Can we follow Jesus into that tension?

3

SALTY CITIZENSHIP

"RAISE YOUR HAND if you don't think a Christian can be a Democrat. Now, raise your hand if you don't think a Christian can be a Republican." A few of my church history classmates raised their hands in response to Dr. Jerry Sittser's first prompt. I don't think any raised their hand in response to the second prompt. Most of us didn't raise our hands, unsure about whether there was a "right" response and not wanting to be asked to explain our opinion. As a college sophomore, I had what I thought were reasonable political views, but I also realized I had given little thought to how my faith and my politics related. A few years later, I was boarding a bus in northern Ghana when a Ghanaian man asked my American friend and me, "Democrat or Republican?" We were taken aback, not expecting to be asked about our political stances halfway around the world. We answered, "Christian." He didn't seem satisfied with that answer, but is it the answer Christians ought to give? Is there a right answer to these questions?

We have already seen the different foundations and values upon which the Kingdom and the country are built and explored some biblical principles for political participation. Now we can apply these ideas to party politics in the United States. Given the foundational differences between Kingdom and country, we cannot expect any political party or system of government to perfectly align with the mission and values of the Kingdom of God. The body of Christ is not a political party and Scripture is not a policy agenda; therefore, no party's platform or ideology perfectly aligns with Christian convictions. Moreover, Christians are not in complete agreement among ourselves about doctrine or its implications for public life. Given the inevitable tensions between Christian faith and party politics, is it appropriate for a Christian to affiliate with a political party? Can a Christian say, "I'm a Republican" or "I'm a Democrat"? This chapter will consider how to be a faithful citizen of the Kingdom of God within the reality of America's political system. Thoughtful partisan affiliation calls us to "salty participation." In contrast, unreflective partisan alignment leads to "bland partisanship."

In his Sermon on the Mount Jesus issued a simple exhortation that is as multidimensional as the seasoning he references: "You are the salt of the earth, but if salt has lost its taste, how can its saltiness be restored? It is no longer good for anything but is thrown out and trampled under foot" (Matthew 5:13). At the risk of overextending Jesus' metaphor, salt gives us a framework for our engagement with politics. Salt in correct proportion makes food taste better; therefore, if we are salt, our participation in civic life should make society more flavorful. Salt is also a preservative; therefore, if we are salt, our participation in political life has a role in preserving the common good. If we lose our saltiness and become bland, our participation falls short of Christian faithfulness and we are no longer useful.

CHRISTIAN PARTICIPATION IN PARTY POLITICS

Have you ever felt your stomach tighten or your heart rate increase when politics comes up in conversation? You are not alone. Recent public health research has found that many Americans credit politics with chronic negative impact on health, including lost sleep, anger, lack of impulse control, compulsive behaviors, and even suicidal thoughts.[1] The deleterious impact of partisanship could easily lead Christians to conclude that we are better off ignoring politics entirely. While many Christians do disengage from politics, whether because of separatist convictions (see chapter four) or to avoid stress and conflict, many also see political participation as an important responsibility and opportunity. Christians in the United States do participate in politics more often than not, so we can begin our

---

[1]Kevin B. Smith, "Politics Is Making Us Sick: The Negative Impact of Political Engagement on Public Health during the Trump Administration," *PLOS One*, January 14, 2022, https://doi.org/10.1371/journal.pone.0262022.

movement toward salty partisanship by examining the current landscape of Christian political participation and the positions of the major political parties.

The state of participation. Self-identified Christians made up about 64 percent of the US electorate and about the same percentage of the general population in 2019.[2] Only about 66 percent of eligible voters cast ballots in 2020.[3] About a quarter of Americans who voted were White evangelical Protestants, and 81 percent of White evangelical Protestants voted for Donald Trump, which demonstrates a very strong alignment between White evangelicals and the Republican Party.[4] Black Protestant voters show a parallel alignment with the Democratic Party, with over 90 percent voting for Joe Biden in 2020. Catholic voters were more evenly divided between Democratic and Republican candidates, as were White mainline Protestants.[5] Christians, like other Americans, also tend to be very stable in our political views. Even if we sometimes vote for a candidate of a different party or split our tickets, our foundational beliefs about economic and moral issues do not change easily after our political opinions form in late adolescence and early adulthood.[6] We may like to think of ourselves as people who rationally consider issues and candidates on their own merits, but most of us have settled political preferences that exert strong influence on our voting behaviors and policy preferences, regardless of party registration.

Our goal does not need to be ridding ourselves of partisan leanings, but rather holding these leanings more conscientiously. This is the

---

[2]John Gramlich, "What the 2020 Electorate Looks Like by Party, Race and Ethnicity, Age, Education, and Religion," Pew Research Center, October 26, 2020, www.pewresearch.org/short-reads/2020 /10/26/what-the-2020-electorate-looks-like-by-party-race-and-ethnicity-age-education-and -religion/.

[3]Drew Desilver, "Turnout Soared in 2020 as Nearly Two-Thirds of Eligibile U.S. Voters Cast Ballots for President," Pew Research Center, January 28, 2021, www.pewresearch.org/fact-tank/2021 /01/28/turnout-soared-in-2020-as-nearly-two-thirds-of-eligible-u-s-voters-cast-ballots-for -president/.

[4]Frank Newport, "Religious Group Voting and the 2020 Election," Gallup, November 13, 2020, https://news.gallup.com/opinion/polling-matters/324410/religious-group-voting-2020 -election.aspx?version=print.

[5]Justin Nortey, "Most White Americans Who Regularly Attend Worship Services Voted for Trump in 2020," Pew Research Center, August 30, 2021, www.pewresearch.org/fact-tank/2021/08/30/ most-white-americans-who-regularly-attend-worship-services-voted-for-trump-in -2020/.

[6]Jon A. Krosnick and Duane F. Alwin, "Aging and Susceptibility to Attitude Change," *Journal of Personality and Social Psychology* 57, no. 3 (1989): 6.

difference between thoughtful partisan affiliation and unreflective partisan alignment. Thoughtful partisan affiliation requires us to examine the parties, their underlying ideologies, and their policy platforms and make an informed decision about whether we agree more with one party or another. Unreflective partisan alignment means identifying with a party without careful consideration, which is often the result of adopting the political alignments of our parents or our ethnic or religious communities. The distinction between affiliation and alignment is important. If we affiliate with a party, our connection to the party is malleable and our identity is not subsumed into it. If we align with a party, we take the party's ideology and policies and bring our beliefs into agreement with them. Thoughtful partisan affiliation can be salty; unreflective partisan alignment will be bland.

The US political system. Faithful citizenship requires us to understand how the US government and political systems actually function. The Constitution of the United States is a remarkable document. Unique for its time in history, it forged the path for liberal democracies around the globe. It is alarming that the majority of Americans have not read the Constitution, considering its significance for shaping our public life, including our religious liberties.[7] The Constitution established the United States as both a liberal democracy and a democratic republic. Liberalism in this context refers to the civil liberties that shape civic life, which include freedoms of expression, association, the press, and religion, as well as free and fair elections and equal rights of citizenship.[8] Liberal democracy contrasts with other models, such as authoritarianism or fascism, which deny the basic tenets of liberalism. Christians benefit from the religious liberties guaranteed in liberal democracy, a topic we will return to in chapter five. The term "democratic republic" refers to the balance of power between individuals and their representatives. US citizens do not directly elect the president, nor do we vote on all legislation. Instead, we vote for electors who choose the president, and we elect representatives to state and federal legislatures, who write and vote on legislation on our behalf. Ideologies

---

[7]According to the Marquette Law School Supreme Court Survey, of 1,423 Wisconsinites surveyed only 610 answered "yes" to the question, "have you personally ever read the entire Constitution, either in school or on your own?" There is good reason to regard this data as representative outside of Wisconsin. In addition, it is likely an overestimate, due to response bias in which a respondent might give what they think is the "right" answer instead of the honest answer.
[8]Fred van Geest, *Introduction to Political Science* (Downers Grove, IL: IVP Academic, 2017), 75-76.

and political parties operate within this constitutional system. The system has its flaws, to be sure, but it is what we have, and nearly all Americans consider it preferable to other options.

Two major political parties operate the systems of government: the Republican Party and the Democratic Party. Other parties exist, such as Libertarian and Green, but it is very difficult for them to compete with the two major parties. Political parties are living organisms. They expand and contract, advance and retreat, change direction and stay the course depending on which people, interest groups, and factions have influence at any given time. Therefore, a party's platform—its statement of legislative priorities—is a moving target. Nevertheless, the parties' ideological positions on economic and social issues have been relatively stable for several decades and can serve as a meaningful starting point for Christians to thoughtfully decide whether to affiliate with one of the parties.

Economic and social ideological categories are central to partisan politics. Positions on economic and social issues exist on a spectrum from liberal (left) to conservative (right). Note that liberal in this context is different from liberal*ism* in the context of liberal democracy defined above. On the economic spectrum, liberals believe the government should intervene with the economy when necessary to promote equality, while conservatives believe the government should allow markets to operate freely as much as possible. On the social spectrum, liberals believe individuals should be allowed to live as they will as long as they do not harm others, while conservatives believe a shared moral foundation is necessary for the stability of society and so peoples' moral behavior should be subject to legal restrictions. Decades ago, economic and social ideologies cut across party lines, so a Democrat might be an economic liberal and a social conservative, or a Republican might be an economic conservative and a social liberal. Today, it is rare to find conservative ideologies among Democrats or liberal ideologies among Republicans, or at least among those who hold public office. Democrat/liberal and Republican/conservative are more or less interchangeable today.[9] A brief overview of each party will help us understand their ideological alignments, so we can begin to consider thoughtful partisan affiliation.

---

[9]For an examination of the alignment between ideology and party, see Joshua N. Zingher, *Political Choice in a Polarized America: How Elite Polarization Shapes Mass Behavior* (New York: Oxford University Press, 2022).

The Democratic Party emerged in 1828 under the influence of Martin Van Buren (president from 1837–1841), who believed a two-party system was necessary as a check on the "disposition to abuse power, so deeply planted in the human heart."[10] Since the 1930s, the party has been characterized by efforts to address economic, social, and political inequality, and it has promoted the idea that government ought to actively promote equality. For Democrats, equality means equal opportunity and equitable outcomes; therefore, they interpret unequal outcomes as symptomatic of unequal opportunity or other systemic injustices. The Democratic Party is often labeled the party of "big government," but in reality, liberal ideology is more about the role of government than the size: "Liberals like an active government when it is used to protect disadvantaged or excluded groups. They mistrust it when it is used by the powerful to restrict those groups."[11] Today these ideological commitments are apparent in positions like protecting and expanding Social Security and support for legal rights for same-sex couples.

The Republican Party formed in 1854 under the leadership of soon-to-be-president Abraham Lincoln. The party of Lincoln leaned conservative economically, but liberal socially, hence the party's opposition to slavery. In the 1960s, the party intentionally adopted social conservatism to gain support from southern voters, an alignment that grew stronger with the rise of evangelical activism in the 1980s and 1990s.[12] The Republican Party today is conservative in its economic and social ideologies. In contrast to economic liberalism, economic conservatism promotes free market capitalism and attempts to limit government intervention in the economy. Economic conservatism emphasizes entrepreneurship, ingenuity, and personal responsibility and generally holds that people have equal opportunities; therefore, unequal outcomes are symptomatic of individual rather than social failures. Out of the free market ideology grows a rejection of redistributive economic policies, and a commitment to preserving traditional social arrangements, such as marriage. Conservatism is often characterized as a preference for "small government," but, as with liberalism, it

---

[10]Quoted in Michael C. LeMaye, *The American Political Party System: A Reference Handbook* (Denver, CO: ABC-CLIO, 2017), 12.
[11]Hans Noel, "What the Parties Stand For," in *Guide to U.S. Political Parties*, ed. Marjorie R. Hershey (Washington, DC: CQ Press, 2014), 62.
[12]Joseph A. Aistrup, *The Southern Strategy Revisited* (Lexington: University of Kentucky Press, 1996), 6-11.

is actually less about size and more about the government's role: "Conservatives like government when it is used to protect traditional values, but they dislike it when it prevents business from thriving."[13] This ideology is apparent today in policies like low tax rates for businesses and efforts to legally define marriage as between one man and one woman.

Third parties, such as the Libertarian or Green parties, operate along the same social and economic ideological axes, but tend to be outliers on one or both axes when compared with the two major parties. Libertarians, for example, espouse maximal liberty, yielding a conservative economic ideology and a liberal social ideology. The Green Party is liberal economically, since its primary platform is environmental protection. For a variety of economic and political reasons, it is rare for third-party or independent candidates to gain traction, and when they do get elected to public office they have to caucus with the Democratic or Republican Party. Independent senators Bernie Sanders (I-Vermont) and Kyrsten Sinema (I-Arizona) caucus with the Democrats in Congress, while Sen Rand Paul (R-Kentucky) describes himself as Libertarian but is a member of the Republican Party. Recent polling shows a strong desire among Americans for a third-party option.[14] Even so, the overwhelming majority of Americans register with or lean toward, and ultimately vote for, either the Democratic or Republican Party.[15]

Two stereotypes about the parties are worth challenging. First, Democrats tend to think of themselves as more concerned about justice and fairness than Republicans are. Jonathan Haidt's research on moral foundationalism demonstrates that in fact liberals and conservatives are equally concerned about fairness; however, they define fairness differently. Liberals equate fairness with equal opportunity that, in a just system, should yield equal rewards. Conservatives equate fairness with proportionality, meaning rewards should be based on a person's effort.[16] The former yields the Democratic focus on systems that produce equal results, while the latter corresponds with the Republican emphasis on individual

---

[13]Noel, "What the Parties Stand For," 62.

[14]Jeffrey M. Jones, "Support for Third U.S. Political Party at High Point," Gallup, February 15, 2021, https://news.gallup.com/poll/329639/support-third-political-party-high-point.aspx.

[15]Pew Research Center, "Political Independents: Who They Are, What They Think," March 14, 2019, www.pewresearch.org/politics/2019/03/14/political-independents-who-they-are-what -they-think/.

[16]Jonathan Haidt, *The Righteous Mind: Why Good People Are Divided by Politics and Religion* (New York: Knopf Doubleday, 2013), 196.

responsibility. We do well to accurately locate the point of disconnect not in the concern about justice or fairness, but rather in different ideas about what justice and fairness actually mean and how they are achieved.

The second stereotype is Republicans tend to think of their conservative ideology as more Christian and regard liberal Democratic ideology as indifferent or even hostile to Christianity. In reality, neither liberal nor conservative ideology is essentially religious. Political scientist Fred van Geest explains, "religious truth does not form a significant basis for either ideology. For liberals, religious truth is a purely private matter. It does not inform their thinking about political authority, rights, or citizenship. For traditional conservatives, religion has a little more public significance, but mainly as a source of social stability and individual virtue."[17] Political ideology is just that: political ideology. It is not religious doctrine and is not intended to advance Christian faith. We find faithful Christians leaning toward liberalism and conservatism, and within the Democratic and Republican parties.

The US government has always been influenced by Christian individuals and Christian values and traditions; however, the government is a political institution, not a religious one. A state is not religious—people are. The purpose of political participation is not to bring about the Kingdom of God through right application of political means, for the country is not and will never become the Kingdom. Christians err when we conflate the country's government with God's Kingdom. It is precisely because church and state are so different that we have to grapple with the inherent tensions between them.

Benefits of thoughtful partisan affiliation. Christians have the opportunity to influence society for the sake of the common good through participation in party politics. When we are motivated by love of neighbor, thoughtful partisan affiliation—such as registering with a political party—can be beneficial. Our motives for party affiliation matter. Even in partisan politics, Paul's instructions apply: "Do nothing from selfish ambition or empty conceit, but in humility regard others as better than yourselves. Let each of you look not to your own interests but to the interests of others" (Philippians 2:3-4). Since we have the opportunity to elect leaders and influence legislation, it is appropriate for Christians to participate in politics to promote shalom. Theologian Richard Mouw notes, "Christians

[17]van Geest, *Introduction to Political Science*, 54.

need to find practical ways for making room in our lives for the concerns of people whose life situations are different from our own," and awareness of such concerns should inform our political behavior.[18] Bearing in mind not all Christians agree about what serves the common good, we can nevertheless enter into thoughtful partisan affiliation as a way to demonstrate love of neighbor through elections and public policy. We can influence policy without partisan affiliation, but affiliation is a necessary step for some types of political engagement.

A practical benefit of thoughtful partisan affiliation is the opportunity to vote in primaries or participate in caucuses. In many states, a voter must be registered with the Democratic or Republican Party to participate in primary elections or caucuses. Primaries or caucuses are important because that is when voters select the party's candidates. Voter turnout tends to be low in primaries, and primary voters tend to be the farthest to the right or left ideologically, giving more extreme candidates a primary advantage. Because the primary electorate tends to represent a party's outliers instead of the moderate majority, candidates cater to the outliers. If an incumbent fears losing their primary to a farther right or left challenger, they adapt to appeal to the more ideologically extreme wings of the party.[19] Thoughtful partisan affiliation and primary voting can be antidotes to the extremism and partisan divisions that currently plague government.

Christians might also want to participate in a local political party organization. Christians can invest time and talent in improving our communities through participating in local political clubs or policy advocacy groups. Local politics is sometimes less polarized and can help us be aware of needs and opportunities in our towns and states. A 2017 study found that voting in local elections was alarmingly low, and active engagement with local party organizations is an even smaller percentage of the electorate, so local participation has the potential for significant impact.[20] We can also build relationships with elected officials and candidates through local organizations, which helps us know them as people, not only as party

---

[18]Richard J. Mouw, *How to Be a Patriotic Christian: Love of Country as Love of Neighbor* (Downers Grove, IL: InterVarsity Press, 2022), 56.

[19]Elaine Kamarck and James Wallner, "Anticipating Trouble: Congressional Primaries and Incumbent Behavior," Brookings, October 29, 2018, www.brookings.edu/research/anticipating-trouble -congressional-primaries-and-incumbent-behavior/.

[20]Brian F. Schaffner et al., *Hometown Inequality: Race, Class, and Representation in American Local Politics* (New York: Cambridge University Press, 2020), 84, 95-96.

representatives. Our thoughtful partisan affiliation through local organizations is a way to add salt to party politics.

Another benefit of thoughtful partisan affiliation is the opportunity to hold public office. Affiliating with either the Democratic or Republican Party is a practical necessity for a successful campaign, at least in our current system. The parties manage the financial resources, professional expertise, and even the demographic data that are essential to modern political campaigns, and it is rare for someone to mount a successful campaign for any office without major party backing. If we do choose to run for office, we run greater risk of becoming bland because of the pressure toward partisan alignment. Those who seek public office should examine their motives and maintain intentional practices of self-examination to prevent thoughtful affiliation from becoming unreflective alignment.

A final benefit of thoughtful partisan affiliation is intellectual honesty. Since most people do lean toward one party or another, we can be honest about our affiliation instead of claiming neutrality. When we state our affiliations, however loose or uncertain they may be, we can amplify our saltiness as people recognize our ability to critique our own political affiliations and resist the hypocrisy that comes with complete party alignment. When we affiliate with a party or support a Republican or Democratic candidate, then critique the party or candidate on matters of Christian concern, this demonstrates our prioritization of faith over politics and adds salt to partisanship.

Risks of partisan affiliation. While there are benefits to participating in partisan politics, there are also risks. A significant risk of partisan affiliation is negative impact on Christian witness. Recent research indicates that politics may be causing people to leave religion, with people who lean liberal being much more likely to be a religious "none" than those who lean conservative.[21] One interpretation of this research is Christianity has become so intertwined with political conservatism that those who lean liberal politically cannot see a path to be both Christian and liberal, and some do not want to be associated with politically conservative Christianity. This is a problem for all Christians, because political identity is trumping Christian identity such that some people see the political and religious as practically synonymous, while others see them as completely

[21]Ryan P. Burge, *The Nones: Where They Came From, Who They Are, and Where They Are Going* (Minneapolis: Fortress, 2021), 53-54.

incompatible. In this way conservatives and liberals alike show a misunderstanding of the place of Kingdom citizenship over and above citizenship in the country.

For those who affiliate with a party to run for public office or influence elected officials, another risk is the seductive force of power and immoral behaviors people might engage in to attain power. As British historian Lord John Dalberg-Acton (1834–1902) wrote, "power tends to corrupt, and absolute power corrupts absolutely."[22] William Wilberforce (1759–1833), who led the fight to ban the slave trade in Great Britain, was concerned that political engagement would lead him into corruption and moral compromise.[23] We should not think Christians are immune to grasping for power or compromising our convictions to gain influence. If anything, we are skilled at justifying our compromises on the grounds that we need to be in power to execute God's will. When power becomes an end in itself, the gospel is corrupted and Christian witness is damaged.

Partisan affiliation also runs the risk of eroding the distinction between Kingdom and country if we attempt to bring about the Kingdom of God through political means. If we affiliate with a political party, we might begin to think of our party in almost messianic terms, as though the policies and priorities of the party are necessary for the preservation of both the country and the Kingdom. When we begin to think the fate of Christianity depends on politics, we put mere human machinations in control of the Kingdom, wresting sovereignty away from God. We must always bear in mind that the country is temporal by definition and the Christian faith is not dependent upon any political entity. Elections and legislation have important consequences, but they are neither an existential threat nor an eternal savior.

Most Christians have ideological and partisan leanings. Our goal is not to stop partisan affiliation, but rather to be more thoughtful about our affiliation and to maintain loyalty to Christ over party. When partisan affiliation becomes unreflective alignment, our political identity subsumes our Christian identity and our political participation becomes bland. But if we maintain the primacy of our Christian identity, we can be salt and light for the world, including the world of partisan politics.

---

[22]Lord Acton, "Letter to Archbishop Mandell Creighton," April 5, 1887, https://history.hanover.edu/courses/excerpts/165acton.html.

[23]Stephen Tomkins, *William Wilberforce: A Biography* (Grand Rapids, MI: Eerdmans, 2007), 14.

BLAND PARTISANSHIP

There are two words that strike fear into the heart of every food-lover and chef: low sodium. We might resign ourselves to the low sodium soup or potato chips, but we know the flavor will disappoint us. My husband took up cooking several years ago, and as he developed his craft, he embraced a simple truth: salt makes things taste better. Once he became more liberal with salt, our kitchen took off. Brownies went from tolerable to delectable with a little sea salt on top. Enchilada casserole had more layers of flavor than layers of meat and tortillas. Salt was a revelation. In her cookbook *Salt, Fat, Acid, Heat*, Samin Nosrat explains, "salt has a greater impact on flavor than any other ingredient. Learn to use it well and your food will taste good. Salt's relationship to flavor is multidimensional: it has its own particular taste, and it enhances the flavor of other ingredients."[24] Ms. Nosrat knows what she's talking about. We don't crave bland food. Neither should we crave bland politics, in which the salt of Christ is so diluted as to be undetectable. Bland partisan alignment is a temptation Christians face when we are politically engaged; therefore me must recognize the risk and intentionally bring the salt.

Becoming bland. Affiliation with a political party has a tendency to devolve into unreflective partisan alignment, characterized by divisiveness, rancor, and even violence if we are not attentive to the forces that pull us toward bland partisanship. A symptom of bland partisanship is when identity becomes so intertwined with political party that party alignment compromises the Christian command to love our neighbor. If it seems like the two parties have become more sharply divided along partisan lines, it's because they have. And Christians have the opportunity to succumb to the bland division, or add much-needed salt.

If our partisanship is bland, we have aligned with our political party so much we fail to contribute anything unique or necessary. When we align with a political party, our brains rail against any incongruence between Christian convictions and political opinions. We might try to resolve this tension by justifying our political opinions on theological grounds. We start looking for biblical proof texts or dubious interpretations to prove that our politics align with our faith. But since political platforms and ideologies are not Christian doctrine, this often leads us to compromise

---

[24]Samin Nosrat, *Salt, Fat, Acid, Heat: Mastering the Elements of Good Cooking* (New York: Simon & Schuster, 2017), 21.

on some of our Christian convictions. If we do not feel tension between our faith and our partisanship, we are likely bland partisans who have bent our faith to align with our politics. If this paragraph brings to mind examples of how *other* Christians compromise or proof text, we should look for the plank in our own eyes first (Matthew 7:3-5).

When we affiliate with a political party, we face internal and external pressures to agree with the party on all aspects of ideology and policy. Political science research suggests we will uncritically align with our party on issues that are not our top priorities; our party alignment shapes our policy positions.[25] For example, if a Christian affiliates with the Democratic Party because of his position on health care, but he does not have an opinion about labor unions, he is likely to align with the party's stance on labor unions. In the 1970s and 1980s, a voter with liberal social attitudes was equally likely to vote for either major party, since the parties were not internally aligned on social ideology.[26] However, in the last few decades, the Democratic and Republican parties have become more ideologically differentiated, leaving little room for ideologically conservative Democrats or ideologically liberal Republicans. We face pressure to align with our party on both the economic and social axis. For example, if a Christian affiliates with the Republican Party because of her conservative social ideology, she is likely to bring her economic ideology into alignment with the party as well. Once we affiliate with a political party, as with any other identity-influencing organization, we face pressure to uncritically align with the party's entire policy agenda and ideology. Such conformity means compromising some convictions and becoming bland.

Powerful psychological forces work against our salty partisanship. Sociologists and psychologists use social identity theory to describe the powerful link between partisanship and identity. Joshua Zingher, a scholar of elections and political behavior, says Americans tend to view "their partisan identity as connected to a larger set of social identities such as race, ethnicity, gender, religion, sexual orientation, social class, and region," which has "led Americans to view the political world as divided into teams

---

[25]Thomas M. Carsey and Geoffrey C. Layman, "Changing Sides or Changing Minds? Party Identification and Policy Preferences in the American Electorate," *American Journal of Political Psychology* 50, no. 2 (April 2006): 464-77.

[26]Zingher, *Political Choice*, 146.

consisting of those on our side and those on the opposing side."[27] This kind of identification can become divisive and even deadly when the groups form around deeply held beliefs and ideologies.

When we affiliate with a group, like a political party, we do four things that forge group identity, according to moral psychologist Christena Cleveland: we gravitate toward similar others, we defend the group's positive identity, we distance ourselves from groups we deem lower status, and finally, we disparage other groups to elevate our own group.[28] When a political party becomes part of our identity, co-partisans become "us" and the other party becomes "them." Once we make us/them distinctions, we elevate our own in-group by denigrating and vilifying members of the other party, who we now view as adversaries.[29] As party becomes identity, the persistent us/them divide produces partisan rancor instead of civil disagreement.

Group-serving bias, also known as confirmation bias, contributes to bland partisanship as we uncritically take in information that promotes our party's positions. Studies have shown that Americans choose news sources whose coverage and commentary are more favorable to our preferred political party. Once we choose partisan information sources like websites, radio, and cable news, we are exposed to more similarly aligned sources and distanced from opposing views.[30] Conservative and liberal media outlets report and comment on the news so differently that people who are immersed in different media inhabit different worlds.[31] Additionally, studies have shown that social media heightens political polarization, while disengagement from social media reduces polarization, since algorithms seem to steep people more deeply into their partisan identities while limiting positive engagement with people of the opposing party.[32] The more group-serving bias one consumes, the less capable one

[27]Alan I. Abramowitz, "Peak Polarization?," in State of the Parties 2022, ed. John C. Green et al. (Lanham, MD: Rowman & Littlefield, 2022), 79.

[28]Christena Cleveland, Disunity in Christ: Uncovering the Hidden Forces That Keep Us Apart (Downers Grove, IL: InterVarsity Press, 2013), 84-85.

[29]Stacy G. Ulbig, Angry Politics: Partisan Hatred and Political Polarization Among College Students (Lawrence: University Press of Kansas, 2020) 36.

[30]Daniel Muise et al., "Quantifying Partisan News Diets in Web and TV Audiences," Science Advances 8, no. 28 (July 3, 2022), https://doi.org/10.1126/sciadv.abn0083.

[31]Muise et al., "Quantifying Partisan News Diets."

[32]Paul Barrett et al., "How Tech Platforms Fuel U.S. Political Polarization and What Government Can Do About It," Brookings, September 27, 2021, www.brookings.edu/blog/techtank/2021/09

is of salty self-examination and the easier it is to uncritically align with a party.

Once partisanship becomes identity and is reinforced by biased information sources, we become susceptible to stereotyping and dehumanizing our political "others." Christena Cleveland explains that the lack of interaction with outgroups leads to "inaccurate perceptions and metaperceptions [that] begin to take on lives of their own by overriding objective reality and distorting our interpretations and memories."[33] Partisan news and entertainment spill over into partisan friendships, workplaces, and churches. The polarization becomes more glaring because *we* don't want to risk being confused with *them,* so we emphasize differences and ignore commonalities across party lines, pushing liberals and conservatives alike toward more extreme positions.[34] This degree of polarization manifests in disparaging and dehumanizing comments, hatred, and even violence. Among Christians, it frequently looks like questioning the faith of brothers and sisters who affiliate with the other party.

Pastors see the impact of bland partisanship, and it is hurting churches. When asked about the impact of political division on their ability to lead their congregations, over half of pastors who had considered leaving the ministry in 2022 responded, "Christians are more loyal to their political views than their faith," according to a study by the Barna group.[35] We become bland partisans when we merge our ideological opinions and policy preferences with our party of choice, tie our identity to the party, and compromise the gospel for the sake of partisan coherence. This can happen without our realizing it, just as I do not realize how hot my space heater makes my office until I get a blast of cold (normal room temperature) air when I step into the hallway. We might not notice the slow changes in our friend groups, social media feeds, or policy opinions, and we might even become defensive when someone points them out to us.

Remaining bland. Once we have lost our saltiness, inertia drags us deeper into partisanship and our own pride resists correction. However, by remaining bland we do grievous damage to the mission and witness of

---

/27/how-tech-platforms-fuel-u-s-political-polarization-and-what-government-can-do-about-it/.

[33]Cleveland, *Disunity in Christ,* 57.

[34]Cleveland, *Disunity in Christ,* 68.

[35]Barna webinar, "Two Trends That Reshaped Ministry in 2022," 28:21 mark, accessed November 28, 2022, https://subsplash.com/demos/media/mi/+d9jcz53.

the church and also to our own souls. Several factors contribute to our remaining bland.

We remain bland by giving our elephants free rein. According to the social intuitionist model of human behavior, intuitions precede strategic reasoning. In other words, our gut comes first and our brain follows.[36] Intuition is like an elephant, and strategic reasoning is like a rider trying to steer the elephant. According to Jonathan Haidt, who studies social intuition, "within the first second of seeing, hearing, or meeting another person, the elephant has already begun to lean toward or away, and that lean influences what you think and do next. Intuitions come first."[37] When we have become bland by merging our identity with a partisan tribe, we are constantly making split-second decisions about whether people are with us or against us politically, then behaving toward them in a way that reinforces our intuition. Social intuition theory says there is little we can do to prevent the elephant from leaning one way or the other, but we do have control over recognizing what our elephant is doing and why, then intentionally steering it in another direction when necessary. To remain bland, all we have to do is remain blind and indifferent to the elephant's leanings.

Bland partisanship frequently goes beyond intuitive leaning to disagreement, hostility, and even visceral hate. If it seems to you like mistrust and hostility are increasingly characteristic of ordinary Americans, that's not just your perception; it is measurably true.[38] To measure hostility, political scientists use a "Feeling Thermometer" on which people rate their feelings toward various groups on a warmth-coldness scale. Democrats and Republicans have been growing more "cold" toward each other for the past thirty years.[39] More concerning, recent research finds a majority of both Democrats and Republicans attribute some actions of the opposing party to "'bad' internal character," and over 10 percent "have thoughts of a desire to get rid of or destroy" members of the opposing party, "to take action in order to take revenge" or "imagine a violent action against" them.[40] According to a survey conducted in February 2021 (the month after the January 6 attack on the US Capitol), 20 percent of Republicans

[36]Haidt, *Righteous Mind*, 61.
[37]Haidt, *Righteous Mind*, 69.
[38]Abramowitz, "Peak Polarization?," 93.
[39]Abramowitz, "Peak Polarization?," 88, Table 5.4.
[40]Ulbig, *Angry Politics*, 67-68.

and over 10 percent of Democrats expressed the belief that political violence is at least a little bit acceptable.[41] Perhaps most disturbing, "twelve percent of Republicans and 11 percent of Democrats said assassinations carried out by their party were at least 'a little bit' justified," the only measure on which Democrats and Republicans showed the same degree of radicalization.[42] The majority of people who imagine violence do not take action, but some do. Nearly half of Americans surveyed report having been insulted and 3 percent report having been physically attacked because of their politics.[43] For Christians, blandness can feel like self-righteousness when we identify an enemy and justify aggression as defense of our faith. The pull toward bland partisanship is pervasive and powerful. Becoming and remaining salty will require intentional and consistent effort.

SALTY PARTY PARTICIPATION

John Danforth (b. 1936) served as a Republican senator from Missouri from 1976 to 1995, and he is also ordained as an Episcopal priest. He made a salty move when he crossed party lines to prevent a Republican filibuster of the Violent Crime Control and Law Enforcement Act of 1994, a flagship piece of legislation for the Clinton White House, because the Republican substitute proposal would greatly expand use of the death penalty. According to Danforth, "I could not go along with the Republican strategy because I did not support the death penalty, and I agreed with some of the proposed social programs."[44] Sen. Danforth wrote of his Republican colleagues' reaction to his vote, "I became a pariah among Republicans. . . . I was at the end of my eighteen years in the Senate, at a time when I had hoped to be borne away by the warm feelings of people I had known so well, and I was getting the cold shoulder. Such is the pressure to stick with the party on defining issues."[45] Some Christians might disagree with Danforth's position on the death penalty or have problems with the 1994 Crime Bill, but regardless of political details, Danforth's action is an example of saltiness—and its potential cost. As salt in the world of politics, Christians ought to add a dimension of flavor that is lacking without us. The flavor

---

[41]Nathan P. Kalmoe and Lilliana Mason, *Radical American Partisanship* (Chicago: University of Chicago Press, 2022), 68.

[42]Kalmoe and Mason, *Radical American Partisanship*, 69.

[43]Kalmoe and Mason, *Radical American Partisanship*, 94.

[44]John Danforth, *Faith and Politics* (New York: Viking Press, 2006), 142.

[45]Danforth, *Faith and Politics*, 142, 143.

may be subtle or surprising, and it may not always be what others are looking for or what they would have chosen to add, but our salty participation makes politics better. Saltiness does not come naturally; we have to cultivate it.

Becoming salty. Salty party participation starts with Christian discipleship. We must begin with our faith, not with our political ideologies or policy positions. This is challenging because we already have political opinions, so we are subject to confirmation bias that reinforces those opinions. We become salty as we grow in Christlikeness and yield ourselves to the values of the Kingdom, which will inevitably conflict with the values of party or country. We also grow in the love of neighbor that enables us to disagree about Christian convictions and values, even within the body of Christ. Political ideologies present us with a lens through which to view reality, but as Christians we are called to view reality through the lens of God's redeeming work in the world, from creation to final restoration. Discipleship trains us to see the world the way the triune God sees it.

Because saltiness begins with discipleship and demonstrates love of neighbor, it rules out behavior that is merely intended to spice things up. We all know people who like to argue for argument's sake, to play devil's advocate, or even simply to see whether they can get people worked up over something. Such people tend to either lack the courage to express their convictions in a way that engenders respect, or they simply lack clear convictions. If the motive is to provoke anger or to "take down" or "own" someone, that is not salty citizenship.

Within the context of discipleship, we become salty as we examine party platforms, ideologies, and policies to determine where we can affiliate and where we need to add flavor. This can be overwhelming, as so many ideas and policies compete for our attention. We will be tempted to outsource our critical thinking to a political party or partisan faction. But our Christian discipleship can help us interpret the issues of the day and develop in us the humility to admit when we lack knowledge or understanding. For many Christians, saltiness begins at a point of disconnect between party and ideology. Many Christians find our faith leading us to conservatism in some areas and liberalism in others, which leaves Christians without an obvious party with which to align. That can actually work to our advantage, as the partisan division can make it clear that total alignment with a party is simply untenable. We are faced with a decision: differ with our party or sacrifice some Christian convictions for the sake of partisan alignment. In such circumstances, we can add salt to our party by expressing our disagreement, even as we continue to clarify our Christian convictions.

We become salty through critical thinking. Moral psychology shows that our brains save time and energy by taking mental shortcuts. We cannot think critically about every single idea or decision we encounter in a day, so our brains categorize information to allow us to jump to conclusions. When it comes to party politics, this leads us to adopt positions or align with ideologies without giving them much thought. Political messaging is an area that especially needs our critical thinking. Most of what we know about a party, its policies, and their impact comes to us through carefully crafted messaging from political professionals. The authors of *Compassion (&) Conviction* caution Christians, "the world is constantly bombarding us with well-researched, targeted messaging aimed at persuading, distracting, or enraging us in regard to cultural and political matters. Without a trained eye, it's hard to discern what motives and hidden agendas lie beneath the surface."[46] We need to train our eyes to recognize political messaging, to differentiate reportage from opinion, to ask what information is being excluded from partisan presentation, and to interpret the biases of various media outlets. We are bombarded by political messaging constantly, so investigating every claim is unrealistic. But it is possible and not that difficult to learn to recognize partisan bias and ask questions that can prevent us from uncritically accepting partisan spin. One simple way to evaluate partisan bias is to ask, *Who does this source want me to fear, and what does this source want me to be angry about?* When a political message triggers our fear or anger, that can signal us to question the bias and the accuracy of the message. We add salt to partisanship when we refuse to consume or spread fear and anger.

More likely than not, we start from a bland posture. We have been influenced by our upbringing, our environment, and political messaging so much that we may not even be aware of how bland we are. We may even have ourselves convinced that our preferred party is fully compatible with Christian faith and that Christians who disagree with our politics are not

---

[46]Justin Giboney et al., *Compassion (&) Conviction: The AND Campaign's Guide to Faithful Civic Engagement* (Downers Grove, IL: InterVarsity Press, 2020), 75.

genuine followers of Christ. We need to take intentional steps to become salty and to stay salty.

Staying salty. Staying salty requires sustained effort. The first and most important thing we must do to stay salty is abide in Christ by staying committed to Christ's body, the church, and by studying Scripture. But simply reading the Bible and going to church do not guarantee saltiness, since we tend to read the Bible through the lens of our own biases and self-sort into churches that agree with us politically. We can counteract these tendencies, though. We can study Scripture with people who see the world differently, whether in a Bible study with diverse people or by reading books and commentaries that represent a range of interpretive lenses. We can choose a church with salty leadership, where different political views are represented and respected. Staying salty also requires checking our own positions and rhetoric against the command to love God and neighbor. We can be honest with ourselves and others about whether love or anger motivate our political behavior. We can pray for the Holy Spirit to reveal to us ways we compromise our faith for partisan alignment, where fear and anger get the better of us, and where we contribute to division instead of shalom.

Staying salty requires us to revisit, revise, and re-evaluate our ideological and policy positions regularly. Research suggests "party revision occurs only under limited conditions," and such revision is much more likely to occur because the party's position shifted than because a person shifted their personal beliefs.[47] Since party platforms shift, we will need to revisit them to consider whether we can continue our affiliation in good conscience. We also re-evaluate our policy positions as we learn more about the intent and impact of legislation. We can evaluate our political views and stand firm in our Christian convictions to make sure we are not succumbing to uncritical partisan alignment.

One way to evaluate how our Christian convictions relate to partisanship is pointing out when the Overton window has shifted around us and doing our part to move that window in a direction that reflects love of neighbor. The Overton window, developed in the 1990s by Joseph Overton, is the range of what is considered politically acceptable and possible, versus what is extreme and unfeasible. From a Christian perspective,

[47]Paul Goren, "Party Identification and Core Political Principles," in *The American Political Party System*, 155-56.

there are some positions or perspectives that we should consider extreme, and others that are within an acceptable range.[48] When the Overton window shifts too far to the right or left, what should be extreme might move into the window of acceptable, or what had been acceptable might move out of the window. For example, the civil rights movement shifted the Overton window so that expressing racist ideas or using racial slurs moved out of the window into the extremities. In the last fifteen years or so, the Overton window has shifted in the opposite direction, through an increase in open expression of White supremacy, for example.[49] The comment threads on social media are a prime location for shifting the Overton window as language or ideas that were considered beyond the pale can become ordinary. One of the easiest ways for Christians to be salty in such an environment is to refuse to move when the Overton window opens to views that are harmful to the common good—not only views we disagree with, but views that cause harm and move society away from shalom. We are salty when we call attention to harmful shifts, refuse to participate in the normalization of damaging ideas or language, and help shift the window for the better.

Earlier in the chapter we met our elephant, which is our gut-level intuition. Now we can return to the rider, which is rational thought, and learn how the rider-elephant dynamic can change to help us remain salty. Jonathan Haidt's research on moral psychology has shown that the elephant is stronger than the rider, but that the rider is not powerless against the elephant. When we realize our elephant is leaning in a particular direction, our rider can be alert to where the elephant is going and correct course when necessary. We are only powerless when we fail to recognize that the elephant is the one setting the course.

If our identity is first and firmly located in Jesus Christ, then we should be able to participate in party politics without succumbing to the temptation to build our identity around partisanship. This requires intentionality and yielding our whole selves—even our psychological wiring—to the transformation of the Holy Spirit. We must intentionally cultivate

[48]Nathan J. Russell, "An Introduction to the Overton Window of Political Possibilities," The Mackinac Center for Public Policy, January 4, 2006, www.mackinac.org/7504.

[49]Ariel Worthy, "White Supremacy Propaganda & Activity at an All-Time High in Texas, U.S., ADL Reports," Houston Public Media, March 9, 2023, www.houstonpublicmedia.org/articles/civil-rights/2023/03/09/445781/white-supremacy-propaganda-activity-at-an-all-time-high-in-texas-u-s-adl-reports/.

dispositions that resist the social forces bending us toward uncritical partisan alignment. Jesus gives us our identity: "you are the salt of the earth." He also gives us a warning: if we fail to be salt, we are "thrown out and trampled under foot" (Matthew 5:13).

The next six chapters examine ten approaches to Christian political engagement. Each approach can become unreflective partisan alignment, if we let it. So we will keep the salt handy as we consider the approaches to Christian citizenship in the Kingdom and the country.

4

KEEPING THE KINGDOM
OUT OF THE COUNTRY

THREE SEPARATIST APPROACHES

"How am I supposed to vote, as a Christian, when I'm choosing between candidates who both seem incompatible with Christianity?"

My students frequently ask a question like this one during presidential election cycles, often as they prepare to vote for the first time. They feel the weight of their responsibility as citizens, the conviction of their Christian faith, and are confused by conflicting advice from various influencers. You can't vote for X and be a true Christian. No real Christian can support Y's policy. If you believe Z, you don't take the Bible seriously.

Such simple absolutes are not helpful or satisfying. Discipleship requires more of us than adopting an either-or mindset that allows us to outsource our critical thinking to our preferred party or pastor. Determining how to live out our dual citizenship is an act of responsible discipleship that requires our whole mind and heart. It is not an easy task, but neither is following Jesus.

Many Christians uncritically adopt one of three approaches to politics. Some passively disengage by choosing not to follow current events or be aware of local or national politics. Whether it is due to lack of time, lack of interest, frustration with the whole political process, or the desire to avoid conflict, many Christians opt for an "ignorance is bliss" approach. Other

Christians aim to enact their interpretation of biblical commands or principles through legislation. A third group of Christians try to keep their faith so private that it has no bearing on their political engagement, often because of their interpretation of church-state separation.

Each of these approaches is simple, and one does not have to peel away many layers to discover how thin and unsubstantial they are. These approaches avoid the question of how to live as dual citizens, rather than faithfully engaging it. Religion and politics can be such intimidating and controversial topics that their relationship can seem paralyzingly complicated, so we oversimplify. But surely Christian citizenship calls us to more than avoiding the question or adopting too-simple answers. Many Christians do not realize other, more faithful, options are available.

In the previous chapters, I outlined some important differences between the Kingdom of God and the United States. We examined the distinction between biblical Israel and America, and how the Bible can inform our political engagement. We also contrasted salty versus bland political participation, and looked at ways Christians participate in partisan politics. With these foundations in place, the next six chapters will introduce ten approaches to Christian political engagement, ranging from complete separation to complete conflation of Kingdom and country. We will evaluate these approaches in their historical and theological contexts and assess their impact on Christian mission and witness. Our exploration begins with three approaches to separatism.

Christian separatism emphasizes the importance of maintaining a clear distinction between the world and the church, where the world includes all that is not yet redeemed by Christ and the church includes believers who have professed Jesus as Lord. This definition has two parts: the world as unredeemed, and the church as an assembly of believers. Because the country is not and will not become the Kingdom of God, the separatist strives to keep the Kingdom out of the country. Christians have applied separatism in different ways and to varying degrees, as we will explore below. While all Christians in America have some engagement with politics, if only through being subject to the laws that politicians enact, Christians do not necessarily have to actively engage in the political process, whether by voting, holding office, serving in the military, or advocating for a policy agenda. In chapter two, we saw biblical examples of engaging with society instead of denying or withdrawing from it, which might set us up to dismiss separatist options from the outset. However, separatists can be active and faithful witnesses to the lordship of Jesus Christ, since separatism is not merely denial or escapism. This chapter explores three separatist approaches. The first two approaches are rooted in the Anabaptist theological tradition, and I will call them "radical isolation" and "prophetic witness." A third approach arises from evangelicalism, and I will call it "strategic withdrawal."

Anabaptist Separatism: Radical Isolation and Prophetic Witness

Anabaptist separatism is a model of political engagement that originated during the sixteenth-century Protestant Reformation. Early Anabaptists in Germany and Switzerland separated from society in general and government in particular, refusing to vote, hold public office, or serve in the military. European immigrants carried Anabaptist beliefs to the American colonies as early as the seventeenth century. Anabaptist separatists make an active choice to maintain the purity of their beliefs by remaining separated from civic life. One does not need to be Anabaptist to adopt this approach to politics.

It is worth noting that separatism is a choice in the United States. Christians in many parts of the world face persecution and oppression that necessitate separatism for the sake of survival, and we should be mindful of our sisters and brothers around the world who worship in isolation and risk death if they profess their faith publicly. Indeed, the experience of persecuted Christians around the world today is not much different from the experience of the Anabaptist Christians of the sixteenth century, who often separated themselves from society as much to keep themselves safe as to live their theological commitments.

Origins of Anabaptist separatism. After Emperor Constantine's conversion to Christianity in the early fourth century, Europe became Christianized. Over the course of several hundred years, its culture and political structures came to be intertwined with the beliefs and practices of the Western Catholic church. In Christianized Western Europe, also known as Christendom, to be Christian meant one was baptized as an infant, participated in the rites of the Church, accepted one's place in society as God's design, and conformed to the dominant culture. Separation of church and state as Americans conceive of it did not exist in concept or practice, and individuals did not choose whether to be Christian or what kind of Christian to be. One was born Christian the same way one was born French or English. Into this context of Christendom, Martin Luther and Ulrich Zwingli launched the Protestant Reformation by proclaiming *sola scriptura*, the principle that Scripture alone should be the source for Christian faith and practice.

Upon reading the Bible according to the *sola scriptura* principle, some Christians came to believe individual profession of faith in Christ was a prerequisite for Christian baptism, and thus one became a Christian through converting, not conforming. Felix Mantz (ca. 1498–1527), a founder of the Swiss Brethren, argued in 1524 that "Christ commanded to baptize those who had been taught, the apostles baptized none except those who had been taught of Christ, and nobody was baptized without external evidence and certain testimony or desire."[1] The radicals declared that only individuals who freely professed faith in Jesus Christ could rightfully receive baptism and call themselves Christian. This belief was an unprecedented departure from centuries of tradition in Christendom. The insistence upon individual believers as the only proper recipients of baptism gained the radicals the nickname "Anabaptist," meaning "rebaptizers," since their detractors accused them of baptizing again people who had already received the sacrament as infants. Like many pejoratives, Anabaptist stuck and mostly lost its negative connotation over time.

In addition to believer's baptism as a defining characteristic, the Anabaptists took seriously the biblical exhortation to personal and communal holiness. They heeded Paul's exhortation to the Corinthian church: "Therefore come out from them, and be separate from them, says the Lord, and touch nothing unclean; then I will welcome you, and I will be your father, and you shall be my sons and daughters, says the Lord Almighty" (2 Corinthians 6:17-18). To this end, the Schleitheim Confession of Faith (1527) called for radical separatism:

> We have been united concerning the separation that shall take place from the evil and the wickedness which the devil has planted in the world, simply in this; that we have no fellowship with them, and do not run with them in the confusion of their abominations. . . . To us, then, the commandment of the Lord is also obvious, whereby He orders us to be and to become

---

[1] "Mantz's Petition of Defense, Zurich (1524)," in *The European Reformations Sourcebook*, 2nd ed., ed. Carter Lindberg (New York: Wiley Blackwell, 2014), 125.

separated from the evil one, and thus He will be our God and we shall be His sons and daughters. . . . From all this we should learn that everything which has not been united with our God in Christ is nothing but an abomination which we should shun.[2]

The call to separatism required avoiding involvement with the state and with society, convictions Anabaptists learned from Scripture as well as from the negative example of several sixteenth-century apocalyptic fanatics.[3]

Anabaptist insistence that the majority of Christendom's people were abominable and their baptisms were invalid led to persecution and martyrdom at the hands of Catholics and Protestants alike. The Zurich City Council issued an order that "no one in our town, country, or domains, whether man, woman, or girl, shall baptize another; and if any one hereafter shall baptize another, he will be seized by our Lords and, according to the decree now set forth, will be drowned without mercy."[4] The Zurich Council sentenced Felix Mantz to execution by drowning in 1527. Meanwhile, in Austria, Michael Sattler (ca. 1490–1527) was convicted as a heretic and sentenced to be "delivered to the executioner, who shall lead him to the place of execution and cut out his tongue, then forge him fast to a wagon and thereon with red-hot tongs twice tear pieces from his body; and after he has been brought outside the gate, he shall be plied five times more in the same manner."[5] The palpable risks to life and limb reinforced the Anabaptists' commitment to separatism as both a theological conviction and a necessity for self-preservation. As Anabaptist communities formed and grew, they came to dot the landscape of rural Europe, outside the cities and just beyond the direct oversight of regional governments. In addition to emigrating to the American colonies, some Anabaptists traveled as far as Siberia or South America to maintain their separatism and safety.

Pacifism also became a central Anabaptist tenet that precluded participation in government and other aspects of civil society, especially the military. The Anabaptists rejected the idea that one could be coerced into

---

[2]John Howard Yoder, ed. and trans., *The Schleitheim Confession* (Scottdale, PA: Herald Press, 1977), 11-12.
[3]Bernard M. G. Reardon, *Religious Thought in the Reformation*, 2nd ed. (New York: Longman, 1995), 196.
[4]"The Council Orders Anabaptists to Be Drowned (1526)," in *The European Reformations Sourcebook*, 126.
[5]"The Trial and Martyrdom of Michael Sattler (1527)," in *The European Reformations Sourcebook*, 129.

Christian faith, which led them to reject other forms of coercion as well, including physical violence. Pilgram Marpeck (1495–1556), a sixteenth-century Anabaptist leader, wrote, "human coercion will destroy all who [support] a human, forcibly imposed faith and all who claim the Word of faith, but who trust and depend upon human protection and power; like Peter, they will be driven to a denial."[6] Consistent with their straight-forward reading of Scripture, Anabaptists understood Christ's commands to "turn the other cheek" and to "put away their swords" as binding instructions for all circumstances (Matthew 5:39 and 26:52). Moreover, self-defense was also unnecessary because our "life is hidden with Christ in God," and, "living is Christ, dying is gain" (Colossians 3:3 and Philippians 1:21). Refusal to serve in the military or otherwise wield the sword was a radical departure from social norms in a European society in which violence was simply a way of life.

Not only should Anabaptists not take up the sword themselves, but the state should not use coercion to promote or defend the church. Menno Simons (1496–1561), namesake of the Mennonite movement, argued that "Christ Jesus and His powerful Word and the Holy Spirit are the protectors and defenders of the church, and not, eternally not, the emperor, king, or any worldly potentate! The kingdom of the Spirit must be protected and defended by the sword of the Spirit, and not by the sword of the world."[7] Following Christ required the Christian to reject violence, whether to coerce others or to defend themselves. As contemporary Anabaptist Johann Christoph Arnold succinctly put it, "Christ forbids us to use force against others, but he clearly demands our readiness to suffer at the hands of others."[8] Thus, the various Anabaptist communities and movements had theological and practical reasons for isolating themselves from society and the government.

Separatism applied to politics in several more ways. First, Anabaptists opposed oath-taking on the basis of Jesus' instruction, "Let your word be 'Yes, Yes' or 'No, No'; anything more than this comes from the evil one" (Matthew 5:37). Since military service, holding political offices, and sometimes even citizenship required taking an oath, Anabaptists exempted

---

[6]Pilgram Marpeck, "Concerning the Lowliness of Christ," in *T&T Clark Reader in Political Theology*, ed. Elizabeth Philips et al. (London: T&T Clark, 2021), 339-40.

[7]Menno Simons, "Reply to Gellius Faber (1554)," in *The Believer and the Powers That Are*, ed. John T. Noonan Jr. (New York: Macmillan, 1987), 63.

[8]Johann Christoph Arnold, *Seeking Peace* (New York: Plume, 2000), 33.

themselves from such activities. Anabaptists also understood government as being of the world, and therefore inherently sinful and corrupt. The world's politics had no place among the holy people of God. Christendom's intertwining of the church with imperial power was at least partly to blame for its apparent abandonment of sound doctrine, so Anabaptists believed themselves to be restoring the true church from centuries of apostasy.

Most Anabaptist traditions in the United States today, including Amish, Mennonite, Hutterite, and Brethren, continue to embrace separatism and orient their communities around holiness in the midst of a sin-sick world, to varying degrees. This includes viewing politics as fundamentally at odds with the holiness of the church and embracing a pacifist ethic that is incompatible with the government's use of violence. Moreover, since the Kingdom of God is fundamentally different from the world, there is no practical or theological reason to attempt to bring the world into conformity with the Kingdom of God. This affirmation has led some Anabaptists to embrace radical isolation, while others adopt a posture of prophetic witness.

Separatism as radical isolation. My dad grew up near Amish country in Pennsylvania. His descriptions of horse-drawn buggies and men in plain dress harvesting crops come to mind when I buy meat and flowers from women in bonnets at my local farmers' market in Indiana. Although the Amish are not the only Anabaptist traditions to avoid civic and political engagement as much as possible, they are the most easily identifiable due to their distinctive dress, language, and culture. While it is a myth that the Amish are completely isolated from the outside world, they do not vote, hold public office, attend public schools, or otherwise participate in wider society except where unavoidable.[9] Amish, Hutterites, Mennonites, and other Anabaptist traditions are isolationist because they believe "the true church [is] an alternative community, distinct from larger society and not responsible for morally propping up the political order," though these traditions do not all practice isolation to the same degree or in the same ways.[10] Since the church is not responsible for society, and society is not the church, by definition, it is logical that some Anabaptist traditions avoid engaging with the political order. Their isolation serves as its own kind of testimony to the nature of the church in contrast to the world, but it is not necessarily concerned about whether the world heeds such testimony.

---

[9]Steven M. Nolt, *The Amish* (Baltimore: Johns Hopkins University, 2016), 4.
[10]Nolt, *The Amish,* 14.

Christians who are not members of radical isolationist religious communities are not likely to embrace this model of separatism for practical reasons. A close-knit community is necessary for creating a self-sustaining alternative society. Christians who are more integrated into society than the isolationists may hold similar theological convictions about the relationship between the church and society, but without the religious and cultural scaffolding of a self-sustaining community, radical isolation is simply not tenable or desirable for most people. Therefore, a prophetic witness approach may be more appealing for Christians who hold an Anabaptist worldview, but who do not seek radical isolation from society.

Separatism as prophetic witness. The prophetic witness model of separatism holds several realities in tension: the Kingdom of God is fundamentally incompatible with the world, and yet the citizens of the Kingdom are called to be *in* the world for the sake of Christian witness *to* the world. The prophetic witness model builds on an Anabaptist vision of the relationship between church and society, but turns outward to bear public witness to the Kingdom of God. Individuals or churches need not be Anabaptist to espouse this aspect of Anabaptist belief and practice, therefore separatism in this case may be more theological than physical. As John Howard Yoder (1927–1997), a leading Mennonite theologian, put it, "the church's responsibility in and for the world is first and always to be the church."[11] Likewise, ethicist Stanley Hauerwas (b. 1940) and practical theologian Will Willimon (b. 1946) explain in their book *Resident Aliens*, "this church knows that its most credible form of witness (and the most 'effective' thing it can do for the world) is the actual creation of a living, breathing, visible community of faith. . . . The overriding political task of the church is to be the community of the cross."[12] The church cannot and should not attempt to transform the world into the Kingdom of God, but rather should *be* the church in such a way that it causes "the world to strike hard against something which is an alternative to what the world offers."[13] God's Kingdom will come, but it will come eschatologically through Jesus, not temporally through political revolution.

---

[11] John Howard Yoder, "The Otherness of the Church," in *Royal Priesthood: Essays Ecclesiological and Ecumenical*, ed. Michael G. Cartwright (Scottdale, PA: Heral Press, 1998), 61.

[12] Stanley Hauerwas and William H. Willimon, *Resident Aliens*, 25th anniversary ed. (Nashville: Abingdon Press, 2014), 47.

[13] Hauerwas and Willimon, *Resident Aliens*, 94.

Nonviolence is a central tenet of the prophetic witness model. For Yoder and other Anabaptist ethicists and political theorists, the commitment to follow Jesus' example of nonviolence shapes all other aspects of political engagement. Government is coercive by its very nature in that it must encourage obedience to the law and discourage lawbreaking, which it often does through violence or the threat of violence. While the government's coercive power is necessary for maintaining order in society, it is at odds with the Kingdom of God, which looks to Jesus for the example of godly conduct. Jesus had multiple opportunities to seize power and force compliance with his ethic, as Yoder notes, and each time "Jesus sees this option as a real temptation," but then rejects it.[14] Jesus faced "the temptation to exercise social responsibility, in the interest of justified revolution, through the use of available violent methods," and in refusing those methods he established the Christian ethic of nonviolence.[15]

In this view, Christians cannot follow Jesus faithfully while also directly contributing to political systems that rely on violence or threats of violence. For Yoder, Hauerwas, and like-minded Christians, Anabaptist or not, the temptation to seize or retain power on the world's terms must be resisted at all costs. When the church succumbs to the temptation Jesus resisted, especially the temptation to violent coercion, the church fails to be the church and trades its witness for "all sorts of moral compromises."[16] While radical isolation is one possible way to refuse to participate in the world's violence, prophetic witness is an option for Christians who cannot reconcile isolation with the mission of the church to the world.

Defining the church as a voluntary gathering of believers is another core tenet of the Anabaptist tradition that influences its prophetic witness. "Christians are not naturally *born*. . . . Christians are intentionally *made*," explain Hauerwas and Willimon.[17] Jesus, writes Yoder, calls the church to "an ethic marked by the cross, a cross identified as the punishment of a man who threatens society by creating a new kind of community leading a radically new kind of life."[18] Though this new kind of spiritual community is set apart, it does not extricate itself from the circumstances in which it exists. Rather, the "creation of an alternative social group" has a

---

[14]John Howard Yoder, *The Politics of Jesus* (Grand Rapids, MI: Eerdmans, 1994), 57.
[15]Yoder, *Politics of Jesus*, 98.
[16]Hauerwas and Willimon, *Resident Aliens*, 27.
[17]Hauerwas and Willimon, *Resident Aliens*, 19. Italics in original.
[18]Yoder, *Politics of Jesus*, 63.

"powerful (sometimes conservative, sometimes revolutionary) impact on society," following the model of Jesus, whose "particular way of rejecting the sword and at the same time condemning those who wielded it *was* politically relevant," so much so that Pilate had him executed because he was a political threat.[19]

The existence of the church *as church* is itself political, even threatening, because it stands in stark contrast to the political structures of the world and unmasks them as perversions of God's design. For this reason, Hauerwas and Willimon say, "the church need not feel caught between . . . whether to be in or out of the world, politically responsible or introspectively irresponsible. The church is not out of the world. There is no other place for the church to be than [in the world]."[20] The church need not enact political revolution, whether through violence or vote, because, as Hendrik Berkhof writes, "the very presence of the church in a world ruled by the Powers is a superlatively positive and aggressive fact."[21] The church's mission is simply to be the church.

Not only does the church not actively use or pursue political power, as Yoder says, "the church concentrates on not being seduced by [the powers]."[22] The outcome of political seduction is what Yoder called "Constantinianism," referring to "the perennial temptation to shift attention away from the task of building up the particular polis of the church in favor of constructing an ideal polis at some supposedly wider level."[23] The Constantinian believes that Christians should "ally ourselves with the powers that surround us as our way of participating in the creating of a society worthy of humankind."[24]

Progressive and conservative Christians are equally susceptible to the Constantinian temptation, although they might ally with "the powers" around different visions of the ideal society. Both conservative and progressive churches, says Hauerwas, "have thought their primary religious duty to the state was and is to provide support and justification for the state that guarantees freedom of religion," with the result that "believer and

---

[19]Yoder, *Politics of Jesus*, 111. Italics in original.

[20]Hauerwas and Willimon, *Resident Aliens*, 43.

[21]Hendrik Berkhof, quoted in Yoder, *Politics of Jesus*, 151.

[22]Yoder, *Politics of Jesus*, 153.

[23]Alain Epp Weaver, "After Politics: John Howard Yoder, Body Politics, and the Witnessing Church," *The Review of Politics* 61, no. 4 (October 1999): 637-73.

[24]John Howard Yoder, "Constantinianism Old and New," in *Royal Priesthood: Essays Ecclesiological and Ecumenical*, ed. Michael G. Cartwright (Scottsdale, PA: Herald Press, 1998), 198.

nonbeliever alike soon begin to think what matters is not whether our convictions are true but whether they are functional."[25] This Constantinian temptation must be resisted if the church is to be the church in and for the world. In an increasingly secular United States, "the decline of the old Constantinian synthesis between the church and the world means that we American Christians are at last free to be faithful in a way that makes being a Christian today an exciting adventure," write Hauerwas and Willimon.[26] Because the church is confident in the eschatological victory of Jesus Christ, she is set free from trying to bring about contemporary political victory through violence or coercion.

The church's witness becomes intentionally prophetic, not only passively so, when it selectively engages civic life in nonpartisan and noncoercive ways. The temptation to power entices Christians to take hold of society and transform it, but Hauerwas explains, "following a crucified Lord entails embodying a politics that cannot resort to coercion and violence; it is a politics of persuasion all the way down. It is a tiring business that is slow and time-consuming, but then we, that is, Christians, believe that by redeeming time Christ has given us all the time we need to pursue peace."[27] Thus, a Christian might participate in a sit-in or a boycott, "not to coerce the 'adversary' but to communicate to him, to 'get through to him,' to bring to his attention moral dimensions of his behavior which he had not recognized . . . to point people's awareness to moral issues."[28] Whether such a witness is effective, in the sense of changing minds or policies, is beside the point. Christians are politically faithful inasmuch as they live according to the ethic of the body of Christ, come what may.

The question of how and whether to engage with specific political actions or issues will depend upon the details of the circumstances and our understanding of the church's relationship with society. Yoder could conceive the possibility of a Christian voting or even holding public office without violating the Christian prophetic witness of nonviolence, although he saw this as an ad hoc possibility, rather than a general axiom of Christian political

---

[25]Stanley Hauerwas, *After Christendom* (Nashville: Abingdon, 1999), 70-71.

[26]Hauerwas and Willimon, *Resident Aliens*, 18.

[27]Stanley Hauerwas, "Church Matters: On Faith and Politics," in *Approaching the End: Eschatological Reflections on Church, Politics, and Life* (Grand Rapids, MI: Eerdmans, 2013), 82.

[28]John Howard Yoder, "The Racial Revolution in Theological Perspective," in *For the Nations: Essays Evangelical and Public* (Eugene, OR: Wipf and Stock, 2002), 118-19.

engagement.[29] Can we vote for the sake of ensuring that competent persons are placed in positions of authority? For Yoder, the answer was maybe. But in the Anabaptist prophetic witness approach, Christians cannot vote with the idea that by doing so we are transforming the world into the church or seeking the power to coerce our neighbors to yield to a Christian ethic.

Application of Anabaptist separatism. In 2006, Charles Roberts opened fire on a schoolhouse in an Amish community in Nickel Mines, Pennsylvania, killing five girls, then himself. Afterward, the Amish community shocked the world by extending forgiveness to the murderer. Some even attended his burial, consoled his grieving mother, and donated money to support his widow and children.

Sociologist Donald Kraybill, author of a book about this event, said:

> I think the most powerful demonstration of the depth of Amish forgiveness was when members of the Amish community went to the killer's burial service at the cemetery . . . Several families, Amish families who had buried their own daughters just the day before, were in attendance and they hugged the widow, and hugged other members of the killer's family.[30]

This was an incomprehensible act for people outside the Amish community, and in that disconnect between the Amish commitment to forgiveness and society's ethic of retribution, the church bore witness to its unique identity. By living its theological commitments in public, the Amish community testified to the failures of the world and the promise of the world to come. Christians don't need a horrific act of violence to practice forgiveness or to reveal the shortcomings of society. Christians can bear prophetic witness to the failure of vengeance, violence, and coercion through simple acts of daily forgiveness and nonviolent peacekeeping.

The Bruderhof Community, founded in Germany in 1920, is one contemporary example of a separatist model of political engagement. The Bruderhof's website says, "we refuse to wield governmental power by serving in high office or in any position such as judge or juror that is vested with power over the life, liberty, or civil rights of another." This does not mean the Bruderhof is indifferent to government, because "at its best, the state represents a relative order of justice in the present sinful world."

---

[29]Weaver, "After Politics," 27.

[30]Joseph Shapiro, "Amish Forgive School Shooter, Struggle with Grief," *All Things Considered*, NPR, accessed October 25, 2022, www.npr.org/2007/10/02/14900930/amish-forgive-school -shooter-struggle-with-grief.

The church's role in relation to the government is to "witness to the state, serving as its conscience, helping it to distinguish good from evil, and reminding it not to overstep the bounds of its God-appointed authority."[31] The residents of the several dozen Bruderhof communities around the world share in common "all property, earnings, and inheritances" and "agree to work wherever [they] are needed, regardless of their preferences or prior training."[32] They understand this way of life as separated from the world for the sake of bearing witness to the gospel as it is reflected in their way of life. While the Bruderhof tends toward isolation, it also welcomes temporary guests to learn its way of life and carry its prophetic witness into the world.

The Simple Way community in Philadelphia is another example of prophetic separatism. This community began in the mid-1990s as a protest when the Catholic diocese of Philadelphia ordered homeless families to vacate an abandoned church building in which they had taken up residence. Local students joined the protest, then some of them pooled their money to purchase a property on which they established an intentional Christian community that became a flagship for the New Monasticism movement.

Regarding the community's purpose and posture toward politics, Shane Claiborne (b. 1975), one of its founders, wrote, "the church is a people called out of the world to embody a social alternative that the world cannot know on its own terms. We are not simply asking the government to be what God has commissioned the church to be . . . The church is not simply suggesting political alternatives. The church is embodying one."[33] The Simple Way and similar communities are often located in urban contexts, and are therefore distinct while being deeply engaged in the world. Some participants in The Simple Way would take an Anabaptist approach to separating from politics, while others would see voting or other political participation as necessary to their mission, but they share the understanding that the church's place in the political world is prophetic, not Constantinian.

One need not be Amish or Anabaptist to embrace the tenets of separatism, especially in its prophetic witness iteration. Nor must one live in

[31]The Bruderhof, "Our Calling," accessed October 31, 2022, www.bruderhof.com/foundations/our-calling#the-way-of-peace.

[32]The Bruderhof, "Life in Community," accessed October 31, 2022, www.bruderhof.com/life-in-community.

[33]Shane Claiborne, *Jesus for President* (Grand Rapids, MI: Zondervan, 2008), 228.

a distinctive community like the Bruderhof or the Simple Way. Many Christians live in cities and suburbs, attend churches of any branch of Christianity, earn a living in their typical jobs, and are not physically separate in any obvious way. Yet they embrace a prophetic witness posture with regard to the relationship between the Kingdom of God and the country, and therefore are reticent to engage directly with electoral politics or the military. This approach is salty, as it adds a missing dimension to a country frequently marked by Christians grasping for influence or hoping to blend in.

EVANGELICAL SEPARATISM: STRATEGIC WITHDRAWAL

Strategic withdrawal calls upon Christians to carefully assess our engagement with politics and public institutions, then strategically withdraw our participation whenever engagement with civic life seems futile or compromises our convictions. It is an evangelical approach because it arises out of the history, theology, and culture of American evangelicalism, but not all evangelicals are separatists and not all who strategically withdraw are evangelical. *Evangelical* is a broad and blurry term these days, but in the context of strategic withdrawal it primarily refers to Protestant Christians who are theologically, socially, and politically conservative. We will encounter several other branches and definitions of evangelicalism in later chapters.

Strategic withdrawal begins with the recognition that culture plays an influential role in forming our moral and religious convictions. Because American cultural values are frequently at odds with Christian values, some Christians strategically withdraw from public life by not participating in electoral politics or attending public schools. This withdrawal does not necessarily rule out attempting to influence public policy; however, this engagement is often limited to moral or educational causes. Evangelical separatism may look similar to isolationist separatism; however, it differs in its theological and historical basis and its degree of isolation. Evangelical separatists are more likely to live differently within society than to isolate from society. Evangelical separatism can be called strategic withdrawal because it is an intentional movement away from certain aspects of the wider culture, often including political action.

Origins of evangelical separatism. Strategic withdrawal has roots in the Puritans of sixteenth- and seventeenth-century England. In the wake of the Protestant Reformation, some English Protestants lobbied Queen Elizabeth, then her successor King James, to "purify" the Church of England from all vestiges of Catholicism, thereby earning the pejorative moniker, Puritans. Some of the Puritans eventually chose a separatist path, which led them to the Netherlands, then from there to New England, where they established colonies patterned on their Christian ideal. We will meet the Puritans again in chapter seven, since their influence spread in multiple directions. The Puritan model of societal formation has inspired Christians whenever America's laws or culture have become detached from conservative Christian values. Strategic withdrawal appears to be cyclical in American history, arising from time to time when the sociocultural context exerts sufficient pressure to motivate some Christians to step back from participation in American public life. Such was the case for some evangelicals in the 1920s to 1960s, when they found themselves theologically and culturally displaced from the center of American society.

One theological motivation for strategic withdrawal in the early twentieth century was evangelicals' embrace of premillennial dispensationalism and biblical inerrancy. Premillennialism is an interpretation of eschatology that anticipates the return of Jesus Christ and the institution of his thousand-year (millennial) reign, with strong emphasis on interpreting the signs of the times to predict Christ's return. John Nelson Darby popularized premillennialism in the early nineteenth century, and it slowly gained popularity in the United States after the Civil War, until evangelicals adopted it on a larger scale in the 1920s.[34]

The stream of premillennialism that became influential among evangelicals was apocalyptic and dispensational. This version of premillennialism believed the world would only get worse as violence, poverty, immorality, and other ills heat to a rolling boil, until Christ returns to rapture the church and judge the world. Evangelicals had been deeply engaged with political and social reform throughout the nineteenth century, as we will see in chapter six. But as historian Randall Balmer explains, premillennial eschatology "relieved evangelicals of the obligations to labor for the amelioration of social ills. Evangelicals increasingly stood in judgment of culture and awaited its destruction, which would follow their

---

[34]George M. Marsden, "The Rise of Fundamentalism," in *Turning Points in the History of American Evangelicalism*, ed. Heath W. Carter and Laura Rominger Porter (Grand Rapids, MI: Eerdmans, 2017), 138.

translation into heaven."[35] Evangelicals largely withdrew from political and social efforts to improve the world, because they came to view such efforts as futile and as possibly delaying Christ's return.

Displacement of evangelicals from mainstream American culture was also a powerful motivation for evangelical withdrawal. In the early 1920s, evangelicals found their moral commitments to be increasingly at odds with the wider culture. The success of the temperance movement largely backfired when alcohol trafficking proliferated. Holiness convictions against dancing, drinking, and gambling faced ridicule during the Jazz Age. A culture that had once taken its cues from the evangelical majority was now seeing those same evangelicals as behind the times.

Darwinian evolution became a lightning rod issue, as it challenged the literal reading of Scripture and, evangelicals feared, threatened the moral foundations of society. After all, if humans were merely evolved primates, then how could humans be said to bear the image of God or to have moral responsibility? Evangelicals launched antievolution campaigns in which they warned against humanity's inevitable descent into moral relativity and atheism if they rejected a literal reading of the biblical account of creation. Presbyterian and revivalist evangelicals became known as fundamentalists when they united to promote fundamental Christian beliefs, including the inerrancy of the Bible and a literalist reading of Genesis.[36]

The antievolution movement peaked with the 1925 trial of John Scopes in Dayton, Tennessee. During the trial, in which John Scopes was found guilty of teaching Darwinian evolution in violation of Tennessee law, *Baltimore Sun* reporter H. L. Mencken (1880–1956) portrayed the people of Dayton and the American south as "poor white trash" who lived under "impudent and ignorant sacerdotal tyranny" and whose once-noble culture had been "broken down, alas, by the hot rages of Puritanism."[37] The negative stereotypes stuck, and the play *Inherit the Wind* (1955) and its 1960 film adaptation solidified the image of fundamentalist Christians as "country hicks out of touch with the modern world."[38]

---

[35]Randall Balmer, *Mine Eyes Have Seen the Glory: A Journey into the Evangelical Subculture in America* (New York: Oxford University Press, 1989), 36.

[36]Peter J. Bowler, *Monkey Trials and Gorilla Sermons* (Cambridge, MA: Harvard University Press, 2007), 175-84.

[37]D. G. Hart, *Damning Words: The Life and Religious Times of H. L. Mencken* (Grand Rapids, MI: Eerdmans, 2016), 135.

[38]Bowler, *Monkey Trials*, 185.

Fundamentalists fortified themselves against the ridicule they experienced and increasingly thought of themselves as "those who were ready to stand up for the fundamental truths of the Bible without compromise," explains historian George Marsden.[39] For fundamentalists, withdrawal seemed the best option for preserving Christian culture and values in the face of a hostile world. They formed a subculture complete with publications, schools, music, and churches that would allow them to limit engagement with the wider society. Some chose to homeschool and form Bible institutes as alternatives to mainstream education. They largely dismissed politics as irredeemably corrupt and anti-Christian, and therefore saw political activity as futile at best, damaging to Christian values at worst.

Having moved away from social and political action, explains historian Wes Markofski, "conservative Protestants refocused their energies on evangelism—preaching the gospel of personal salvation from sin and God's judgment through faith in Jesus Christ."[40] *Fundamentalist* and *evangelical* were mostly interchangeable terms until Harold Ockenga founded the National Association of Evangelicals in 1942 "as a fresh voice for biblical, Christ-centered faith that was meant to be a 'middle way' between the fundamentalist American Council of Christian Churches and the progressive Federal Council of Churches."[41] While not all fundamentalist evangelicals withdrew to the same degree or in the same ways, evangelicals would not emerge as a significant voting bloc until the mid-1970s.

Separatism as strategic withdrawal. Some evangelicals exerted significant influence on American politics throughout the twentieth century, especially through anti-Communism.[42] However, political engagement did not characterize fundamentalist or evangelical Christians broadly. Evangelicals began to emerge from withdrawal to advocate against federal interference in racially segregated private schools in the 1960s, then against the Supreme Court's 1973 decision to legalize abortion in *Roe v. Wade*.[43]

---

[39]Marsden, "Rise of Fundamentalism," 148.

[40]Wes Markofski, *New Monasticism and the Transformation of American Evangelicalism* (Oxford: Oxford University Press, 2015), 43.

[41]National Association of Evangelicals, "Our History," accessed May 30, 2023, www.nae.org /history/.

[42]See Daniel K. Williams, *God's Own Party: The Making of the Christian Right* (New York: Oxford University Press, 2010), chapters 1-2 on evangelical political engagement in the early twentieth century.

[43]Randall Balmer, *Evangelicalism in America* (Waco, TX: Baylor University Press, 2016), chapter 8.

The 1980s and 1990s witnessed a remarkable increase in evangelical political engagement, fueled by a loose confraternity of conservative evangelicals known as the religious right or the Christian right. We'll examine
the history of the Christian right in more detail in chapter seven.

It is apparent that American social mores are increasingly out of step
with evangelicalism.[44] The Supreme Court's 2015 decision in *Obergefell v.
Hodges* in favor of same-sex marriage reignited contention among evangelicals. When the Supreme Court overturned *Roe v. Wade* in June 2022,
the public reaction showed that evangelical opposition to legal abortion is
broadly unpopular.[45] Evangelicals had long taken for granted a basic
agreement between evangelical values and US law. As American policy
and culture shift, some evangelicals do not see a legislative path to bringing
the United States into alignment with their convictions. Some recent evangelicals also saw Donald Trump's legal and moral troubles as evidence that
national politics are a lost cause. In light of this situation, some evangelicals call for a strategic withdrawal of Christians from various areas of
public life.

One version of this strategic withdrawal is what Rod Dreher, a politically and theologically conservative journalist, calls *The Benedict Option*,
in his 2017 book by that title. Dreher advocates for "a radical new way of
doing politics, a hands-on localism" as "the best way forward for Orthodox
Christians seeking practical and effective engagement in public life without
losing our integrity, and indeed our humanity."[46] Dreher took his title
from philosopher Alasdair MacIntyre's (b. 1929) *After Virtue*, in which he
called for "the construction of local forms of community within which
civility and the intellectual and moral life can be sustained through the

---

[44]For example: Gabriel Borelli, "About Six-in-Ten Americans Say Legalization of Same-Sex Marriage
Is Good for Society," Pew Research Center, November 15, 2022, www.pewresearch.org/short
-reads/2022/11/15/about-six-in-ten-americans-say-legalization-of-same-sex-marriage-is-good-for
-society/; Hannah Hartig, "About Six-in-Ten Americans Say Abortion Should Be Legal in All or
Most Cases," Pew Research Center, June 13, 2022, www.pewresearch.org/short-reads/2022/06/13
/about-six-in-ten-americans-say-abortion-should-be-legal-in-all-or-most-cases-2/; Andrew
Chung and Lawrence Hurley, "Most Americans Oppose Businesses Refusing to Serve Gay People:
Reuters/Ipsos Poll," Reuters, June 4, 2018, www.reuters.com/article/us-usa-court-baker-poll
/most-americans-oppose-businesses-refusing-to-serve-gay-people-reuters-ipsos-poll-idUSKCN
1J02WN.

[45]Pew Research Center, "Majority of Public Disapproves of Supreme Court's Decision to Overturn
Roe v. Wade," July 6, 2022, www.pewresearch.org/politics/2022/07/06/majority-of-public
-disapproves-of-supreme-courts-decision-to-overturn-roe-v-wade/.

[46]Rod Dreher, *The Benedict Option* (New York: Sentinel, 2018), 78.

new dark ages which are already upon us. . . . We are waiting not for a Godot, but for another—doubtless very different—St. Benedict."[47]

In *The Benedict Option*, a *New York Times* bestseller, Dreher laments that "conservative Christians, once comfortably established in the Republican Party, are politically homeless," and cautions, "if conservative church leaders aren't extraordinarily careful in how they manage their public relationship to the Trump administration, anti-Trump blowback will do severe damage to the church's reputation."[48] Dreher, who converted from Catholicism to Eastern Orthodoxy in 2016, and others like him call for a strategic withdrawal from politics, because "no administration in Washington, no matter how ostensibly pro-Christian, is capable of stopping cultural trends toward desacralization and fragmentation that have been building for centuries."[49] This withdrawal is for the sake of protecting the church's space to do "the work of charity, culture building, and conversion," and it is strategic because "Christians cannot afford to vacate the public square entirely."[50]

To this end, the primary arena for strategic entry into politics, according to Dreher, is at "the state and local level, engaging lawmakers with personal letters . . . and face-to-face meetings," in order to "secure and expand the space within which we can be ourselves and build our own institutions."[51] Political action and advocacy are strategically focused on protecting religious liberty and maintaining the operational independence of Christian churches and institutions.

A key aspect of strategic withdrawal is the formation of communities where Christians can live out their moral convictions and limit the impact of society's increasing secularization. Dreher encourages Christians to

---

[47]Alasdair MacIntyre, *After Virtue*, 2nd ed. (Notre Dame, IN: University of Notre Dame Press, 1984), 263. MacIntyre himself critiqued Dreher's book, saying, "when I said we need a new St. Benedict, I was suggesting we need a new kind of engagement with the social order, not any kind of withdrawal from it. I should add by the way it's also the case that by and large the people who have put forward this [the Benedict Movement] appear to have conservative views politically, and I'm well known for holding that conservatism and liberalism are mirror images of each other; one should have nothing to do with either of them. I mean, the moment you think of yourself as a liberal or a conservative you're done for." Alasdair MacIntyre, "Common Goods, Frequent Evils," The Common Good as Common Project Conference, Nanovic Institute for European Studies at Notre Dame, March 27, 2017, www.youtube.com/watch?v=9nx0Kvb5U04&t=4088s.

[48]Dreher, *Benedict Option*, 80, 81.

[49]Dreher, *Benedict Option*, 81.

[50]Dreher, *Benedict Option*, 82.

[51]Dreher, *Benedict Option*, 87, 86.

form self-sustaining communities to the degree possible, and offers practical steps that include starting a Christian business that employs Christians, patronizing church member businesses, choosing careers that are less likely to place one in morally compromising situations (e.g., skilled trades), and disconnecting from television, social media, and video games.[52] The goal of Benedict Option communities is to create the environment in which people can be formed in Christian beliefs and virtues, what Dreher calls "a thick Christian culture," in contrast to the malformation the world has to offer.[53] Homeschool or parochial schools are essential to this project, as are proximity to the local church and a close-knit social network of like-minded people.

One example of a strategically withdrawn community is Alleluia Community in Augusta, Georgia. Alleluia Community began in the 1970s when a group of families formed a covenant community to share a common life of prayer, worship, and service. The community organizes its life to help its members "advance in sanctity." As one of the community's leaders describes it, "those we live with 'rub against us' and show us our weaknesses and imperfections, but they can also build us up with their strengths. A community also makes it possible to evangelize, which is an integral part of a Christian life."[54] Not everyone who strategically withdraws will do so in community, but without intentional community, strategic withdrawal could easily become apathetic disengagement.

The outworking of strategic withdrawal could look quite similar to the prophetic witness or even isolationist approach to separatism. The key difference is the underlying theology of the relationship between the church and the government. Anabaptist separatism conceives of the church as essentially incompatible with the world, and it therefore does not use the tools of government to bring the church's influence to bear upon society. Evangelical separatism, on the other hand, conceptualizes the church as being edged out of its rightful place at the center of society, including an influential role in government. Where Yoder and Hauerwas see Christendom as a theological aberration, Dreher sees it, or at least some version of it, as an ideal, as evidenced by his 2021 move to Hungary, where he is a

[52] Rod Dreher, interview with Matthew Lee Anderson et al., "'The Benedict Option' with Rod Dreher," *Mere Fidelity*, podcast audio, April 26, 2017, https://merefidelity.com/podcast/27653/.
[53] Dreher, *Benedict Option*, 121.
[54] "Interview with the Alleluia Community," Happy Are You Poor, accessed November 4, 2022, https://happyareyoupoor.com/podcast/interview-with-the-alleluia-community/.

strong supporter of Prime Minister Viktor Orbán's efforts to form an il-liberal Christian democracy.[55] Thus, evangelicals and like-minded Christians who strategically withdraw are also likely to strategically engage when the political circumstances appear favorable to their success.

EVALUATION OF SEPARATIST APPROACHES

The Anabaptist and evangelical approaches to separatism have their strongest appeals in their ability to clearly differentiate between the church and the world, and their commitment to Christian formation as an essential function of the church. We are all being discipled by something, transformed by the various influences with which we engage. The separatist models recognize that engagement with civic life and American culture has strong potential to become malformative. Philosopher James K. A. Smith writes that even seemingly insignificant daily routines, "are actually thick formative practices that over time embed in us desires for a particular vision of the good life," and society's vision of the good life often proves "antithetical to being a disciple of Jesus."[56] Americans have neither a shared faith nor a shared definition of the good, contributing to a culture of moral relativity and egoistic hedonism. As Alasdair MacIntyre asserted, "in a society where there is no longer a shared conception of the community's good as specified by the good for man, there can no longer either be any very substantial concept of what it is to contribute more or less to the achievement of that good."[57]

Recognizing this formative role of politics can lead some Christians toward separatism for the sake of being formed by Christian community and Scripture instead. This kind of alternative formation happens best in community, which is why so many of the contemporary examples in this chapter are from Christian intentional communities that are influenced by monasticism. Christian formation is whole life formation, and political life should not be segmented out as if it as somehow untouched by one's faith. Discipleship in these contexts has the potential to be more holistic and effective, as the church sees the formation the world offers as inherently falling short of Christian discipleship.

---

[55]Annika Brockschmidt, "The 'Dreher Affair' Highlights the Right's International Networks," Religion Dispatches, February 23, 2023, https://religiondispatches.org/the-dreher-affair-highlights -the-rights-international-networks/.

[56]James K. A. Smith, *Desiring the Kingdom: Worship, Worldview, and Cultural Formation* (Grand Rapids, MI: Baker Academic, 2009), 83-84.

[57]MacIntyre, *After Virtue*, 232.

One considerable drawback of separatism is that it risks neglecting present human needs that public policy can address. While there are limits to what the government can do, public policies can cause real harm or accomplish real good in people's lives. Policies that affect social welfare programs, city zoning, law enforcement, public education, health care, and more often have a disproportionate impact on economically depressed communities and people of color. Disengagement is more possible for those who do not feel their basic needs or safety threatened by public policy, or who have communal safety nets to soften the impact. Evangelical separatists may be especially susceptible to an insularity that fosters "narrowness, prejudice and moral arrogance," as David Brooks wrote in his review of *The Benedict Option*.[58] Therefore, separatism runs of the risk of actual or perceived disregard for the needs of our neighbors, which can reflect negatively on the church's witness.

Faithfully Separatist

Separatism can be a faithful approach to following Christ in the world when it is an intentional choice motivated by a desire for Christian formation and theological consistency. Separatism should lead us to deeper engagement with the needs of our neighbors and greater determination to meet those needs directly, instead of relying on the state. I am reminded of a team of midwestern Mennonites I met in Mississippi while helping with relief work after Hurricane Katrina. Their separatist posture toward government did not isolate them from the needs of their neighbors, whom they traveled hundreds of miles to assist in a time of dire need. Separatist models can serve as testimonies to the unique nature of the church and her uncompromising witness in the world. They can also challenge Christians to take stock of our influences and the ways we bend our identity toward the dominant culture. They can show us that we might be more discipled by the world than we realized. They can help us recognize the allure of power and prestige and challenge us to focus more on upholding the Kingdom than supporting the country.

---

[58]David Brooks, "The Benedict Option: Commentary," *New York Times*, March 14, 2017, www .nytimes.com/2017/03/14/opinion/the-benedict-option.html.

5

KEEPING THE COUNTRY OUT OF THE KINGDOM

TWO SEPARATIONIST APPROACHES

"WE'RE STARTING A WEEKLY WORSHIP SERVICE for students. We'll meet in the choir room. Sign up if you want to come!"

It was my junior year of high school, and a group of seniors felt inspired to launch a worship time during the school's study period. They called it Shirley Praise in honor of a beloved school administrator who was a Christian and who had passed away suddenly the previous summer. So many students signed up to attend the worship gathering that it moved from the choir room to the auditorium.

Every week students nearly filled our small auditorium to sing praise songs, give testimonies, and pray together. A student leader sometimes encouraged us to invite our friends, but also to tone down our evangelism, or else the school might have to shutter Shirley Praise. The administration, though generally supportive of Shirley Praise, wanted to avoid it becoming a cause of complaint among students, which might raise church-state separation issues. This was a public high school, so the administration could not give a Christian gathering preferential treatment.

Occasionally I wondered why we were allowed to have what amounted to an evangelical church service in a public school, during school hours, using school facilities, but mostly I was just happy to sing another chorus of "In the Secret."

In the United States we commonly describe the relationship between the church and state as "separation." Church becomes an umbrella term for anything faith-based, from formal religious institutions to individual religious convictions, and state refers to any function of the government, from public schools to business regulation to elections. Separation of church and state sounds simple. Take your faith in one hand and your politics in the other, then avoid clapping. But is that possible? Is it even desirable? In a country that grants people the right to influence legislation and elect leaders, Christians have an opportunity to exercise those rights. How can, or how should, Christian convictions influence which candidates we vote for, what legislation we support, or which policies we protest? And how does that influence fit with church-state separation?

This chapter examines two Christian approaches to separation of church and state. The first is historic Baptist separation, which is rooted in the Baptist distinctive of soul liberty. The second is Two Kingdoms separation, which originated with Martin Luther's political theology during the sixteenth-century Protestant Reformation. While both approaches promote separate roles for the church and the government, they have slightly different visions for the interaction between the two and for the role of Christianity in civil government. Both have their benefits and drawbacks for Christians to consider as we discern how to faithfully live out our faith convictions in political contexts.

SEPARATION OF CHURCH AND STATE

The concept of separation of church and state is so deeply embedded in Americans' minds that it is difficult for us to imagine a state-sponsored church in the United States. We take it for granted today that the government has no right to influence our religious beliefs, so we might not realize how radical and complicated religious liberty was when the United States adopted it as a constitutional principle. All of the European countries or empires from which the early American colonists came had some kind of religious establishment, meaning religion and region went together, and the leader of one often also had authority over the other. In that context one's religion had more to do with where one lived than what one believed. Religious practice was a matter of public concern, societal conformity, and legal enforcement, not primarily a matter of personal choice. Penalties for diverging from the official religion could vary from social ostracism to monetary fines, to imprisonment, to death, as we saw with the Anabaptists in the previous chapter. Some colonies continued this type of legal establishment, while others opted for religious toleration.

While some colonists came to the New World to escape religious establishment and persecution, others re-created or expanded the establishment system. The Virginia colony, for example, adopted the Church of England as its official church, while Puritans modeled the Massachusetts Bay Colony after John Calvin's religious establishment in Geneva.[1] In each case, establishment meant the church and its clergy were funded by taxes and religious minorities were suppressed. Virginia and Massachusetts Bay Colony each banned Quakers, for example.[2] Some colonies that did not have an official church, such as Delaware, still required men to "profess to believe in Jesus Christ, the savior of the world" to be eligible for public office.[3] Toleration and religious pluralism were far from the minds of most early residents of the American colonies, making it all the more remarkable that within a few generations the new country would adopt a constitutional amendment guaranteeing religious liberty.

Separation of church and state as we think of it today was by no means a foregone conclusion as the Founders developed the Constitution. Indeed, it was quite challenging for men with different personal beliefs and religious affiliations to determine what role, if any, religion ought to have in the new US government. Ultimately, Thomas Jefferson's disestablishment position won the day. He argued, since God did not coerce people into religious belief, neither should the government. Moreover, where the government is actively involved with the functions of the church, the result is

---

[1] Try though they did, Virginia and other Anglican colonies were not able to re-create the English system, in large part because they were under the authority of the bishop in London and had no local bishop. See Charles H. Lippy et al., *Christianity Comes to the Americas: 1492-1776* (New York: Paragon House, 1992), 288-98.

[2] See "An Act for the Suppressing the Quakers, Virginia (1659)," in *The Sacred Rights of Conscience*, ed. Daniel L. Dreisbach and Mark David Hall (Indianapolis: Liberty Fund, 2009), 113-14; "An Act Made at a General Court, Held at Boston, the 20th of October, 1658," in *Sacred Rights of Conscience*, 110-12.

[3] "The Charter of Delaware—1701," The Avalon Project, Yale Law School, https://avalon.law.yale.edu/18th_century/de01.asp.

likely to be hypocrisy on the part of religious leaders who are determined to remain in the government's good graces.[4]

The phrase "separation of church and state" did not appear in the founding documents, but it has become common parlance for people describing American church-state relations. Thomas Jefferson coined the phrase in his "Letter to the Danbury Baptist Association," in which he assured a Baptist congregation in Connecticut that the religion clauses build a "wall of separation between church and state."[5] But not everyone understood the First Amendment the way Jefferson did. Indeed, several states retained state-level religious establishment into the early nineteenth century, with Massachusetts being the last state to end its religious establishment in 1833. American shorthand references to separation of church and state therefore gloss over a much more complex history.

The First Amendment includes two deceptively simple religion clauses: first, "Congress shall make no law concerning an establishment of religion," and second, "or prohibiting the free exercise thereof." The "Establishment Clause" limits the government's interference in religion, while the "Free Exercise Clause" ensures individual and collective rights to religious beliefs and practices. One issue underlying the First Amendment debates was the influence of clergy in politics. Some clergy opposed intervention in politics because, as Abraham Bishop wrote in 1801, "the siding with a party in a cause of contention, involves engendered strife, and is a root of bitterness, which will poison religious intercourse at its source."[6]

For his part, Thomas Jefferson, whose anticlericalism was well-known, sought to limit the influence of clergy, whom he accused of "tyranny over the mind of man."[7] Religious dissenters, such as Baptists, urged separation for the sake of religious liberty and ecclesial purity. As a dissenter in Virginia wrote in 1777: "The State, I say, has always corrupted the Church. . . . The very establishment corrupts the Church. And such a Church will consequently corrupt the State."[8] Thus, protecting the state from the church

---

[4] Thomas Jefferson, "A Bill for Establishing Religious Freedom, Virginia (1779 and 1786)," in *Sacred Rights of Conscience*, 251.

[5] Thomas Jefferson, "Letter from Thomas Jefferson to Messrs. Nehemiah Dodge, Ephraim Robbins, and Stephe S. Nelson (January 1, 1802) (final version)," in *Sacred Rights of Conscience*, 528.

[6] Quoted in Philip Hamburger, *Separation of Church and State* (Cambridge, MA: Harvard University Press, 2004), 131.

[7] Hamburger, *Separation of Church and State*, 148.

[8] Hamburger, *Separation of Church and State*, 55.

and the church from the state yielded a constitutional amendment that attempted to guarantee mutual liberties from undue influence.

Separation of church and state eventually became shorthand for a complicated and controversial principle. What exactly counts as establishment? In what ways can religious practices be limited? Can religious beliefs influence public policy? US courts are frequently called upon to decide whether the government has shown undue support for a religion or has wrongly limited a person or group's free exercise. While the majority of people in the United States affirm the principle of separation, the details of particular cases or positions are much more complicated.[9] Issues like prayer or Bible study in public schools or nativity displays on municipal property are perennially before the courts. Christians are regularly making judgments about what we can or cannot say or do as we navigate the place of our convictions in our schools, workplaces, and voting booths. Likewise, Christians navigate whether deeply held religious beliefs can or should have a seat at the tables where public policy is written.

The basic question of separation at the personal level is, How and under what circumstances should our Christian beliefs influence our engagement with the political process? Historic Baptist separation and Two Kingdoms separation offer subtly different answers to that question. Each approach has similar convictions about the complementary roles of church and government, but they draw different boundaries around when and how Christians can directly influence government.

HISTORIC BAPTIST SEPARATIONISM

Historic Baptist Separationism focuses on the church's and individuals' free exercise and seeks to influence government in ways that strengthen the church's independence from state interference. The government's role vis-à-vis religion is to safeguard free exercise and to otherwise leave faith up to the people and institutions that practice it. This approach arises from Baptist history, but not all Baptist individuals or churches today approach politics in this way.

Origins of historic Baptist separationism. The historic Baptist commitment to the separation of church and state arises from the doctrine of

---

[9]Gregory A. Smith, "In U.S., Far More Support Than Oppose Separation of Church and State," Pew Research Center, October 28, 2021, www.pewresearch.org/religion/2021/10/28/in-u-s-far -more-support-than-oppose-separation-of-church-and-state/.

soul competency and the experience of persecution in Great Britain. Soul competency, also known as soul liberty, is a core tenet of the Baptist faith, and yields a strong commitment to religious liberty in law and culture. Baptist theologian David Garland explains, "'Soul competency' refers to the God-given freedom and ability of persons to know and respond to God's will. It assumes that God allows human beings to make choices, and that they are held accountable for their choices."[10] Soul competency applies to doctrinal beliefs and other matters of conscience, and therefore has far-reaching theological and political implications for the Baptist's engagement with society.

Roger Williams (ca. 1603–1683), a Puritan-turned-Baptist in the New England colonies, articulated soul competency in his vigorous rejection of Anglican and Puritan religious establishment in the American colonies. He argued, "next to the saving of your own *soules* (in the lamen-table *shipwrack of Mankind*) your taske (as *Christians*) is to save the Soules, but as *Magistrates,* the *Bodies* and *Goods* of others."[11] In other words, Christians are responsible for their own souls and for evangelism, while government officials are only responsible for others' physical and economic safety, even when government officials are Christians. This division of roles is important because, according to the historic Baptist tradition, violating soul competency by demanding religious conformity, whether through laws or creeds, corrupts both individual faith and the church.

Baptists' belief in soul competency led them to separate from the legally established Church of England in the seventeenth century. The Church of England was under the authority of the monarch and mandated the use of the Book of Common Prayer, both of which violated the Baptist conviction that an individual's faith could not be prescribed by the government or religious hierarchies. In the "London Baptist Confession of Faith," Baptists affirmed a duty to follow the law, respect the magistrates, and do "whatever is for the well-being of the commonwealth," but they also insisted "we cannot do anything contrary to our understandings and consciences" and pledged passive resistance to government action and to "die a thousand deaths, rather than to do anything against the least tittle of the truth of God, or against the light of our own consciences."[12] Their sole

---

[10]David E. Garland, "Conforming to Christ's Spirit, Not to the Crowd," in *Distinctly Baptist*, ed. Brian C. Brewer (Valley Forge, PA: Judson Press, 2011), 32.

[11]Roger Williams, "The Bloudy Tenent of Persecution, 1644," in *Sacred Rights of Conscience*, 149.

[12]"The First London Baptist Confession of Faith (1646)," in *Sacred Rights of Conscience*, 34.

loyalty was to God and the sole source of their faith was Scripture, not laws or creeds.

While it is a common adage that colonists came to the New World for religious freedom, it is most true of the Baptists, who rejected the very notion of religious establishment and demanded religious liberty for all, not only for themselves. When Roger Williams founded the Rhode Island colony in 1636, the colony's charter promised residents that they were secure "in the free exercise and enjoyment of their civil and religious rights," and should not be "punished, disquieted, or called in question, for any differences in opinion in matters of religion."[13] The principle of soul competency was planted and took root in the colonies as the population grew, religious homogeneity became less tenable, and a desire for liberty blossomed.

Applying historic Baptist separation, past and present. The historic Baptist principle of soul liberty directly influenced the debates that led to the ratification of the First Amendment and the ongoing work of applying it in the late eighteenth century and beyond. For example, in the 1780s, Baptists and other like-minded dissenters in Virginia united in their opposition to public taxes being used to fund Episcopal ministers' salaries. The dissenters argued that such use of taxes constituted establishment in the form of privileging one denomination over another.[14]

As politicians and clerics alike debated the relationship between church and state, the principle of freedom of conscience, rooted in the conviction of soul liberty, ultimately won the day. John Leland, a Baptist minister in Virginia, wrote in 1791, "religion is a matter between God and individuals: the religious opinions of men not being the objects of civil government, nor in any way under its control."[15] Regarding the stability and well-being of the state, Leland further explained that immigrants would be hesitant to come to the United States "with their arts and wealth" if they could not "enjoy their religious sentiments without exposing themselves to the law," and moreover, religious establishments "keep from civil office the best of men."[16] The Baptist articulation of soul competency thus contributed to the country's ideals of individual liberties and a limited role for government.

---

[13]"Charter of Rhode Island and Providence Plantations (1663)," in *Sacred Rights of Conscience*, 115.
[14]Hamburger, *Separation of Church and State*, 90.
[15]John Leland, "The Rights of Conscience Inalienable (1791)," in *Sacred Rights of Conscience*, 337.
[16]Leland, "Rights of Conscience," 339.

Historic Baptist separation maintains that the government should have no authority over religious practices or individual faith, therefore people who hold this view are attentive to possible government incursion on religious liberty. A few examples from the Supreme Court illustrate how the collision of faith and government has played out and help us consider how separation of church and state might inform our own political engagement today. In the case *Minersville School District v. Gobitis* (1940), the children of the Gobitis family objected to saluting or pledging allegiance to the American (or any other) flag because of their convictions as Jehovah's Witnesses. The children were expelled from school when they refused to salute the flag. Their attorney argued before the US Supreme Court that they had the right not to salute the flag as part of their "free exercise" of religion.

Perhaps surprising to contemporary readers, the court decided against the Gobitises, on the grounds that the government had a compelling interest in promoting patriotism and national unity. The lone dissenter, Justice Harlan Stone (served 1925–1941), disagreed on the basis that the government did not have a compelling reason to force children to make statements that contradicted their religious convictions. He wrote in his dissent, "by this law, the state seeks to coerce these children to express a sentiment which, as they interpret it, they do not entertain, and which violates their deepest religious convictions. It is not denied that such compulsion is a prohibited infringement of personal liberty, freedom of speech and religion, guaranteed by the Bill of Rights, except insofar as it may be justified and supported as a proper exercise of the state's power over public education."[17] While Stone was not Baptist, his dissent was consistent with a historic Baptist separationist approach to religious liberty.

For a more recent example of historic Baptist separation in the courts we can turn to *Ramirez v. Collier* (2022). John Ramirez was a death row inmate in Texas who petitioned to have his pastor be allowed to lay hands on him and audibly pray during his execution, which the state of Texas refused to allow. Ramirez appealed, and his execution was stayed while the Supreme Court heard arguments for and against Ramirez's religious request. The Baptist Joint Committee for Religious Liberty (BJC), the Ethics and Religious Liberty Commission of the Southern Baptist Conventions (ERLC), and several other Christian advocacy organizations jointly filed a brief in support of Ramirez on religious liberty grounds. They argued that

---

[17] *Minersville School District v. Gobitis*, 310 U.S. 586 (1940).

the state did not have a compelling interest to refuse Mr. Ramirez's request and that the state was not enforcing the law in the least restrictive way possible.[18]

For its part, the BJC demonstrated historic Baptist separation when it described its own commitments in the brief: "BJC deals exclusively with religious liberty issues and believes that vigorous enforcement of both the Establishment and Free Exercise clauses is essential for protecting religious liberty for all Americans."[19] Similarly, the ERLC explained, "religious freedom is an indispensable, bedrock value for Southern Baptists. The Constitution's guarantee of freedom from governmental interference in matters of faith is a crucial protection upon which SBC members and adherents of other faith traditions depend as they follow the dictates of their conscience in the practice of their faith."[20]

These Baptist and other Christian organizations apply historic Baptist separation by insisting that the government not violate the Free Exercise clause. The Supreme Court agreed in an eight-to-one decision in support of Ramirez's petition. Chief Justice John Roberts wrote the opinion of the court, in which he acknowledged the validity of laying on hands and audible prayer as religious practices and the sincerity of Ramirez's beliefs. The court concluded that Ramirez would suffer spiritual harm if he were "unable to engage in protected religious exercise in the final moments of his life."[21] The court's decision is thus consistent with historic Baptist separation, which emphasizes separation of church and state for the sake of safeguarding religious liberty.

Historic Baptist separation was evident in some Christians' reasons for staying out of the civil rights movement in the 1960s. The National Association of Evangelicals concluded "that civil rights 'is not the business of the church; so the NAE has strictly stayed out of this area.'" In response to Martin Luther King Jr. planning a march from Selma to Birmingham, "the NAE again demurred, this time stating that the association 'has a policy of not becoming involved in political or sociological affairs that do not affect

---

[18]Brief for the Christian Legal Society et al., as Amici Curiae, p. 7, *Ramirez v. Collier*, 595 U.S. 21-5592 (2022).

[19]Brief for the Christian Legal Society et al., as Amici Curiae, p. 2, *Ramirez v. Collier*, 595 U.S. 21-5592 (2022).

[20]Brief for the Christian Legal Society et al., as Amici Curiae, p. 3, *Ramirez v. Collier*, 595 U.S. 21-5592 (2022).

[21]*Ramirez v. Collier*, 595 U.S. 21-5592 (2022).

the function of the church or those involved in the propagation of the gospel."[22] Some Black Christians responded similarly, criticizing King and other civil rights leaders for their political action. Such critiques exemplify a dialectical model of the Black church, which includes a contrast between the priestly and prophetic roles of clergy and the other-worldly versus this-worldly theological emphases of churches.[23]

Another example of historic Baptist separation at work in public life is when a person or politician states they have personal religious convictions, but those convictions are separate from their political actions. The first Catholic president of the United States, John F. Kennedy, is an example of this distinction. During his presidential campaign, Kennedy received a letter from a woman who believed a Catholic could not be president because the Catholic Church rejected separation of church and state. Kennedy's response is consistent with historic Baptist separation:

> I have absolutely no hesitancy in stating to you that without reservation I subscribe to the principles of the First Amendment to the Constitution, guaranteeing as they do to every American the freedom to worship or not to worship as he pleases. . . . I can conceive of no situation in which my religious convictions could interfere or conflict with the faithful exercise of any responsibility I might be called upon to assume in public life.[24]

For Kennedy, and many other religious elected officials, one's personal faith is valuable and need not be hidden; however, it is not the basis for governing. Where personal views and the law conflict, the elected official is obliged to uphold the law. Most Christians are not elected officials, so do not necessarily separate faith from politics as clearly as Kennedy did. But Christians demonstrate the same idea when they express sentiments like, *I personally do not agree with that because of my faith, but I don't think I should impose my beliefs on others.* This approach to separation does not negate personal convictions, but it does limit when and how faith operates in the public square.

---

[22]J. Russell Hawkins, "A Conversation with Four Historians on the Response of White Evangelicals to the Civil Rights Movement," ed. Justin Taylor, The Gospel Coalition, July 1, 2016, www.thegospelcoalition.org/blogs/evangelical-history/a-conversation-with-four-historians-on-the-response-of-white-evangelicals-to-the-civil-rights-movement/.

[23]C. Eric Lincoln and Lawrence H. Mamiya, *The Black Church in the African American Experience* (Durham, NC: Duke University Press, 2001), 12.

[24]Quoted in Shaun Casey, *The Making of a Catholic President: Kennedy vs. Nixon, 1960* (New York: Oxford University Press, 2009), 20-21.

Historic Baptist separationists can lean conservative or progressive regarding the role of government, and therefore they can be found among supporters of all candidates and parties. People who affirm this Baptist approach, not all of whom are Baptists, generally believe ideas that are inherently religious should not be imposed legally, especially where the privileged belief would suppress other's sincerely held convictions. Historic Baptist separationists particularly emphasize religious liberty, but may not always agree about its application. For some, separationist focus on religious liberty leads to protecting small business owners who refuse to provide services for same-sex couples on religious grounds. For others, separation requires government and businesses to operate as businesses, not as religious entities, regardless of religious convictions.

Abortion is a fiercely contested example. Some historic Baptist separationists argue that the point at which a life has human rights is a matter of religious conviction, and therefore the government should allow abortion, at least very early in pregnancy. Others argue, on the basis of soul competency, that abortion is a matter of personal conscience in which the government should not intervene. Others argue that the point at which life begins is a matter of scientific certainty and universal moral law, and therefore argue on the basis of reason that abortion ought to be illegal. In all cases, a solely religious foundation for beliefs about beginning of life are not considered grounds for legislation.

Two Kingdoms Separationism

Two Kingdoms separationism has different historical roots and theological foundations than historic Baptist separation, and it has not exerted the same direct influence on American history as historic Baptist separation has. The two separationist approaches can look similar in practice, but the Baptist approach emphasizes religious liberty while this approach emphasizes distinct roles for church and state. Martin Luther (1483–1546) developed the Two Kingdoms separation approach during the Protestant Reformation. He identified the church and the government as two kingdoms, both under God's authority, but ordained by God for different purposes. The different functions lead to the principle that church and government should not interfere with each other, but rather fulfill their unique functions in accord with God's design.

Origins of Two Kingdoms separationism. Martin Luther's Two Kingdoms theology drew heavily on Saint Augustine's distinction between the City of God and the City of Man. Luther emphasized God's sovereignty in ordaining the church and civil government as two essential spheres that give order to the world. The church is responsible for souls—salvation, worship, morality. The state is responsible for bodies—maintaining order and punishing evildoers. Luther developed this theology out of necessity. When he shook the foundations of Western Europe by questioning the authority of the pope in his *Ninety-five Theses* (1517), the church and the empire had been inextricably linked for hundreds of years. In the so-called Holy Roman Empire, pope and emperor had danced in an uncomfortable lockstep since at least 800, when Pope Leo III presided over the coronation of Emperor Charlemagne.

In Luther's Germany, the nobility often were beholden to the local clergy, a situation ripe for abuse. Luther decried that the clergy "made decrees and declared that the temporal power had no jurisdiction over them, but that on the contrary, the spiritual power is above the temporal."[25] The union of church and empire was corrupt, but decoupling church from empire was inconceivable. Although Luther had no intention of breaking with the Catholic church, their theological differences were irreconcilable, and Luther's followers petitioned Emperor Charles V for permission to form a new church in 1530. But how could two versions of Christianity, what we now call denominations, coexist in a single empire? Anticipating a break with the Catholic church, Luther developed a political theology that made room for more than one Christian church to exist within the empire.

Luther formulated his "two governments doctrine" to differentiate the church(es) from the empire, which would allow each sphere to operate under God's authority instead of under each other's. According to Luther, "God has ordained two governments: the spiritual, by which the Holy Spirit produces Christians and righteous people under Christ; and the temporal, which restrains the un-Christian and wicked so that . . . they are obliged to keep still and to maintain an outward peace."[26] If the church or the

[25]Martin Luther, "To the Christian Nobility of the German Nation Concerning the Reform of the Christian Estate (1520)," in *The European Reformations Sourcebook*, 2nd ed., ed. Carter Lindberg (New York: Wiley Blackwell, 2014), 34.

[26]Martin Luther, "Temporal Authority: To What Extent It Should Be Obeyed," in *Martin Luther's Basic Theological Writings*, ed. Timothy F. Lull (Minneapolis: Fortress, 1989), 665.

government stepped outside their prescribed spheres of authority, they violated God's design; therefore, citizens were not obligated to obey civil authority if it transgressed the boundaries of its divinely ordained sphere. Luther instructed his followers,

> If your prince or temporal ruler commands you to side with the pope, to believe thus and so, or to get rid of certain books, you should say, " . . . Gracious sir, I owe you obedience in body and property; command me within the limits of your authority on earth, and I will obey. But if you command me to believe or to get rid of certain books, I will not obey; for then you are a tyrant and overreach yourself, . . ."[27]

When the temporal government overstepped its boundaries by making religious demands, the people were justified in their refusal to comply. Luther could not have anticipated the battles waged and lives lost when some used this idea to justify attempting to overthrow the government in the so-called Peasants War (1525).

Luther likewise limited the authority of the church to the spiritual sphere. He pointed out that, "although [Christ] sanctions the sword, he did not make use of it."[28] The spiritual government should not use the sword—that is, the tools of the world—to compel people to live like Christians, since no one can be compelled to be Christian.[29] And besides, Luther added, "[spiritual rulers] are so busily occupied with the spiritual sword, the Word of God, that they must perforce neglect the temporal sword and leave it to others who do not have to preach."[30] Luther saw danger in Christians giving their convictions the force of temporal law. He warned, if Christians take it upon themselves to make the law of Moses the law of the land, "they will be compelled by such a commandment to engage in rebellion, in murdering and killing, as works which God has commanded them to do."[31] As the state should not direct the law of the faith, so the church should not direct the law of the land. By articulating Two Kingdoms separation, Luther attempted to free both the church and the state from the corruptions that resulted from their mingling.

---

[27]Luther, "Temporal Authority," 685-86.
[28]Luther, "Temporal Authority," 667.
[29]Luther, "Temporal Authority," 666.
[30]Luther, "Temporal Authority," 675.
[31]Martin Luther, "Against the Heavenly Prophets (1525)," in *The European Reformations Sourcebook*, 66.

Luther's Two Kingdoms was not fully actualized in Reformation-era Europe. Church and state continued to be intertwined as kingdoms and empires continued to dictate which version of Christianity would be officially recognized and supported in their realms. The result was a Catholic-Protestant patchwork, the remnants of which are still visible today in the regional religious majorities of Western and Central Europe. However, Two Kingdoms separation paved the way for further developments that could be enacted, including John Calvin's political theology.

Applying two-spheres separation. Luther's Two Kingdoms doctrine was not directly influential in the United States' founding, but inasmuch as the doctrine is similar to historic Baptist separation it is consistent with some of the country's founding principles. One key difference between Luther's Two Kingdoms and the separationism of the Founders is that Luther understood civil government as instituted by and deriving its authority from God, not from the "consent of the governed." This is an important distinction as it shapes the way Two Kingdoms separation is and is not in alignment with the American system of government. Nevertheless, a Christian can hold to this approach as the ideal, while acknowledging that it is not the same kind of separation as the First Amendment introduced.

Luther's Two Kingdoms separation envisions Christians serving in government or other public roles in an intentionally Christian way as service to God and neighbor. Luther explains, "if the governing authority and its sword are a divine service . . . then everything that is essential for the authority's bearing of the sword must also be divine service. There must be those who arrest, prosecute, execute, and destroy the wicked, and who protect, acquit, defend, and save the good."[32] It is not enough that the ruler be called a Christian. The ruler who acts consistent with God's design must "aim at the common good and prosperity, not seeking their own gain and profit or following their own desires, pleasures, and delights."[33] The Christian need not leave their faith convictions behind in entering public service; rather, their faith should guide them to understanding public service as a Christian duty that they can carry out as a service to God and neighbor. At the same time, the Christian who is guided by faith into

---

[32]Luther, "Temporal Authority," 677.
[33]Martin Luther, *Table Talk* DCCXIX, trans. William Hazlitt (Gainesville, FL: Bridge-Logos, 2004), 439.

public service understands their role as advancing the common good, not advancing their religious beliefs.

Many Christians enter politics or public service because they believe God has called them to do so as an aspect of their stewardship of the world. A Christian in public service who adopts Two Kingdoms separation acknowledges the limited sphere of government action, even as they see their service to the state as ultimately service to God. In general, Christians with a Two Kingdoms separation view will enter politics because of their faith, but will not use their political office to promote Christian beliefs or policy agendas where such promotion would encroach upon the proper role of the church. Likewise, Christians who are not in public service expect their elected officials to preserve justice and peace, while maintaining separate spheres for faith and politics.

Two Kingdoms separationists might favor limiting government's role on the grounds that a smaller government is less likely to transgress the boundaries of its sphere. The role of government is to preserve and enact justice, which primarily means maintaining peace and order, such as through law enforcement and military protection. Conversely, some Two Kingdoms separationists might favor an expanded role for government for the sake of actively promoting justice. When government is charged with doing justice, that includes maintaining peace and order, but it can also include efforts to promote equity and the general health and well-being of society as a whole. Two Kingdoms separation has not been very influential in the United States, at least not directly, but a closely related Calvinist approach has been. We will examine that approach, called principled pluralism, in chapter seven.

EVALUATION OF HISTORIC BAPTIST AND TWO KINGDOMS SEPARATION

Separationism can be a faithful approach to Christian political engagement, with a few caveats. One key strength of both separationist approaches is the clear distinction between the church and the government, between the Kingdom of God and the country. As established in chapter one, the United States is not, has never been, and will not become the Kingdom of God. Neither historic Baptist nor Two Kingdoms separation confuse or conflate the country, with its structures and laws, with the Kingdom. By preventing the conflation of the Kingdom of God and the country, separation can maintain the unique identity and function of both. Separation is a model by which Christians can seek the common good within a religiously diverse society, safeguarding religious liberty for all people.

Separation also promotes a generally positive view of government. Since government is ordained by God, Christians need not think of it as inherently evil. It is flawed, prone to corruption, and not always trustworthy, but its existence is not contrary to God's will. While we must be vigilant against injustice and overreach, we need not regard the government or its agents or agencies as our enemies. Christians with this approach are, therefore, free to participate in elections, to hold public office, and to generally seek the shalom of our cities through civic engagement. It matters that we see government as having a positive function, even though it is not carried out perfectly, because some people who believe the government is evil, Christian and non-Christian alike, have been radicalized and have used anti-government ideology as justification for violence.[34]

Separation has also allowed Christianity to thrive in the United States in large part because the Constitution protects religious liberty. Religious disestablishment opened up a religious marketplace in which previously established denominations declined, but religious upstarts like Methodists and Baptists grew rapidly.[35] When French statesman Alexis de Tocqueville (1805–1859) toured the United States in 1831, he expected people living without religious establishment would have abandoned religion. In turn, the irreligious culture would "enervate the soul, relax the springs of the will, and prepare a people for servitude. Not only does it happen, in such a case, that they allow their freedom to be taken from them; they frequently themselves surrender it."[36] Would religion inevitably decline in the United States, making its inhabitants susceptible to the very tyranny against which they had rebelled less than sixty years earlier? To the contrary, de Tocqueville found a country bursting at the seams with religion. The 1830s saw the rise of revivalism, the founding of new churches and denominations, and innumerable preachers—both women and men—free

---

[34]Tore Bjørgo and Kurt Braddock, "Anti-Government Extremist: A New Threat?," *Perspectives on Terrorism* 16, no. 1 (December 2022): 2-8, 3-4.

[35]Roger Finke and Rodney Stark, *The Churching of America 1776–2005: Winners and Losers in Our Religious Economy* (New Brunswick, NJ: Rutgers University Press, 2005), 55.

[36]Alexis de Tocqueville, *Democracy in America*, ed. Richard D. Heffner (New York: Mentor, 1956), 151.

to proclaim the gospel (or altogether new religions) from traveling stages and train cars and along the riverways that carried physical and spiritual goods from New York to Chicago and all points in between.[37]

Religious liberty is also a challenge for separationist approaches because Christians do not always agree about when a person's religious liberty is being threatened, or they may not agree about what properly falls within the spiritual versus temporal spheres. For example, after the Supreme Court's 2015 *Obergefell v. Hodges* decision made same-sex marriage legal nationwide, Kim Davis, a county clerk in Kentucky, refused to sign any marriage licenses to avoid signing licenses for same-sex couples. Davis was sued, a district judge ordered her to sign legal marriage licenses, and she was jailed for contempt of court when she refused.[38] For some Christians, Davis was a hero of religious liberty. For other Christians, she was refusing to fulfill the obligations of a job she had chosen to do.[39] Christians of good faith disagree. Religious liberty is at the heart of separation, but it is not as clear-cut as we might like.

Two Kingdoms separation can also lead to political withdrawal. Not all matters of concern to Christians will affect religious liberty, so that might lead some Christians into a functional separatism, disengaging from politics unless and until the "wall of separation" is threatened. We saw this kind of separatism with some fundamentalist Christians in the early twentieth century, as explained in the previous chapter. Some Christians may find it appealing to disengage from politics if faith is not directly implicated, but if we can limit matters of faith so strictly, we likely have an anemic understanding of what it means to follow Christ wholly. It may also come across as hypocritical to the wider world, who could perceive Christians as only concerned about our own self-protection and indifferent to other groups who are helped or harmed by government policies.

A related drawback is that separation does not provide a clear path for when and how faith convictions might be brought to bear on public policy. Strict separationism has often been understood as religion having no

---

[37]See Sydney E. Ahlstrom, *A Religious History of the American People*, 2nd ed. (New Haven, CT: Yale University Press, 2004), 415-45.

[38]Lauren Hodges, "Kentucky Clerk's Office Continues To Refuse Marriage Licenses," NPR, August 27, 2015, www.npr.org/sections/thetwo-way/2015/08/27/435185521/kentucky-clerks-office -continues-to-refuse-marriage-licenses.

[39]Katie Rogers, "Outside Courthouse, Kim Davis Is Seen as a Villain and a Hero," *New York Times*, September 3, 2015, www.nytimes.com/2015/09/04/us/outside-courthouse-kim-davis-is-seen-as -a-villain-and-a-hero.html.

place at all in the public square. Some separationists believe religious arguments cannot be introduced to debates about governance, and when a person has religious convictions on a subject, they must also offer secular or natural law arguments. In some cases, this is not a problem. Murder, for example, can be outlawed without resorting to religious convictions, even though many people root their opposition to murder in their religious faith. But other issues of Christian conviction are more complicated. Christians disagree among one another about whether a compelling secular case can be made for banning abortion or for teaching creationism in public schools, for example. In such cases, must we adopt political positions at odds with our faith or withhold our faith-based arguments from public discourse? Must Christians lock away our faith-based rationale as the price of participation in the democratic process? Such a radical bifurcation of religion and politics is not necessary or beneficial for the Kingdom or the country.

On a larger scale, separation's emphasis on separate roles for church and state can mean the church does not have a path for intervening in extreme circumstances of government failing in its purpose. 1930s Germany provides a cautionary example. When Adolf Hitler became chancellor in 1933, the German Christians, a pro-Nazi faction of the German Protestant Church, believed he was, as one German Christian put it, "the liberator and savior whom God has sent" to revive Germany.[40] The German Christians praised Hitler's creation of a Reich Church, which brought the Protestant churches under the state's authority.

The Confessing Church, led by Martin Niemöller (1892–1984), Karl Barth (1886–1968), and others, was committed to preserving doctrinal orthodoxy against the government's incursions. The Barmen Declaration exemplifies this courageous defense of orthodoxy.[41] Karl Barth wrote, "our theological existence is our existence in the church, as those who have been called to be the church's preachers and teachers," and so "for a theologian to become a politician or a church-politician can well mean the loss of his theological existence."[42] Inasmuch as Nazism threatened the church's

---

[40]Reinhold Krause, "Speech at the Sports Palace in Berlin," in *A Church Undone: Documents from the German Christian Faith Movement, 1932–1940*, ed. Mary M. Solberg (Minneapolis: Fortress Press, 2015), 253-54.

[41]"The Barmen Declaration, 1934," in *Documents of the Christian Church*, 4th ed., ed. Henry Bettenson and Chris Maunder (New York: Oxford University Press, 2011), 357-59.

[42]Karl Barth, "Theological Existence Today" in *A Church Undone*, 84, 87.

confession of faith, the Confessing Church resisted, some suffering imprisonment, exile, and death. The Confessing Church called upon German clergy "not to accept any instructions from the present Reich Church government and its authorities and to withdraw from cooperation with those who want to continue to obey this government."[43]

But the Confessing Church focused only on government actions that infringed upon the church's spiritual sphere. The *Kirchliches Jahrbuch*, a publication of the Protestant church in Germany, noted, "against anti-Semitism [the Confessing Church] uttered no word, and even at the time of the Jewish persecutions and of their extermination it could not bring itself to stand up against these acts of terrorism in the Third Reich."[44] Adherence to Two Kingdoms separation perhaps saved the German Protestant church from completely collapsing into heresy, but it likely also prevented Confessing Church leaders from directly confronting Hitler's government or defying its unjust laws.

Frustration with this separation-induced inaction led Dietrich Bonhoeffer (1906–1945) to disassociate from the Confessing Church and join a resistance network in working to overthrow Hitler's regime. As a Lutheran, Bonhoeffer presupposed Two Kingdoms separation. However, the crisis of Nazi action against Jews and others was so grievous that Bonhoeffer believed it superseded the constraints of the Two Kingdoms doctrine. Thus, he wrote, the church's role in the current crisis was "not just to bandage the victims under the wheel, but to put a spoke in the wheel itself."[45] For Bonhoeffer, Two Kingdoms separation was a sound foundation, but it reached its limits when the actions of the state were so heinously harmful to humanity that the church could not in good conscience refrain from intervening in the political sphere. Bonhoeffer's example can teach Christians to carefully consider what the limits of the spheres are and under what circumstances the church can or should attempt to exert influence on the state.

---

[43]Quoted in Renate Wind, *Dietrich Bonhoeffer: A Spoke in the Wheel*, trans. John Bowden (Grand Rapids, MI: Eerdmans, 1991), 91.

[44]Ruth Zerner, "German Protestant Responses to Nazi Persecution of the Jews," in *Perspectives on the Holocaust*, ed. Randolph L. Braham (Dordrecht, The Netherlands: Springer Science and Business Media, 1983), 60.

[45]Dietrich Bonhoeffer, "The Church and the Jewish Question," in *The Bonhoeffer Reader*, ed. Clifford J. Green and Michael P. DeJonge (Minneapolis: Fortress Press, 2013), 374.

Faithfully Separationist

A Christian can follow Christ faithfully while also maintaining a separationist approach to politics. The liberty of the church as an institution and of individual believers to share the gospel has directly contributed to the church's thriving in the United States, and some view Christian efforts to gain political power as a cause for recent declines in Christian adherence. Thus, separation appears to be beneficial for the mission and witness of the church. Separation is a valuable principle for Christians living in a diverse society. It pushes us to be aware of our rights under the First Amendment and how those same rights apply to Americans who do not share our faith commitments. It also requires us to consider ways we can influence American society through means other than public policy. It requires us to clarify the role of the church and the role of the government, and to be aware of when either is overstepping its role.

However, separation also can be used as an excuse to bifurcate our spiritual and temporal lives to such a degree that our Christian faith becomes a purely private matter that has no bearing on our politics, allowing us to think whatever we want politically without considering points of tension or contradiction with Christian convictions. A faithful separationist will thoughtfully navigate the complexities of faith-based positions on policy issues, with an eye toward safeguarding religious liberty for the sake of Christian witness.

6

BRINGING THE KINGDOM
INTO THE COUNTRY

SOCIAL GOSPEL APPROACHES

"THE HANDS AND FEET OF CHRIST" was emblazoned on more than one of my high school mission trip T-shirts. As a youth group kid, the summer mission trip was an annual highlight. It was an opportunity to bond with my small youth group, learn to install drywall and subflooring, build things that surely were not up to code, get as much paint on clothes as on walls, laugh and cry from exhaustion, and see new parts of the country and the world. We were doing the work that God put Christians on earth to do, building the Kingdom by building homes and churches.

I assumed all mission trips entailed this kind of manual labor, until I made friends who had evangelized on Las Vegas street corners, hosted inner city Vacation Bible School programs, or put on Passion Plays around the world. Some friends informed me that my mission trips were not actually mission trips, since we were not inviting people to ask Jesus into their hearts. It turns out I was not just a youth group kid. I was a mainline Protestant youth group kid, which meant being the hands and feet of Christ entailed bringing about the Kingdom of God through transforming the material world.

Most Christians believe that our faith should influence society in some way; some believe that way should be directly through politics. Christians throughout American history have attempted, and sometimes succeeded, to directly influence society's laws and values. But, as we saw in the previous chapter and as we know from experience, not all Christians have the same political opinions or priorities. This chapter and the next each examine approaches to applying Christian values and convictions to politics directly; however, different theological and ideological convictions yield different political goals. This chapter explores the nineteenth-century social gospel and its various twentieth- and twenty-first-century iterations, including the civil rights movement, the evangelical left, and mainline Protestantism. Each historical and contemporary social gospel approach emphasizes care for the poor, economic justice, and moral reform, although their methods and moral emphases differ.

The Social Gospel

The social gospel is the belief that Christianity should be social; that is, it has implications for society, including morality, politics, and economic systems. The social gospel teaches that Christians can and should make the Kingdom of God a reality "on earth as it is in heaven" through personal and social righteousness. In this approach, interpersonal persuasion is an important method of reform, but it is also sometimes necessary for the government to infuse Christian virtues and values into culture, law, and the economy. For example, social gospelers might persuade a factory owner that his factory should have fire exits and also lobby the government to require windows and doors. In the latter nineteenth and early twentieth centuries, Christians like Washington Gladden (1836–1918), Walter Rauschenbusch (1861–1918), and Frances Willard (1839–1898) preached a social gospel that called for the moral reform of society in the wake of the Industrial Revolution. More recent inheritors of the social gospel tend to be less optimistic about the possibility of realizing the Kingdom of God on earth through social reform but are no less committed to the idea that Christianity has immediate social and political implications.

Origins of the social gospel. While the social gospel has deep roots in the social reforms of the Reformation era, its most significant theological forerunner was John Wesley (1703–1791), who brought the Anglican and Catholic concept of works of mercy into the Methodist movement. Works of mercy are ways of expressing love of neighbor by offering individual charity or working to improve social conditions. John Wesley described works of mercy as actions directed "to the souls or bodies of men," such as "feeding the hungry, clothing the naked, entertaining the stranger, visiting those that are in prison, or sick, or variously afflicted."[1] Wesley understood works of mercy as means of grace, which are "outward signs, words, or actions" through which God conveys "preventing, justifying, or sanctifying grace."[2] Acting on love of neighbor, in the Wesleyan perspective, is not simply a good behavior that we ought to add to our beliefs; it is essential to working out our salvation.

Works of mercy can include working within government systems to bring about justice for the poor and oppressed, like Wesley's support for abolishing the slave trade. It can also include interpersonal acts of charity, like Wesley's frequent visits to prisoners. In the early nineteenth century, Methodism was one of the fastest growing branches of Christianity in the United States and overtook Calvinism as the dominant theological perspective.[3] This theological shift was fueled by revival preachers, such as Phoebe Palmer (1807–1874) and Charles Grandison Finney (1792–1875), who emphasized personal and social holiness.

In the United States, the social gospel grew out of the early nineteenth-century abolition movement. Charles Finney, known as the father of modern revivalism, expounded the union of personal and social reform when he declared, "now the great business of the church is to reform the world. The church of Christ was originally organized to be a body of reformers. The very profession of Christianity implies the profession and virtually an oath to do all that can be done for the universal reformation of the world. . . . It is amazing to see what excuses are made by ministers for remaining silent in respect to almost every branch of reform."[4] This union of personal and social holiness was characteristic of Methodism and became

---

[1] John Wesley, "The Scripture Way of Salvation," in *John Wesley's Sermons: An Anthology*, ed. Albert C. Outler and Richard P. Heitzenrater (Nashville: Abingdon, 1991), 378.

[2] John Wesley, "The Means of Grace," in *John Wesley's Sermons*, 160.

[3] In 1776, only 2.5 percent of Americans were Methodist; by 1850, 34.2 percent were. The next largest branch of Christianity in 1850 was Baptist, with 20.5 percent of the population. Roger Finke and Rodney Stark, *The Churching of America 1776–2005: Winners and Losers in Our Religious Economy* (New Brunswick, NJ: Rutgers University Press, 2005), 56; cf. Catherine A. Brekus, "The Evangelical Encounter with the Enlightenment," in *Turning Points in the History of American Evangelicalism*, ed. Heath W. Carter and Laura Rominger Porter (Grand Rapids, MI: Eerdmans, 2017).

[4] Quoted in Randall Balmer, "'An End to Unjust Inequality in the World': The Radical Tradition of Progressive Evangelicalism," *Church History and Religious Culture* 94 (2014): 505-30, 511.

a distinctive element of nineteenth-century evangelicalism.[5] The successful abolition of the "hell-begotten system" of slavery, as Finney called it, spurred optimism about the church's potential to reform society so thoroughly that the Kingdom of God would be realized in the United States.

In the late 1800s, socioeconomic and theological forces combined with post–Civil War optimism to make possible the movement called the social gospel. The socioeconomic precursor to the social gospel was rapid industrialization and urbanization and the resulting explosion of poverty juxtaposed against the massive wealth of the captains of industry. The American values of individualism and entrepreneurship that made industrialization possible also, according to historian Maury Klein, "divorced economic power from social responsibility. The individual had few obligations to society beyond those imposed by his own conscience or the minimal and often ambiguous restraints of law. He could amass as much wealth and property as possible and do whatever he pleased with it without regard for the broader consequences of his actions."[6]

Industrialization and urbanization occurred more quickly than people and infrastructure could keep up, leading to environmental pollution, dangerous working conditions, slums, disease, crime, poverty, and corruption.[7] Some Christians viewed rising wealth inequality as a natural result of economic progress and an opportunity for Christian society to emerge through the voluntary benevolence of the very rich. Some saw wealth as a sign of God's blessing and associated success in business with personal virtue. Social gospel advocates saw the situation differently.[8]

Writing in 1907, Walter Rauschenbusch lamented, "my millions live from hand to mouth. Those who toil longest have least. My thousands sink exhausted before their days are half spent. My human wreckage multiplies."[9] Social gospelers, as proponents of this theology came to be called, saw a need for an infusion of Christian virtue. Washington Gladden

---

[5]Douglas M. Strong, "Introduction to the Second Edition (2014): A Tradition of Integrated Faith," in Donald W. Dayton and Douglas M. Strong, *Rediscovering an Evangelical Heritage: A Tradition and Trajectory of Integrating Piety and Justice*, 2nd ed. (Grand Rapids, MI: Baker Academic, 2014), 13.

[6]Maury Klein, *The Genesis of Industrial America: 1870–1920* (Cambridge: Cambridge University Press, 2007), 132.

[7]Klein, *Genesis*, 155-56.

[8]Christopher H. Evans, *The Social Gospel in American Religion: A History* (New York: New York University Press, 2017), 27.

[9]Walter Rauschenbusch, *Christianity and the Social Crisis* (Louisville, KY: Westminster John Knox, 1991), 212.

preached the need for Christians to adopt a "spirit that thinks less of personal power or gain or glory than of the common good. . . . Where this spirit abounds, there is always unity and fruitfulness; where this spirit is not, there is confusion and all kinds of evil."[10]

Rauschenbusch, Gladden, and others surveyed the injustices of their time, attributed them to capitalism, and came to believe Christianity ought to transform people's physical circumstances, not only their souls.[11] Doctrine and theory took a backseat to action, as Washington Gladden proclaimed, "the essence of Christian teaching needed to be translatable to the social realities faced by men and women living in a modern industrial society, and if doctrine could not hold up to that test, then it was suspect."[12] The social gospelers preached a message that had specific this-worldly implications for politics and economics and promoted government intervention where moral suasion was insufficient.

Two theological developments undergirded the social gospel: classical Protestant liberalism and postmillennialism. Major German thinkers of the nineteenth century, such as Immanuel Kant (1724–1804) and Friedrich Schleiermacher (1768–1834), applied post–Enlightenment rationalism to Christian Scripture and doctrine, yielding emphases on ethics and human reason. Liberalism's this-worldly focus downplayed, or in some cases rejected, dogmatic positions that could not be empirically proven, such as the bodily resurrection and return of Jesus Christ and the divine inspiration of the Bible. Theologians Stanley Grenz and Roger Olson explain, liberal theologians "saw the task of theology as identifying the kernel, the 'essence of Christianity,' and clearly separating it from the husk of cultural ideas and expressions that encased it. For many liberal theologians that husk included miracles, supernatural beings such as angels and demons, and apocalyptic events."[13] It would be difficult to overstate the influence of the liberal turn in theology on all branches of Christianity in the United States and Western Europe, and on the social gospel in particular.

The ethical emphasis of theological liberalism contributed to social gospelers' preaching personal and social morality as a Christian response to the

---

[10]Washington Gladden quoted in Evans, *Social Gospel*, 23.

[11]Evans, *Social Gospel*, 24.

[12]Evans, *Social Gospel*, 34.

[13]Stanley J. Grenz and Roger E. Olson, *20th Century Theology: God and the World in a Transitional Age* (Downers Grove, IL: InterVarsity Press, 1992), 52.

materialism and greed of the industrial age. Rauschenbusch, Gladden, and others preached moral reform to the wealthy for the sake of the poor, and believed if the wealthy were unwilling to reform, the government should step in with regulations to aid the victims of unfettered capitalism. Such reform was possible, they believed, because history was advancing toward universal prosperity, a belief commonly shared among theological liberals. Rauschenbusch expressed this optimism in his book *Christianity and the Social Crisis* (1907): "Knowledge has unlocked the mines of wealth, and the hoarded wealth of to-day creates the vaster wealth of to-morrow. Man has escaped the slavery of Necessity and is free."[14] Industrial technology had propelled humanity forward and opened new horizons of opportunity, if only humanity would infuse capitalism with Christian morality.

Another theological tenet of the nineteenth-century social gospel was postmillennial eschatology. Arising out of liberal theology, postmillennialism is the idea that humans bring about the reign of Christ by moving society into alignment with the moral values of the Kingdom of God. In contrast to premillennialism, which expects the world to descend into deeper crisis until Christ finally returns, postmillennialism expects humanity to bring about Christ's metaphorical return by inaugurating the Kingdom from earth. In this theology, Christ reigns through the church, but does not return to earth bodily. Rejecting premillennial pessimism and a solely personal and spiritual understanding of salvation, social gospel eschatology promoted the idea that the country would become the Kingdom of God.

Walter Rauschenbusch taught postmillennialism as "the ideal of a social life in which the law of Christ shall prevail, and in which its prevalence shall result in peace, justice and a glorious blossoming of human life," and "in which the worth and freedom of every least human being will be honoured and protected; in which the brotherhood of man will be expressed in the common possession of the economic resources of society; and in which the spiritual good of humanity will be set high above the private profit interests of all materialistic groups."[15] Rauschenbusch wrote *A Theology for the Social Gospel* at the dawn of the First World War. By the end of the Second World War, postmillennial optimism was largely abandoned.

---

[14]Rauschenbusch, *Christianity*, 211.

[15]Walter Rauschenbusch, *A Theology for the Social Gospel* (Louisville, KY: Westminster John Knox, 1997), 224.

Contemporary versions of the social gospel tend to retain the commitment to social change but set aside postmillennial eschatology.

The social gospel and the Progressive Era. The social gospel was influential in American politics during the Progressive Era, from roughly the 1870s to the early 1900s.[16] Social gospel preachers called for nothing less than the Christianization of American society, from personal piety to public policy. The social gospelers' vision for Christianization was shaped by the ascendant ideology of Christian socialism, an idea with moral and economic elements. Frances Willard (1839–1898) was among the most famous and influential social gospelers on this moral battle front. Willard was the face and voice of the temperance movement and served as president of the Women's Christian Temperance Union (WCTU) from 1879 until her death in 1898. Describing her understanding of Christian socialism, she wrote that Christians must "invest our lives to make conditions as equal as we can, believe in, pray for, work towards, the Brotherhood, when all men's weal shall be each man's care."[17]

To this end, the WCTU and like-minded Christian organizations promoted a wide range of reforms consistent with Christian socialism. In addition to the WCTU's focus on abstinence from alcohol, social gospelers supported labor unions, worker rights, government regulation of business, provision for urban poor, prevention of animal cruelty, equality between spouses, and raising the age of sexual consent.

On the economic front, Christian socialism saw in Jesus' teachings the ideal of human equality, which implied a right to a sustainable economic livelihood.[18] Therefore, social gospelers promoted redistribution of wealth and criticized capitalism as an unjust system that thrived on—even depended upon—the vice of greed. Washington Gladden described the relationship between workers and their employers as a conflict in which "the laborer wants to get all he can for his labor, the employer wants to give for it no more than he must; and between the two there is an unceasing struggle for advantage and mastery."[19] He called on employers to regard

---

[16]See Heather Cox Richardson, "Reconstructing the Gilded Age and the Progressive Era," in *A Companion to the Gilded Age and Progressive Era*, ed. Christopher McKnight Nichols and Nancy C. Unger (New York: Wiley, 2017), 7-11.

[17]Quoted in Christopher H. Evans, *Do Everything: The Biography of Frances Willard* (Oxford: Oxford University Press, 2022), 216.

[18]Evans, *Social Gospel,* 40.

[19]Washington Gladden, *Working People and Their Employers,* ATLA Historical Monographs Collection (Boston: Lockwood, Brooks, and Company, 1876), 34, https://search.ebscohost.com

business as a high calling from God that requires conscience and benevolence alongside entrepreneurship.[20] Gladden and other social gospelers also promoted the right for workers to form labor unions and negotiate for higher wages, among other reforms intended to level the economic playing field.

In the years after World War II, the social gospel was overwhelmed by the surge in Christianity-infused patriotism and the Cold War era's suspicion of communism. The brutality of the world wars brought postmillennial optimism to an abrupt end. The success of Willard's temperance fight largely backfired with the unintended consequences of the Eighteenth Amendment, further reducing the influence of the social gospel. The nineteenth-century evangelical emphasis on social reform splintered, with some evangelicals turning inward toward fundamentalism, others embracing cultural Christianity or civil religion, and others carrying aspects of the social gospel into other Christian traditions.

RECENT ITERATIONS OF THE SOCIAL GOSPEL

The social gospel's political advocacy for social and economic justice continues in several Christian traditions. Three influential American Christian traditions with social gospel roots or affinities include the Black civil rights movement, the evangelical left, and mainline Protestantism.

The social gospel and the civil rights movement. The version of the social gospel that Gladden, Rauschenbusch, and Willard expounded was firmly embedded within White Protestantism and, lamentably, did little to address racial inequities. For example, White social gospelers were reluctant to condemn lynching of Black Americans, partly due to their own complicity with racism and partly for fear of alienating their target audience.[21] Black theologians had developed a parallel social gospel during the Progressive Era that shared many tenets of its White counterpart but applied the social gospel to racial justice. Historian Gary Dorrien explains:

> Like the white social gospel and Progressive movements, [the black social gospel] espoused principles of social justice, conceived the federal government as an indispensable guarantor of constitutional rights, struggled

---

/login.aspx?direct=true&AuthType=ip,sso&db=h7h&AN=36936567&site=eds-live&custid=s8
876267&profile=eds&scope=site&kw=true&acc=false&lpId=NA&ppId=divp3&twPV=true&x
Off=0&yOff=0&zm=fit&fs=&rot=0&docMapOpen=true&pageMapOpen=true.
[20]Gladden, *Working People*, 38.
[21]Evans, *Social Gospel*, 45.

with industrialization and economic injustice, and grappled with the Great Migration. Like the white social gospel, it also wrestled with modern challenges to religious belief. But the black social gospel addressed these things very differently than white progressives did, for racial oppression trumped everything in the African American context and refigured how other problems were experienced.[22]

Both White and Black social gospelers drew from the well of their respective abolitionist movements, but the Black social gospel continued to focus on the liberation of Black Americans while the White social gospel focused on economic and moral issues to the exclusion of racial equity. Even as the White social gospel largely faded or transformed after the world wars, the Black social gospel continued into the civil rights movement and its contemporary successors.

The Black social gospel that developed in the early twentieth century drew heavily on Walter Rauschenbusch's theology as well as W. E. B. Du Bois's (1868–1963) social theories and activism. Du Bois gained a following among White and Black social gospel leaders in response to his book *The Souls of Black Folk* (1903), which Washington Gladden praised.[23] Du Bois spearheaded the Niagara Movement, which demanded "the abolition of discrimination in public accommodation, the right to social freedom, and the rule of law applied equally to rich and poor, capitalists and laborers, and whites and blacks."[24] Du Bois thus forged a link in a chain of Black social gospel activists that is unbroken to the present day. That chain includes theologians who combined Black social gospel hermeneutics and activism with aspects of White social gospel theological liberalism.

Benjamin Mays (1894–1984) was one of the country's most influential African American educators in the early twentieth century and helped revive interest in the theology of the social gospel and the writings of Walter Rauschenbusch. Mays integrated social gospel ideas at Morehouse College, where he became president in 1940. In a pamphlet explaining Morehouse College's goals, he wrote that the Morehouse man's

destiny is tied up, and inevitably so, with the great mass of people who do the ordinary work of the world and need their souls lifted by contact and

---

[22]Gary J. Dorrien, *The New Abolition: W. E. B. Du Bois and the Black Social Gospel* (New Haven, CT: Yale University Press, 2015), 2.
[23]Dorrien, *New Abolition*, 218-19.
[24]Dorrien, *New Abolition*, 237.

fellowship with the more privileged among us. . . . A community-minded
college would go a long way toward assisting the student to move away from
the erroneous conception of absolute freedom of the individual—the
old idea that the "selfish interest of the individual" is alone to be taken
into consideration.[25]

Among these Morehouse men was a student named Martin Luther King Jr.
Mays was also a driving force for the social gospel among Black Baptists,
amid intramural disagreement about whether evangelicals should focus
only on individual souls, or also on societal transformation.[26]

One of Benjamin Mays's students at Morehouse was Howard Thurman
(1899–1981), whose social gospel development continued at Rochester
Theological Seminary, where Walter Rauschenbusch had been a professor.
In his 1943 commencement address at Garrett Biblical Institute, Thurman
exhorted graduates in a social gospel key: "It is mandatory that we work
for a society in which the least person can find refuge and refreshment. . . .
You must lay your lives on the altar of social change so that wherever you
are there the Kingdom of God is at hand."[27] He set the agenda for the Black
social gospel with his 1949 book *Jesus and the Disinherited*. Thurman
began the book by asking "what the teachings and the life of Jesus have to
say to those who stand, at a moment in human history, with their backs
against the wall."[28] He challenged his readers to consider the Christian's
"obligation to administer to human need."[29] The end of racial segregation
would require political action, not only individual changes of heart.[30]
Thurman proposed a solution to racial inequality based on the love ethic
in Jesus' teachings, which requires Christians to have contact with their
enemies so they cease to be enemies. Such contacts are opportunities,
wrote Thurman, for the "privileged and the underprivileged to work on
the common environment for the purpose of providing normal experiences of fellowship," which would in turn motivate White Americans to
take political action toward racial equality.[31] Thurman would see the end
of legal segregation during his lifetime, in no small part because he

---

[25]Quoted in Randal Maurise Jenks, *Benjamin Elijah Mays: Schoolmaster of the Movement* (Chapel
Hill: University of North Carolina Press, 2012), 148.

[26]Evans, *Social Gospel*, 169.

[27]Quoted in Evans, *Social Gospel*, 190.

[28]Howard Thurman, *Jesus and the Disinherited* (Boston: Beacon Press, 1976), 1.

[29]Thurman, *Jesus and the Disinherited*, 3.

[30]Thurman, *Jesus and the Disinherited*, 88.

[31]Thurman, *Jesus and the Disinherited*, 87, 88.

mentored a young graduate student at Boston University named Martin Luther King Jr., who in later years often carried with him a copy of *Jesus and the Disinherited.*[32]

Mays's and Thurman's best-known student, Martin Luther King Jr. (1929–1968), took the social gospel with him from Morehouse to Crozer Seminary, where he read Rauschenbusch's *Christianity and the Social Crisis.* King wrote of the book, it "left an indelible impression on my mind," although he also criticized nineteenth-century White social gospelers for their silence on issues of racial justice and their naive belief in inevitable social progress.[33] King believed with Rauschenbusch that God was at work in human history to bring about social change, and that the people who led social change would need to prepare to suffer for their convictions, as Jesus had.[34] He espoused an ethical view of Jesus' teaching, influenced by theological liberalism, that emphasized social justice activism to reform oppressive systems and downplayed Jesus' divinity.[35] He agreed with Rauschenbusch that American capitalism was exploitative and could not be harnessed as a vehicle for liberation.[36] He saw economic and racial injustice through a socialist lens, like his Black and White social gospel predecessors.[37] He also emphasized the role of the Christian church as a moral authority for bringing about justice in America.

King's understanding of the social implications of Christianity come through in his assertion that "our hope for creative living lies in our ability to reestablish the spiritual ends of our lives in personal character and social justice. Without this spiritual and moral reawakening we shall destroy ourselves in the misuse of our own instruments."[38] For King, social reform was part and parcel of the Christian faith, not an optional addendum. He wrote in *Stride Toward Freedom* (1958),

> A religion true to its nature must also be concerned about man's social conditions. . . . This means, at bottom, that the Christian gospel is a two-way road. On the one hand, it seeks to change the souls of men, and thereby

---

[32]Evans, *Social Gospel*, 166.
[33]King quoted in Ralph Luker, *The Social Gospel in Black and White* (Chapel Hill: University of North Carolina Press, 1991), 322.
[34]Evans, *Social Gospel*, 181.
[35]Gary J. Dorrien, *Breaking White Supremacy: Martin Luther King, Jr. and the Black Social Gospel* (New Haven, CT: Yale University Press, 2018), 275.
[36]Dorrien, *Breaking White Supremacy*, 263.
[37]Dorrien, *Breaking White Supremacy*, 443.
[38]Martin Luther King Jr., *Strength to Love* (Philadelphia: Fortress Press, 1963), 76.

unite them with God; on the other hand, it seeks to change the environ-mental conditions of men so that the soul will have a chance after it is changed. Any religion that professes to be concerned with the souls of men and is not concerned with the slums that damn them, the economic condi-tions that strangle them, and the social conditions that cripple them is a dry-as-dust religion.[39]

King's view of Christianity's social reform implications is clear in his "Letter from Birmingham Jail" (1963), in which he criticized churches that "commit themselves to a completely otherworldly religion which makes a strange, un-Biblical distinction between body and soul, between the sacred and the secular."[40] Consistent with the social gospel, King saw Christianity as having immediate social, political, and economic implications.

Along with the social gospelers of the nineteenth century, King saw American churches as the nation's conscience, responsible for bringing American law and culture into alignment with Christian morality, re-sulting in what King often called the beloved community. The National Baptist Convention agreed, in contrast with other Baptist conventions and congregations at the time that adopted a historic Baptist separa-tionist approach examined in the previous chapter. Reflecting on the history of the National Baptist Convention, which is the largest Black Baptist organization in the United States, former convention president Joseph Jackson wrote, "the National Baptist Convention is by origin, structure, and mission a strictly religious body; but it is a religious body with concerns that relate it to human suffering, human needs, and human aspirations. Therefore, it is by nature related to the civil rights struggle."[41]

Thus, King and the branch of the civil rights movement he led promoted direct political action, including protest, voting, and running for public office. The message took effect and "by 1984 there were approximately 450 Black mayors. . . . Upwards of 340 were ministers, nearly all of them Bap-tists. For most of these preacher-mayors, the civil rights era had not ended;

---

[39]Martin Luther King Jr., *Stride Toward Freedom: The Montgomery Story* (Boston: Beacon Press, 2010), 23.

[40]Martin Luther King Jr., "Letter from Birmingham Jail—April 16, 1963," in *African American Religious History: A Documentary Witness*, ed. Milston C. Sernett (Durham, NC: Duke University Press, 1999), 531.

[41]Joseph H. Jackson, "National Baptist Philosophy of Civil Rights," in *African American Religious History*, 517.

it lived and grew through them."[42] Rather than the church being isolated or separated, the church's proper role in society included transforming society through both moral persuasion and political activism.

The civil rights movement and its social gospel convictions persist into the twenty-first century as minoritized Christians and their allies continue to advocate for moral transformation of the nation's laws. Leaders in faith and politics like the late Senator John Lewis (1940–2020, D-Georgia 1987–2020) and Christian Community Development Association founder John M. Perkins (b. 1930) steadily labored for social reform as the nation largely turned to other issues in the final decades of the twentieth century. In 2015, Rev. William Barber (b. 1963) founded Repairers of the Breach, whose mission is to "build a moral agenda rooted in a framework that uplifts our deepest moral and constitutional values to redeem the heart and soul of our country."[43]

As part of Repairers of the Breach's work, Barber inaugurated "Moral Monday" demonstrations in Washington, DC, in 2018. He explains that this movement intends to "awaken people to deep consciousness first, and then to engage them to use this new consciousness as a guidance system for framing a Movement that shifts the center of gravity of political discourse and action away from its accommodation to domination, and back to the deepest moral values of our faith."[44] Barber is a frequent guest on national news and is probably the most recognized Black Christian activist today.

Senator Raphael Warnock (D-Georgia, b. 1969) is another inheritor of the Black civil rights and social gospel tradition. Warnock has not only been a US senator since 2021, he also served for over sixteen years as the senior pastor of Ebenezer Baptist Church, the very church Dr. King once led. In his book *The Divided Mind of the Black Church* (2014), Warnock laments his observation that in contemporary Black churches, "personal piety is given far more sustained and systematic attention than liberation." He urges, "part of what the black church needs is a deeper understanding of the relationship between the ministry of social activism,

---

[42]Gary Dorrien, *A Darkly Radiant Vision: The Black Social Gospel in the Shadow of MLK* (New Haven, CT: Yale University Press, 2023), 5.

[43]"About Us," Repairers of the Breach, accessed February 6, 2023, www.breachrepairers.org /about-us.

[44]William J. Barber, *Forward Together: A Moral Message for the Nation* (St. Louis: Chalice Press, 2014), viii.

embodied in the civil rights movement, and the reality of a liberationist faith rooted not only in the black church's history but in scripture."[45] In his ministry, writing, and government service, Warnock embodies the connection between the social gospel, civil rights, and Black Christian political participation today.

The social gospel and the evangelical left. Vietnam War era political division gave birth to a movement of evangelicals who rejected the jingoism and xenophobia that characterized Cold War evangelicalism. This evangelical movement promoted social and economic justice, opposed the Vietnam War and the nuclear arms race, and reclaimed some of the social gospel convictions of Progressive Era evangelicalism. These theologically conservative, socially liberal Christians came to be called the "evangelical left." They are evangelical in the sense that David Bebbington famously defined it: marked by conversionism, activism, biblicism, and crucicentrism.[46] They are left-leaning in terms of political ideology, especially regarding economic policy.

Today the evangelical left is a broad network of pastors, scholars, churches, and organizations who unite evangelical theology and personal piety with commitment to social and economic justice. While people affiliated with the evangelical left hold a wide range of stances on social and economic issues, they tend to promote an expansive and consistent pro-life ethic. This ethic calls for Christians to view all life as sacred, with implications for everything from abortion to border policy to affordable health-care access to economic welfare programs, among many other issues.

Jim Wallis (b. 1948) and Ronald Sider (1939–2022) each founded influential evangelical left organizations in the 1970s. For Wallis, Sider, and others, theological liberalism—a defining tenet of the nineteenth-century social gospel—was a failure, but the Christian call to transform society remained intact. Jim Wallis's work began in the civil rights and anti-Vietnam War movements of the late 1960s.[47] He founded a community and publication in 1971 called Sojourners, which advocated for peace and

---

[45]Raphael G. Warnock, *The Divided Mind of the Black Church: Theology, Piety and Public Witness* (New York: New York University Press, 2014), 177.

[46]David W. Bebbington, "The Nature of Evangelical Religion," in *Evangelicals: Who They Have Been, Are Now, and Could Be*, ed. Mark A. Noll, David W. Bebbington, and George M. Marsden (Grand Rapids, MI: Eerdmans, 2019), 34.

[47]David R. Swartz, *Moral Minority: The Evangelical Left in an Age of Conservatism* (Philadelphia: University of Pennsylvania Press, 2012), 49.

justice through nonviolent direct action.[48] Today, Sojourners is "an ecumenical Christian media and advocacy organization that works towards social and racial justice" and seeks to "transform individuals, communities, the church, and the world by articulating the biblical call to racial and social justice, life and peace, and environmental stewardship."[49] In his book *God's Politics* (2009), Wallis argued "the religious and political Right gets the public meaning of religion mostly wrong. . . . And the secular Left doesn't seem to get the meaning and promise of faith for politics at all."[50]

Ronald Sider founded Evangelicals for Social Action (now Christians for Social Action) in 1973. The social gospel influence is evident in its founding document, "The Chicago Declaration of Evangelical Social Concern," which says,

> We must attack the materialism of our culture and the maldistribution of the nation's wealth and services. We recognize that as a nation we play a crucial role in the imbalance and injustice of international trade and development. Before God and a billion hungry neighbors, we must rethink our values regarding our present standard of living and promote a more just acquisition and distribution of the world's resources.[51]

Sider's landmark 1978 book *Rich Christians in an Age of Hunger* issued a blistering critique of Christian negligence toward the poor and challenged Christians to examine the impact of consumption and capitalism on local and global poverty. He revised aspects of his argument in later editions but maintained a belief that, "God wants every person and family to have equality of economic opportunity."[52] Throughout his ministry, Sider insisted, "biblical understanding of distributive justice calls for dramatic transformation in every society on this planet."[53] Wallis and Sider ushered several generations of Christians into a socially oriented vision for the role of Christianity in culture and politics.

---

[48]Swartz, *Moral Minority*, 61.

[49]"About Sojourners," Sojourners, accessed October 9, 2023, https://sojo.net/about/about -sojourners.

[50]Jim Wallis, *God's Politics: Why the Right Gets It Wrong and the Left Doesn't Get It* (New York: Harper Collins, 2009) 3.

[51]"Chicago Declaration of Evangelical Social Concern," appendix to David R. Swartz, *Moral Minority*, 267-69.

[52]Ronald J. Sider, "Preface to the Sixth Edition," in *Rich Christians in an Age of Hunger*, 6th ed. (Nashville: W Publishing, 2015), xiv.

[53]Ronald J. Sider, *The Scandal of Evangelical Politics: Why Are Christians Missing the Chance to Really Change the World?* (Grand Rapids, MI: Baker Books, 2008), 126.

Contemporary leaders of the evangelical left include Tony Campolo (b. 1948), Shane Claiborne (b. 1975), Brian McLaren (b. 1956), and Rachel Held Evans (1981–2019), among many other pastors and writers. In 2007 Tony Campolo, a pastor and sociology professor, and Shane Claiborne, an activist and leader of the New Monasticism movement, founded Red Letter Christians. Its mission statement reads: "staying true to the foundation of combining Jesus and justice, Red Letter Christians mobilizes individuals into a movement of believers who live out Jesus' counter-cultural teachings."[54] Campolo and Claiborne have been two of the best known and most influential leaders of the evangelical left for several decades.

Brian McLaren, a leading figure in the Emerging Church movement, is known for his 2004 book *A Generous Orthodoxy*, which encourages Christians to integrate orthodoxy with orthopraxy. He writes of the essential relationship between faith and practice, "so-called orthodox understandings of the Trinity that don't lead so-called orthodox Christians to love their neighbors in the name of the Trinity (including those neighbors who don't properly understand the Trinity) are more or less worthless, which trivializes their orthodoxy."[55] His writing and ministry emphasize a Kingdom ethics, where Christians "practice a liberating *generosity toward the poor* to dethrone greed and topple the regime of money," along with traditional spiritual disciplines of prayer and fasting as acts of "ceaseless rebellion against the tyrannical trinity of money, sex, and power."[56]

Rachel Held Evans was a writer whose evangelical upbringing and education gave her an insider's perspective as she critiqued the conservative political alignments of her own theological tradition. Through her books, blog, and active presence on social media, she became a voice for many millennial Christians who were frustrated by what they saw as conservative evangelical hypocrisy, but who did not want to abandon faith in Jesus. Held Evans wrote about an instance of backlash against her social gospel politics, "I've been a democrat for all of four months now, and what has surprised me the most is how passionately conservative evangelicals oppose social reforms that benefit the poor. I understand why Christians have moral objections to abortion, and I know a lot of good Christian

---

[54]"Our Mission and Our Story," Red Letter Christians, accessed June 5, 2023, www.redletter christians.org/our-mission-our-story/.

[55]Brian D. McLaren, *A Generous Orthodoxy* (Grand Rapids, MI: Zondervan, 2004), 31.

[56]Brian D. McLaren, *The Secret Message of Jesus: Uncovering the Truth That Could Change Everything* (Nashville: W Publishing, 2006), 134. Italics in original.

people who have very good reasons for voting Republican. . . . But since when is laissez-faire economics a biblical principle?"[57]

She especially advocated for women and ethnic minorities who were, and are, frequently marginalized within evangelicalism. Her personal journey of faith led her to the Episcopal Church, a journey she shared in her book *Searching for Sunday* (2015). Held Evans died unexpectedly after a brief illness in 2019, but her legacy continues to influence Christians of the evangelical left, especially those who wrestle with what it means to follow Jesus and not be politically conservative.

Today, where we see evangelical theological convictions fueling commitment to social and economic justice, we recognize the hallmarks of the evangelical left. It has never been a unified voting bloc the way the Christian right has been, so it does not garner the same media attention as its conservative counterpart. The evangelical left is also not united in stances on all controversial social issues such as same-sex marriage or abortion. The convictions that animate the evangelical left are disseminated through conferences like the Christian Community Development Association Conference, InterVarsity Christian Fellowship's Urbana Mission Conference, Church Anew, and Wild Goose Festival, and through the scholarship and teaching of Christian leaders in universities and local churches.

The social gospel and mainline Protestantism. The legacy of the social gospel continues to be evident in mainline Protestant denominations, many of which were directly influenced by theological and political liberalism over a century ago. Denominations like the United Methodist Church, United Church of Christ, Presbyterian Church (USA), Episcopal Church, and others can tend to emphasize Jesus' moral example and Christian responsibility to bring the Kingdom of God into the present through social activism. Denominational faith statements, leadership, and members do not necessarily espouse the tenets of theological liberalism that are at odds with historic orthodoxy (such as the rejection of biblical inspiration or the bodily resurrection), but the liberal influence comes through in preaching and publications. Many mainline Protestant churches demonstrate a theological commitment to social and economic equality that sits comfortably with liberal social and economic ideology.

---

[57]Rachel Held Evans, "'Socialist' Propaganda (with biblical support!)," *Rachel Held Evans* (blog), June 8, 2008, https://rachelheldevans.com/blog/article-1212898761.

The Social Principles of the United Methodist Church, for example, include support for collective bargaining and union formation; the right to a living wage, quality education, and health care; corporate responsibility to stakeholders; and equal rights for women, among many other positions consistent with the social gospel.[58] While not identical in their scope or language, other mainline Protestant denominations hold similar social positions and understand these positions as part of their gospel witness.

Many mainline Protestant denominations advance their social concerns through political lobbying. The Presbyterian Church (USA), for example, maintains a ministry at the United Nations in New York City, where denominational representatives hold special consultative status on the United Nations Economic and Social Council. The denomination's mission agency identifies advocacy and social justice as cornerstones of its work.[59] The United Methodist Church's General Board of Church and Society is headquartered in Washington, DC, less than 300 feet from the Supreme Court. Its website includes links where members can contact their government representatives about issues such as gun control legislation, care for the environment, and immigration reform.[60]

The United Church of Christ promotes Just World Covenants, through which local congregations can learn about and commit to advocacy around issues like creation care, access for people with disabilities, global peace, and welcoming immigrants.[61] It is common for pastors in these denominations to participate in public protests, to testify before their state legislature, to lobby state and federal representatives, and to encourage their congregants to do the same. While not all members of mainline Protestant congregations align with the stated social positions of their denominations, in general the governing bodies of mainline Protestant denominations promote social positions that lean liberal politically. This political orientation has contributed to multiple denominational ruptures, yielding many historically mainline denominations with both liberal and conservative branches.

---

[58] The United Methodist Church, "Our Social Principles," in *The Book of Discipline of the United Methodist Church—2016*, accessed February 6, 2023, www.umc.org/en/content/our-social-principles.

[59] "Advocacy and Social Justice," Presbyterian Church (USA) Presbyterian Mission, accessed March 15, 2023, www.presbyterianmission.org/what-we-do/advocacy-social-justice/.

[60] "Take Action," Church and Society: The United Methodist Church, accessed March 15, 2023, www.umcjustice.org/what-you-can-do/advocacy/take-action.

[61] "Just World Covenants," The United Church of Christ, accessed March 15, 2023, www.ucc.org/just_world_covenants/.

Additional iterations of the social gospel. In addition to the influential social gospel movements explored above, we should be aware of two others: Roman Catholic and Latino/a social gospel approaches. While the social gospel is historically a Protestant theological movement, the nineteenth-century socioeconomic context also yielded parallels in the Roman Catholic Church. Pope Leo XIII's 1891 encyclical *Rerum Novarum* applied Catholic theology to the challenges of industrialization and the resulting increase in global economic inequality. The opening lines of *Rerum Novarum* are in harmony with the language of Protestant social gospelers: "The elements of the conflict now raging are unmistakable, in the vast expansion of industrial pursuits and the marvelous discoveries of science; in the changed relations between masters and workmen; in the enormous fortunes of some few individuals, and the utter poverty of the masses; . . . as also, finally, in the prevailing moral degeneracy."[62]

Rerum Novarum "inaugurated a century-long tradition of papal teaching on matters of labor and economics that has been followed by six subsequent papal encyclicals that have updated its teachings in new historical circumstances not only addressing the practical questions of their day, but doing so in a manner which questions them from the theological perspective of Catholic doctrine," explains Catholic theologian Vincent Miller.[63] Due to the rampant anti-Catholic sentiment in the United States in the nineteenth century, Catholic social teaching had little political influence at that time. However, Catholic social teaching continues to inform many Catholics, including Pope Francis, whose pontificate has elevated this aspect of Catholic thought.

Latino/a social gospel movements are rooted in Catholic Latin American liberation theology and the Protestant *Misión Integral* ("integral mission") movement. Both movements began in the context of political and economic conflict across Latin America in the 1960s and had similar goals and emphases, while drawing on differing Catholic and Protestant theological traditions. Liberation theology's leading theologian, Peruvian Catholic priest Gustavo Gutierrez (b. 1928), taught that liberation includes freedom from sin and also political liberation. Liberation theology emphasizes

---

[62]Catholic Church and Pope Leo XIII, *Rerum Novarum: Encyclical of Pope Leo XIII on Capital and Labor*, www.vatican.va/content/leo-xiii/en/encyclicals/documents/hf_l-xiii_enc_15051891 _rerum-novarum.html.

[63]Vincent J. Miller, "Clues to the Encyclical II: A Long Tradition of Papal Teaching on Social, Economic, and Political Matters," *America: The Jesuit Review* (June 4, 2015).

this-worldly liberation that "expresses the aspirations of oppressed peoples and social classes, emphasizing the conflictual aspect of the economic, social, and political process which puts them at odds with wealthy nations and oppressive classes."[64]

Misión Integral similarly emphasized the political implications of Jesus' teachings, but from an evangelical Protestant theological perspective. Ecuadorian theologian René Padilla (1932–2021), known as the father of *Misión Integral*, explained, "the proclamation of the gospel and the demonstration of the gospel that gives itself in service form an indissoluble whole. One without the other is an incomplete, mutilated gospel and, consequently, contrary to the will of God. From this perspective, it is foolish to ask about the relative importance of evangelism and social responsibility."[65] Liberation theology and *Misión Integral* make their way into the US conversation about faith and politics through a variety of streams, but primarily through the academic work of scholars such as Robert Chao Romero, Ada María Isasi-Díaz, Miguel De La Torre, and others.

EVALUATION OF THE SOCIAL GOSPEL

The social gospel was and continues to be enthusiastically embraced by some Christians and vociferously rejected by others. Some historical and recent criticisms of the social gospel are worth our consideration. First, like several other approaches to political engagement, the social gospel is liable to Constantinianism. Social gospel Christians can wrest power from God by treating human-led political action and social transformation as the sole means of accomplishing God's will. Some social gospel adherents, especially in the nineteenth century, directly stated as much in their arguments for the creation of a society in which the Kingdom of God becomes present reality. Frances Willard believed women could cleanse the country of its sins if only they could vote to end moral ills like pornography and gambling.[66] Others did not go so far as to believe that humans bring about the Kingdom, but belied a reliance on human action to the neglect of God's intervention or eschatological hope.

---

[64]Gustavo Gutierrez, *A Theology of Liberation*, revised edition, trans. and ed. Sr. Caridad Inda and John Eagleson (New York: Orbis, 1988), 24.

[65]René Padilla quoted in Robert Chao Romero, *Brown Church: Five Centuries of Latina/o Social Justice, Theology, and Identity* (Downers Grove, IL: IVP Academic, 2020), 159.

[66]Evans, *Do Everything*, 6.

Rauschenbusch, for example, wrote of the Kingdom of God in terms of present-day ethical and spiritual progress brought about by human action.[67] Christians can agree with the social positions and political advocacy while maintaining the centrality of Jesus Christ, but some social gospel movements past and present functionally restrict God's work to what humans can accomplish.

Brothers Reinhold (1892–1971) and H. Richard Niebuhr (1894–1962), two of the most influential American Christian thinkers of the twentieth century, criticized the social gospel. Reinhold Niebuhr valued the social gospel because "wherever religion concerns itself with the problems of society, it always gives birth to some kind of millennial hope, from the perspective of which present social realities are convicted of inadequacy, and courage is maintained to continue in the effort to redeem society of injustice."[68] However, he rejected Rauschenbusch's social gospel, and argued "there is indeed a very rigorous ethical ideal in the gospel of Jesus, but there is no social ethic in the ordinary sense of the word in it, precisely because the ethical ideal is too rigorous and perfect to lend itself to application in the economic and political problems of our day."[69]

Reinhold Niebuhr found the social gospel impractical and guilty of neglecting racial inequality, as well as being too optimistic about human nature. As an alternative, he developed Christian Realism, a political theology that takes seriously humanity's limitations, especially the consequences of sin, and concludes that God's victory over evil is through Christ's death and resurrection, not through human efforts. However, lest Christians retreat from the world, he also taught that humans are made in the image of God, and therefore have ethical capacity and responsibility for improving the world, even if only in limited ways.[70]

H. Richard Niebuhr's criticism of the social gospel focused on its institutionalization and its tendency toward theological liberalism. The social gospel's ideal of a Christianized society was to be realized through legal and ecclesial institutions. Moral reform became so closely intertwined

---

[67]Rauschenbusch, *Theology*, 225.

[68]Reinhold Niebuhr, *Moral Man and Immoral Society* (Louisville, KY: Westminster John Knox, 2021), 61.

[69]Reinhold Niebuhr, "The Ethic of Jesus and the Social Problem," in *T&T Clark Reader in Political Theology*, ed. Elizabeth Philips et al. (New York: T&T Clark, 2021), 297.

[70]John Marsden, "Reinhold Niebuhr and the Ethics of Christian Realism," *International Journal of Public Theology* 4 (2010), 483-501, 489-94.

with the mechanics of law, economy, and labor that, Niebuhr wrote, "to be reconciled to God now meant to be reconciled to the established customs of a more or less Christianized society."[71] Thus the Christianization of society was reduced to moral conformity. The social gospel's emphasis on moral reform often went hand-in-hand with theological liberalism's reduction of Jesus to merely a great moral teacher. Perhaps Niebuhr's most blistering critique on this point was his assertion that, in the social gospel "a God without wrath brought men without sin into a Kingdom without judgment through the ministrations of a Christ without a Cross."[72] So in the Niebuhr brothers' final analysis, the social gospel was not the gospel of Jesus Christ the Son of God, but merely a political message of social reform.

A related critique is that adherents to the social gospel can become bland in their partisanship. Almost half of mainline Protestants and over 80 percent of Black Protestants identify as Democrats.[73] When we notice bloc party identification, we often also see a temptation toward bland partisanship, and the risks that come with it, such as embracing a party's entire platform, even when planks of it are incompatible with Christian convictions. Christians on the left are as prone to uncritical partisan alignment as those on the right. As Justin Giboney of The AND Campaign notes, Christians whose social justice convictions lead them to uncritical partisan alignment "will end up denying biblical doctrine at some point to keep up with this ever-evolving [progressive] ideology. When Christians allow progressive ideology to diminish the role of Scripture and deny the timelessness of truth, we trade solid ground for sinking sand (Matthew 7:24-27)."[74]

Christians debate whether laboring for social reform is a distraction from gospel proclamation, or a necessary part of it. In general, mainline Protestant churches are less concerned about individual conversion to faith in Jesus Christ and more engaged in social justice work than evangelical churches are. Political scientist John Green explains, "The idea of

[71]H. Richard Niebuhr, *The Kingdom of God in America* (New York: Harper Torchbooks, 1959), 181.
[72]Niebuhr, *Kingdom of God*, 193.
[73]Ryan P. Burge, "Are Mainline Protestants Democrats?," Religion in Public, September 10, 2019, https://religioninpublic.blog/2019/09/10/__trashed/; Pew Research Center, "Faith Among Black Americans," February 16, 2021, www.pewresearch.org/religion/2021/02/16/religion-and -politics/.
[74]Justin Giboney et al., *Compassion (&) Conviction: The AND Campaign's Guide to Faithful Civic Engagement* (Downers Grove, IL: InterVarsity Press, 2020), 51-52.

spreading the word in the mainline tradition is much broader than simply preaching the good news. It also involves economic development. It involves personal assistance, charity, a whole number of other activities."[75] The heart of the issue is the question of what exactly Christians mean by justice and by what methods Christians ought to pursue it. One critique of contemporary iterations of the social gospel is that they are no different from secular movements for social justice, and that there is thus nothing uniquely Christian about them; in other words, critics would say they are social, but are not gospel.

In a similar vein, some Christians differentiate social justice from biblical justice, and in linking the social gospel with social justice disconnect it from biblical Christianity. This critique arises from the non-Christian or anti-Christian philosophies that undergird some social justice movements. Black Lives Matter, for example, became controversial among Christians in part because two of the organization's three founders self-identified with Marxist ideology and the organization's original beliefs statement included goals associated with Marxism.[76] For many Christians who align with contemporary iterations of the social gospel, support for the Black Lives Matter movement is consistent with their biblical justice convictions. Other Christians see such support as beyond the pale because Black Lives Matter is at odds with biblical justice due to its Marxist underpinnings, among other reasons.

The social gospel's leaning toward economic liberalism makes it subject to the same critiques one might level at liberal economic policy. Do redistributive economic policies inhibit growth and innovation by deincentivizing entrepreneurship? Do economic safety nets create cycles of dependence and harm recipients in the long term? Today's social gospel adherents look to flawed systems as root causes of poverty, crime, violence and other social ills, and they prescribe economic reform as one means by which society might alleviate such problems. In contrast, some Christians

---

[75]Frontline, "The Jesus Factor," interview with John Green, December 5, 2003, www.pbs.org /wgbh/pages/frontline/shows/jesus/interviews/green.html.

[76]The nonprofit organization Black Lives Matter, whose website is blacklivesmatter.com, is separate from other organizations or individuals that use the term *Black Lives Matter*. The two founders who self-identified as Marxist are Patrice Cullors and Alicia Garza, neither of whom are currently leaders in the organization. Cullors initiated the Twitter hashtag #BlackLivesMatter in 2012. The "beliefs" page no longer exists. See Tom Kertscher, "Is Black Lives Matter a Marxist Movement?," *PolitiFact*, July 21, 2020, www.politifact.com/article/2020/jul/21/black-lives-matter -marxist-movement/.

reject the notion of systemic injustice in favor of an emphasis on individual responsibility and generosity. This has become a flashpoint of the culture wars, in which contemporary advocates of the social gospel's aims are mocked as "social justice warriors" or "woke."

Weighed against the above critiques, a significant advantage of the social gospel is that it takes seriously Christians' ability to affect our communities, countries, and the world for the better, here and now. Karl Marx famously accused Christianity of being the opiate of the masses, by which he meant that Christianity taught people to focus on eschatological hope to the neglect of their present circumstances. The social gospel is an ironic antidote to Marx's claim, since Christian socialism inspired some social gospelers to address present injustices.

The social gospel's commitment to the equality and dignity of all people militates against a privatized or spiritualized faith that is disconnected from people's lived reality. Moreover, neglect of justice is neglect of a topic of vital concern throughout Scripture. The so-called *Slave Bible* illustrates the centrality of justice as a biblical theme. Published in 1807 for distribution among enslaved persons in the West Indies, the *Slave Bible* omitted sections that White Christians thought might introduce enslaved persons to theological ideas of liberation and equality. The result was omission of about 90 percent of the Old Testament and about 50 percent of the New Testament.[77] To take Scripture seriously is to take justice seriously. The social gospel can compel Christians to act on the biblical injunction to do justice in this time and place.

FAITHFULLY SOCIAL GOSPEL

Christians can faithfully pursue the social gospel's goals of justice and equality, while being thoughtful about the potential theological and practical pitfalls. The social gospel's postmillennial optimism about humanity's ability to perfect society can be balanced with a realistic understanding of sin and the limitations that come with it. Christians who find footing in the social gospel do not agree with each other on all aspects of complex policy issues, but they tend to agree that Christianity can promote equality through political and economic reform. Adherents to the social gospel might thoughtfully affiliate with a political party and may find themselves leaning toward liberal economic and/or social ideologies.

---

[77]Anthony Schmidt, interview by Michel Martin, *All Things Considered*, NPR, December 9, 2018.

As with any approach that can lead to partisanship, social gospel adherents must be salty and avoid the temptation to uncritical partisan alignment. The social gospel presupposes that Christianity can and should lead directly to social, political, and economic reform, and therefore requires political engagement and even activism. Christians can be political activists, but they must resist the temptation to grant eternal power to temporal systems. Elections and laws have real consequences, but they cannot upend or bring about God's ultimate plan for the eternal restoration of shalom. A faithful social gospel Christian will thoughtfully contribute to politics, without contributing to the political rancor that fuels news and social media. A faithful social gospel Christian will ground her or his activism in Scripture and will pursue justice in ways that reflect a uniquely Christian vision of God's justice and righteousness.

7

KEEPING THE COUNTRY UNDER THE KINGDOM

TWO CALVINIST APPROACHES

AS A THEOLOGY PROFESSOR, I get to help nursing, exercise science, elementary education, and business majors understand what theology has to do with their career paths. When I ask them how their faith can influence the way they do their job, I hear responses like, "I could offer to pray for my patients," or "I could invite my students to church," or "I could lead a Bible study for my employees."

These suggestions reflect a division between sacred and secular that was foreign to the biblical world and to most people prior to the Enlightenment. My students, seemingly by default, think of the world of church and spiritual disciplines as sacred, and their jobs as secular. They might conceive of inviting someone from their secular life into their sacred life, but do not easily merge the two by regarding their work itself as sacred.

Many of us make these sacred-secular distinctions, leading us to isolate God from the better part of our daily lives. Dorothy Sayers wrote of work, "it should be looked upon, not as a necessary drudgery to be undergone for the purpose of making money, but as a way of life in which the nature of man should find its proper exercise and delight and so fulfill itself to the glory of God."[1]

---

[1]Dorothy Sayers, "Why Work?," in *Letters to a Diminished Church* (New York: Thomas Nelson, 2004), 118.

This connection between work and God's glory results from the recognition that work is a fulfillment of God's instruction to the first humans to "be fruitful." The role of humans in glorifying God in the world, including the world of politics, is the starting point for this chapter's two Calvinist approaches to Christian political engagement.

God's relationship with humanity begins with a command to steward the created world, recorded in Genesis 1:28 and 2:15. The call to care for creation, sometimes called the dominion mandate or creation mandate, extends to humanity's responsibility for the flourishing of all of creation, including the systems and structures that humans will build. As Old Testament scholar J. Michael Thigpen puts it, "flourishing and justice are part and parcel of the creation mandate. Humanity's rule is designed to facilitate flourishing and to enact justice."[2]

Humanity was created to be partners in God's ongoing creative work. John Calvin (1509–1564) consistently built his theology around God's sovereignty and understood humans as mediators of God's authority, with a covenant responsibility to superintend society for the sake of God's glory and human flourishing. The two Christian approaches to government examined in this chapter, direct Christian influence and principled pluralism, share a focus on responsibility to steward the world, including the political world, but they take that responsibility in different directions. The direct Christian influence model encourages Christians to exert significant influence over government to bring public policy into alignment with Christian ethics and values. The principled pluralism model emphasizes the distinctions between different spheres in society and encourages Christians to safeguard the church's sphere and to influence other spheres for the common good.

CALVINIST POLITICAL THEOLOGY

Does God choose the president? It's a common and valid question for Christians, and one that people answer differently. For the Calvinist, the answer is *sort of*. Elections occur under God's sovereign authority, and so their results are within God's will, not opposed to it. In the Calvinist understanding of God's providence, God is the direct or indirect cause of

---

[2]J. Michael Thigpen, "Flourishing and Justice as 'Subduing' the Earth," Oikonomia Network, October 5, 2020, https://oikonomianetwork.org/2020/10/flourishing-and-justice-as-subduing -the-earth/.

everything that happens, not merely a complicit bystander. As Reformed theologian Daniel Migliore explains, "God governs the course of nature and history down to the smallest details."[3] Calvinist theology emphasizes the sovereignty of God, and the political realm is not exempt from God's providential superintendence.

John Calvin, leader of one branch of the sixteenth-century Protestant Reformation, grounded his theology in a strong affirmation of God's sovereignty. Because God is sovereign, all that happens is consistent with God's will and is the result of God's direct or indirect action. Human government is a mediator of God's power and has no authority except that which God grants it. Civil rulers are charged with overseeing society in accordance with God's law. Accordingly, the Genevan Confession (1536) states, "Because there is one only Lord and Master who has dominion over our consciences, and because his will is the only principle of all justice, we confess all our life ought to be ruled in accordance with the commandments of his holy law in which is contained all perfection of justice, and that we ought to have no other rule of good and just living."[4] In Calvinism, government is an agent of God's dominion, responsible for restraining and punishing sin, while encouraging and incentivizing godliness. Because God's laws promote human flourishing, governing society in accordance with those laws is the best way to secure the common good.

John Calvin's theology. Calvin's theology starts with God's sovereignty and proceeds to humanity's sinful original nature, which Calvin described as "a hereditary depravity and corruption of our nature, diffused into all parts of the soul, which first makes us liable to God's wrath, then also brings forth in us . . . what Paul often calls sin."[5] Given the "naked and destitute" and "rotten" state of human nature that resulted from the "contagion" of sin, it follows that disaster is imminent if people are left entirely to our own devices.[6] Because rationality is also marred by sin, reason "is subject to so many errors, dashes against so many obstacles, is

---

[3]Daniel L. Migliore, *Faith Seeking Understanding: An Introduction to Christian Theology*, 3rd ed. (Grand Rapids, MI: Eerdmans, 2014), 126.

[4]John Calvin, "The Genevan Confession (1536)," in *Calvin: Theological Treatises*, ed. and trans. J. K. S. Reid, vol. XXII of *The Library of Christian Classics* (Philadelphia: Westminster Press, 1954), 26-27.

[5]John Calvin, *Institutes of the Christian Religion*, Library of Christian Classics, ed. John T. McNeill, trans. Ford Lewis Battles (Philadelphia: Westminster Press, 1960), 2.I.8.

[6]Calvin, *Institutes* 2.I.7.

caught in so many difficulties, that it is far from directing us aright."[7] Only those whom the Holy Spirit has regenerated "sometimes ask that their hearts be conformed to obedience to God's law."[8] Given the human condition, government is necessary to restrain vice and promote virtue. However, those who govern are merely sin-sick humans. Humanity cannot be trusted to govern itself and must therefore be subject to God's law. People must submit to God, or at least obey God's law as mediated through human laws, for humanity to flourish.

With God's sovereignty and human sinfulness as his starting point, Calvin set forth a political theology in his *Institutes of the Christian Religion* (1559), in which several sections address the purpose and function of civil government.[9] Calvin made a distinction between civil and spiritual government similar to the Lutheran Two Kingdoms theology examined in chapter five; however, Calvin saw church and government as partners with different roles that served the same goal.[10] Calvin wrote, "civil government has as its appointed end . . . to cherish and protect the outward worship of God, to defend sound doctrine of piety and the position of the church, to adjust our life to the society of men, to form our social behavior to civil righteousness, to reconcile us with one another, and to promote the general peace and tranquility."[11] For Calvin, civil government was a gracious gift of God to restrain "the insolence of evil men" whose "wickedness is so stubborn" that it requires oversight by a body through which God mediates the authority to exact punishment.[12]

Calvin was working in a city-state governed by an elected council, not in a kingdom or empire as many other Reformers were, which gave him a unique vantage point on the role of magistrates. Calvin argued that magistrates "have a mandate from God, have been invested with divine authority, and are wholly God's representatives."[13] Magistrates uphold the law, which should be aligned with the law of God. According to Calvin, one can know God's law through God's general revelation in natural law. Thus, the magistrate who governs in accordance with natural law will

---

[7]Calvin, *Institutes* 2.II.25.

[8]Calvin, *Institutes* 2.II.27.

[9]See Calvin, *Institutes* 4.XX.

[10]Bernard M. G. Reardon, *Religious Thought in the Reformation*, 2nd ed. (New York: Longman, 1995), 160.

[11]Calvin, *Institutes* 4.XX.2.

[12]Calvin, *Institutes* 4.XX.2.

[13]Calvin, *Institutes* 4.XX.4.

govern toward the proper goal of submission to God.[14] Serving in civil government, wrote Calvin, is "a calling, not only holy and lawful before God, but also the most sacred and by far the most honorable of all callings in the whole life of mortal men."[15] Calvin believed that magistrates who understood their role as holy vocation would govern justly and resist corruption.[16]

Calvin recognized the possibility, even the probability, that sinful men would sometimes be corrupt, lazy, and wicked rulers. However, he maintained that even "they who rule unjustly and incompetently have been raised up by [God] to punish the wickedness of the people," and "should be held in the same reverence and esteem by his subjects, in so far as public obedience is concerned, in which they would hold the best of kings if he were given to them."[17] Calvin suggested that God might raise up a citizen to resist or punish a wicked ruler on a rare occasion, but an entire populace opposing the government was tantamount to opposing God.[18] Some elements of Calvin's political theology are better suited to different historical and political contexts than others, so we turn now to several historical attempts to apply Calvin's ideas.

Applying Calvin's political theology in Geneva and New England. John Calvin went from obscurity to notoriety when he led the Swiss city-state of Geneva's transition to Protestantism. The city council needed a Protestant theologian to reform Geneva when the city council voted to become Protestant in 1535. Calvin, a Frenchman, had converted to Protestantism in the early 1530s and had begun to write a systematic Reformed theology, making him the perfect, albeit reluctant, candidate for reforming Geneva.

Sixteenth-century Europe had no paradigm for church-state separation, individual religious liberty, or confessional pluralism. Religious uniformity was understood to be essential to the stability and welfare of any society; therefore, the Genevan church leaders required citizens to sign a confession of faith, or else leave the city.[19] Calvin's goal in reforming Geneva was to build a godly commonwealth where anyone who submitted to the

---

[14]Calvin, *Institutes* 4.XX.16.

[15]Calvin, *Institutes* 4.XX.4.

[16]Calvin, *Institutes* 4.XX.6.

[17]Calvin, *Institutes* 4.XX.25.

[18]Calvin, *Institutes* 4.XX.30.

[19]R. Ward Holder, *Crisis and Renewal: The Era of the Reformations* (Louisville, KY: Westminster John Knox, 2009), 150.

law of the land was thereby also submitting to the law of God, thus fulfilling the dominion mandate. Personal convictions were important, but they would follow after conformity.

Creating a godly commonwealth required moral reform and a system to enforce morality. Apparently, the citizens of Geneva had a reputation for relaxed morals, so Calvin created a Consistory to rein them in.[20] The Ecclesiastical Ordinances adopted by the city required the Consistory representatives to be "men of virtuous lives, honest, without reproach and beyond all suspicion, above all God-fearing and of good spiritual prudence. And, they should be elected in such a manner that there will be some of them in each quarter of the city, so that their eyes will be everywhere."[21] The Consistory had jurisdiction over moral and marital cases, including violations of church polity, such as church attendance, drunkenness, and premarital cohabitation, and had authority to excommunicate those found to be in violation.

A small sampling of Consistory records gives a sense of its purview: "relapses to Catholicism (39 instances); blasphemy (28); general disrespect and complaining about Calvin and his rule (62); games of chance (36); immorality (13); insulting French immigrants (9); dancing and unseemly singing (12); absence from worship and catechetical instruction (10); issues of faith (7) . . ."[22] As intrusive as this may seem, Calvin's intent was for the Consistory to help people live the way God intended.[23] John Knox, who led Scotland's reformation, called Geneva "the most perfect school of Christ that ever was in this earth since the days of the Apostles."[24] The government's role in building a moral society remains central to Calvinist approaches to politics.

English Puritans carried Calvin's political theology to the New England colonies in the seventeenth century. The Puritans, so-called because of their desire to purify the Church of England from Catholicism, had adopted Calvinism in Geneva, where some of them had fled during the anti-Protestant reign of Queen Mary ("Bloody Mary," as she is still known,

---

[20]Reardon, *Religious Thought*, 157.

[21]"The Ecclesiastical Ordinances of 1541," in *The European Reformations Sourcebook*, 2nd ed., ed. Carter Lindberg (New York: Wiley Blackwell, 2014), 162.

[22]Carter Lindberg, *The European Reformations* (Malden, MA: Wiley Blackwell, 2010), 249.

[23]Robert M. Kingdon, "The Geneva Consistory in the Time of Calvin," in *Calvinism in Europe: 1540–1620* (Cambridge: Cambridge University Press, 1994), 34.

[24]John Knox quoted in Lindberg, *European Reformations*, 234.

r. 1553–1558). Upon returning to England during the reigns of Queen Elizabeth I (r. 1558–1603) and King James I (r. 1603–1625), Puritans had hoped to reform the country's religion, but instead faced rejection and persecution. Some emigrated to the Netherlands, then to the Massachusetts Bay Colony, where they attempted to re-create and improve upon Calvin's Geneva.

John Winthrop (1588–1649) laid the theological foundation for the Massachusetts Bay Colony in his "Model of Christian Charity" speech, delivered in 1630 during the voyage to New England. Drawing on the analogy of the body of Christ from 1 Corinthians 12, Winthrop described the company of Puritans as "one body in Christ" who would share each other's strength and weakness, joy and sorrow, well-being and woes.[25] In the Puritans' ideal society, people would live according to Christian love, with the participants "becoming a part of [Christ's] body and being knit with it in the bond of love," said Winthrop.[26] However, because original sin leads people to self-love, only those who had experienced "new birth" were capable of that love; therefore, only reborn Christians would be able to fully participate in Puritan society.[27] The Puritans understood themselves as a covenant community from which God expected obedience and promised to bless the colony in return.[28] Since only reborn Christians were capable of obedience, only church members would be eligible for citizenship in the Puritan colonies, lest God withhold blessing due to sin in the community.

As in Geneva, the Massachusetts Bay Colony's civil and ecclesial governments worked in tandem to create and preserve a community of saints. The elders of the local congregations functioned like Geneva's Consistory, determining the colony's moral values and watching for violators.[29] The success, stability, and divine blessing of the colonies "depended on the way a congregation's members accepted censure, advice, and consolation."[30] To contemporary ears this may sound inquisitorial, but we must remember that Puritans believed the success and stability of the whole community depended on everyone's covenant obedience. Those whom the church elders

---

[25]John Winthrop, "A Modell of Christian Charity (1630)," *Hanover Historical Texts Collection*, https://history.hanover.edu/texts/winthmod.html, accessed May 30, 2023. Spelling updated.

[26]Winthrop, "Modell of Christian Charity."

[27]Winthrop, "Modell of Christian Charity."

[28]Winthrop, "Modell of Christian Charity."

[29]John Butler, "Religion in England's First Colonies," in *Religion in American Life* (New York: Oxford University Press), 54.

[30]Butler, "Religion," 55.

perceived as a threat to the covenant, such as Anne Hutchinson (1591–1643) or Mary Dyer (1611–1660), were a threat to the assurance of God's blessing.

By the 1780s, strict Puritanism had loosened to cultural Congregationalism, yet Massachusetts retained elements of its Puritan roots in its state constitution. The 1780 Massachusetts Constitution declared, "the happiness of a people, and the good order and preservation of civil government, essentially depend upon piety, religion, and morality." The legislature had the right to require towns to "make suitable provision, at their own expense, for the institution of public worship of God, and for the support and maintenance of public Protestant teachers of piety, religion, and morality," which is consistent with the Puritan understanding of the connection between public morality and divine blessing.[31] Even as Puritan congregations declined and New England secularized over the decades, the expectation that the country should be a crucible for forming virtue and that its prosperity depended upon the faith and morality of its inhabitants became embedded in American identity.

The Puritan idea that God has covenanted to bless America on the condition of the country's faithfulness has become part of American religious and political rhetoric. Some transfer God's covenant with Israel to the United States as a new Jerusalem, while others retain the idea that magistrates should govern according to the law of God. Today, Calvin's political theology is most evident in two divergent approaches to faith and politics: direct Christian influence and principled pluralism.

DIRECT CHRISTIAN INFLUENCE

We can think of direct Christian influence as a politically conservative corollary to the social gospel. Both approaches want American law to reinforce Christian values, but they grow from different theological roots and emphasize different Christian values, leading to divergent political ideologies. Those who hold a direct Christian influence position regard Christianity as the best foundation for American law and culture, so they believe it is biblical and desirable for Christians to try to legally establish Christian values.[32] Many Christians in the United States believe the

---

[31]"Massachusetts Constitution (1780)," in *The Sacred Rights of Conscience,* ed. Daniel L. Dreisbach and Mark David Hall (Indianapolis: Liberty Fund, 2009), 246.

[32]Harold O. J. Brown, "The Christian America Position," in *God and Politics: Four Views on the Reformation of Civil Government,* ed. Gary Scott Smith (Phillipsburg, NJ: Presbyterian and Reformed, 1989), 127.

government ought to uphold Christian values, whether implicitly or explicitly, because biblical morality is what's best for individual and collective well-being. Therefore, many Christians see it as a violation of Christian conscience to support policies or candidates that do not reinforce Christian values. But which Christian values? In this case, *Christian values* is often shorthand for conservative Christian positions on sexual ethics, marriage, religious liberty, and a biblically based civil society.[33] The direct Christian influence approach sees Christian values as the necessary foundation for a stable and godly society, and warns that civil instability results from the country's shift away from Christian values.

Wayne Grudem (b. 1948), one of the best-known advocates for this approach, argues in *Politics According to the Bible* that "Christians *should* seek to influence civil government according to God's moral standards and God's purposes for government as revealed in the Bible (when rightly understood)."[34] As we have already seen with the social gospel and its recent iterations, however, Christians do not all agree about which biblical values ought to inform civil law or even what Christian morality means in every situation. Grudem addresses this challenge by saying those who rightly understand the Bible include evangelicals and conservative Catholics, among whom *"there are vastly more areas of widespread agreement than disagreement, both today and throughout history*, regarding the main teachings of the Christian faith and the methods of proper interpretation."[35] Not all Christians who adopt a direct Christian influence approach are theologically Calvinist, but this model is most consistent with and has historical roots in Calvinism, especially through American Puritanism.

Direct Christian influence in the United States' founding. The desire to use the Bible as the foundation for American law and culture arises from the belief that America was founded on Christian principles. Christianity has historically held a privileged and majority position in the country that ought to be maintained. Thus, the role of Christianity in America's founding has become a significant point of historical justification for direct Christian influence.

---

[33]See, for example, the issues promoted by the Family Research Council, www.frc.org/.
[34]Wayne Grudem, *Politics According to the Bible* (Grand Rapids, MI: Zondervan, 2010), 55. Italics in original.
[35]Grudem, *Politics*, 55. Italics in original.

During the revolutionary period, loyalists and patriots alike cited Scripture as the reason for their revolutionary action or resistance.[36] Some of the Founding Fathers understood the United States as uniquely ordained by God for a divine purpose, the success of which depended upon the Christian faithfulness of the populace. For example, John Witherspoon, a Presbyterian minister and member of the Continental Congress, preached at the end of the Revolutionary War, "Their state is so little to be envied, who are free as citizens, but slaves as sinners. All temporal comforts derive their value from their being the fruits of divine goodness, the evidence of covenant love, and the earnest of everlasting mercy. It is therefore our indispensable duty to endeavour to obtain the sanctified improvement of every blessing, whether public or personal."[37]

Samuel Sherwood, a Congregational minister, described the newly established United States as a providential gift from God to the church, which God himself had planted "as a choice vine, in this once howling wilderness. He brought her as on eagles wings from the seat of oppression and persecution 'to her own place,' has, of his unmerited grace, bestowed liberties and privileges upon her, beyond what are enjoyed in any other part of the world."[38] Thomas Reese, a Presbyterian minister in South Carolina, argued for "the utility, even necessity of religion, to the well being, we might venture to say, to the very existence of civil society," since Christianity alone could inculcate virtues in the populace.[39] Witherspoon, Sherwood, and Reese are representative of the popular view, consistent with Calvin's theology of God's providence, that America's founding was divinely ordained for the church, and that America's blessedness depended upon covenant obedience to God.

Many of the first state constitutions granted a central place for Christianity. South Carolina's 1778 Constitution, for example, declared, "the Christian Protestant religion shall be deemed . . . the established religion of this State" and went on to list specific beliefs a group must affirm to be called a Christian church.[40] In the decades following the US Constitution's

---

[36]Mark Noll, *In the Beginning Was the Word* (Oxford: Oxford University Press, 2016), 296-307.

[37]John Witherspoon, "Sermon Delivered at a Public Thanksgiving After Peace (1782)," in *Sacred Rights of Conscience*, 288.

[38]Samuel Sherwood, "The Churches Flight into the Wilderness," in *Critical Issues in American Religious History: A Reader*, ed. Robert R. Mathisen (Waco, TX: Baylor University Press, 2001), 126.

[39]Thomas Reese, "An Essay on the Influence of Religion in Civil Society (1788)," in *Sacred Rights of Conscience*, 318.

[40]"South Carolina Constitution of 1778, Article XXXVIII," in *Sacred Rights of Conscience*, 244.

ratification, states gradually removed Christian establishment from their constitutions. It was left to Christian individuals to advocate for Christianity as the proper legal foundation of the country.

The presidential election of 1800 witnessed just such advocacy. Rev. William Linn, a Dutch Reformed clergyman from New York, wrote and widely distributed his "Serious Considerations on the Election of a President," denouncing Thomas Jefferson's candidacy on the grounds of "his disbelief of the Holy Scriptures; or, in other words, his rejection of Christian Religion and open profession of Deism."[41] Although the Constitution ruled out religious tests, Linn's concern was that Jefferson's deism would harm society since, "If there be no God, there is no law" and without belief in God to stop him, "[my neighbor] will soon pick my pocket, and break not only my *leg* but my *neck*."[42] The concern that a lack of Christian faith equates to a lack of morality continues to motivate Christians to restrain vice by force of Bible-based laws.

As American society has become increasingly secularized since the 1960s, questions about the role of Christianity in America's founding have become flashpoints of debate. Was America founded as a Christian nation? Historian Mark David Hall argues that "America's founders drew from their Christian convictions to create a constitutional order that benefits *all* Americans, not just Christians."[43] Hall's argument is useful for representatives of the Calvinist view: America had a Christian founding, and Christian values benefit all Americans. Advocates of direct Christian influence often base their position on the idea that Christian values are part of the country's DNA and therefore contend that Christianity ought to have a unique place in law and culture, even as other religions are legally tolerated. Debates about the role of Christianity in America's founding became heated in the late twentieth century as politically conservative evangelicals sought historical justification for directly influencing the government.

The direct Christian influence of the religious right. While Christians have always sought to directly influence the government in a variety of ways, direct Christian influence came to define conservative evangelicalism

---

[41]William Linn, "Serious Considerations on the Election of a President: Addressed to the Citizens of the United States (1800)," in *Sacred Rights of Conscience*, 482.

[42]Linn, "Serious Considerations," 486.

[43]Mark David Hall, *Did America Have a Christian Founding? Separating Modern Myth from Historical Truth* (Nashville: Thomas Nelson, 2019), XXVII.

in the latter part of the twentieth century. Among evangelicals, direct Christian influence on public policy has been a relatively recent phenomenon after a period of isolation in the early twentieth century (see chapter four). Americans often wonder how White evangelicals came to be so strongly aligned with the Republican Party, while White mainline Protestants and Catholics are more politically divided.

Historian Randall Balmer has documented the efforts of evangelical political organizers such as Paul Weyrich to enliven evangelical political engagement. Their strategy was to foment evangelicals' frustration with government, then direct that frustration toward a selection of political causes, starting with tax exemption policies, and later shifting to abortion and a host of ideologically related issues.[44] By Weyrich's own account, it was the Internal Revenue Service's denial of tax exemption for racially segregated Christian private schools, most significantly Bob Jones University, that "brought the fundamentalists and evangelicals into the political process."[45] The evangelical political base further expanded when abortion emerged as a political issue in the 1970s. Opposition to abortion became a conservative litmus test that united evangelical Christians as a voting bloc that conservative Republican candidates could rely on for support. The Christian right coalesced in the late 1970s as a loose fraternity of conservative Christian political advocacy organizations that united to move evangelicals toward political conservatism and the Republican Party for the sake of exerting direct Christian influence.

Evangelical political organizations under the umbrella of the Christian right have been incredibly influential in American politics since the early 1980s, when they united behind Ronald Reagan's 1980 presidential campaign, denying Jimmy Carter a second term. Ironically, Carter was well-known for his church involvement and family values, while Reagan seldom attended church and was the first divorced man to win the presidency.[46] The 1970s had been a time of crisis and social upheaval, prompting theologian Richard John Neuhaus to lament "the enforced privatization of religion" that "systematically excluded from policy consideration the operative

---

[44]Randall Balmer, "Re-create the Nation," in *Evangelicalism in America* (Waco, TX: Baylor University Press, 2016).

[45]Balmer, "Re-create the Nation," 113.

[46]Clyde Wilcox, *Onward Christian Soldiers?: The Religious Right in American Politics*, 4th ed. (Boulder, CO: Westview Press, 2010), 124.

values of the American people, values that are overwhelmingly grounded in religious belief."[47]

Evangelicals found their long-held values challenged by the women's rights and gay rights movements, and found themselves displaced from the center of society as the United States became less Christian in belief and practice. Consistent with the Calvinist concern that a lack of shared morality is destabilizing for society and harmful to human flourishing, Christian leaders like Billy Graham (1918–2018), Pat Robertson (1930–2023), Jerry Falwell Sr. (1933–2007), and others began to flex their political muscles in hopes of restoring Christian values to a central place in American culture and law. Charles Colson (1931–2012), who became a Christian while imprisoned for his role in the Watergate scandal, explained in his 1987 book *Kingdoms in Conflict*, "Christians have an obligation to bring transcendent moral values into the public debate" even as they recognize that "being biblically motivated and informed may give wisdom, [but] it does not necessarily assure political success."[48]

Since the 1980s, White evangelical Christians have grown in political influence, even as they have declined as a percentage of the overall population.[49] This inverse relationship makes sense: as Christian social influence and status decrease, the sense of political urgency increases. Whereas for many decades Christians could assume that the law of the land was basically consistent with conservative Christian values, that is no longer a safe assumption. And from a Calvinist direct Christian influence perspective, that is a serious problem for society as a whole. Consistent with the belief that the stability of society depends upon people upholding God's law, "the Religious Right emphasized the importance of moral behavior to the preservation of American democracy" and believed that "the health of an evangelical Christian worldview was the health of the nation, and that the rise of pluralism of belief led to decay of American culture," explains historian Matthew Bowman.[50]

---

[47] Quoted in Steven P. Miller, *The Age of Evangelicalism: America's Born Again Years* (Oxford: Oxford University Press, 2014), 88.

[48] Charles Colson, *Kingdoms in Conflict* (Grand Rapids, MI: Zondervan, 1987), 279, 283.

[49] "PRRI 2021 Census of American Religion, Updates and Trends: White Christian Decline Slows, Unaffiliated Growth Levels Off," Public Religion Research Institute, April 27, 2022, www.prri .org/spotlight/prri-2021-american-values-atlas-religious-affiliation-updates-and-trends-white -christian-decline-slows-unaffiliated-growth-levels-off/.

[50] Matthew Bowman, *Christian: The Politics of a Word in America* (Cambridge, MA: Harvard University Press, 2018), 201.

Exerting Christian influence in politics, in this view, is not merely grasping for power. Rather, direct Christian influence preserves the general well-being and stability of a country. When Christianity loses influence, society becomes chaotic. We can recognize this view when Christians share messages on social media claiming school shootings would not happen if prayer and Bible reading were restored to public schools.[51] I experienced this personally after the 1999 mass shooting at Columbine High School, after which I wore a shirt to school that declared, "1963: The Supreme Court bans prayer in school. Today I'm bringing it back!"

Today, the religious right is a fluid network of politically conservative organizations that base their policy positions on their biblical interpretation, especially regarding issues like abortion, same-sex marriage, gender identity, individual and corporate religious liberty, and pro-business economic policies. The early organizations that formed the religious right, such as Jerry Falwell's Moral Majority and Pat Robertson's Christian Coalition, have waned, but direct Christian influence continues through well-funded and well-connected advocacy organizations including the American Family Association, the Heritage Foundation, and the Family Research Council, among others.

EVALUATION OF DIRECT CHRISTIAN INFLUENCE

Not every Christian who seeks to directly influence politics is politically conservative or Calvinist, but White evangelicals have become a reliable conservative political base. The direct-influence approach has strengths, but also significant challenges, starting with disagreement about biblical interpretation. Wayne Grudem addresses this issue by suggesting that Christians who interpret Scripture correctly are those "who take the whole Bible to be the trustworthy Word of God (that is, among mainstream evangelical interpreters at least, as well as among many conservative Roman Catholic interpreters)."[52] Thus, Grudem defines correct interpretation as evangelical and conservative. As we have already seen with the social gospel, some Christians' interpretation of Scripture leads them to different political positions than those of Christian conservatives, even among

---

[51]Bryan Fischer, "Why School Shootings: Not Enough God, Not Enough Guns," *American Family Association*, February 15, 2018, www.afa.net/the-stand/culture/2018/02/why-school-shootings -not-enough-god-not-enough-guns/.

[52]Grudem, *Politics*, 56.

Christians who trust the Bible as the Word of God. There simply is not a Christian biblical political consensus; and since the country is not, has never been, and will not become the Kingdom of God, we cannot expect a Christian consensus to be imposed in the country. Such lack of consensus does not mean Christians should not continue working to bring biblical values to bear on society, but advocates of direct Christian influence should be mindful that Christians who come to different political conclusions can do so on the basis of Scripture.

We can evaluate direct Christian influence based on its mixed results in American history. Christians, including conservative evangelical Christians, have used the Bible to defend positions that the vast majority of Christians today (including conservative evangelicals) find morally repugnant. The fight against the civil rights movement is a chastening example. In *The Bible Told Them So*, historian Russell Hawkins demonstrates that many southern evangelicals rejected desegregation on supposedly biblical grounds. Speaking at the Southern Baptist Convention in opposition to the Supreme Court's 1954 ruling in *Brown v. Board of Education*, Pastor W. M. Nevins declared, "I do not believe the Bible teaches and I do not believe that God approves amalgamation of the races." His colleague Arthur Hay added, "Negroes are descendants of Ham [and] we whites must keep our blood pure."[53]

Views like those of Nevins and Hay did not win in the official proceedings of the SBC, but neither were they outliers among southern evangelicals. It was common for southern evangelicals to put forth denominational resolutions claiming "God had segregated the races for his own purposes, given this arrangement divine sanction, and instructed the faithful through scripture not to pursue racial integration."[54] Wayne Grudem suggests that this negative example does not mean Christians should refrain from applying the Bible to civil society. He points out that "the American civil rights movement that resulted in the outlawing of racial segregation and discrimination was led by Martin Luther King Jr., a Christian pastor, and supported by many Christian churches and groups."[55]

---

[53]J. Russell Hawkins, *The Bible Told Them So* (Oxford: Oxford University Press, 2021), 20-21.
[54]Hawkins, *Bible,* 45.
[55]Grudem, *Politics,* 50.

While this is true, neither King nor many of the Christians who supported the civil rights movement were conservative evangelicals, but rather embraced a social gospel that Grudem rejects as a liberal distortion of Scripture. Though historical misuse of Scripture is not a sufficient argument against direct Christian influence, it does raise questions about which type of Christian influence, which approach to Scripture, and which stances on issues should be considered right. For Grudem, the conservative evangelical consensus is a good guide to right application of Scripture, but history demonstrates that evangelical conservatives have not always interpreted Scripture faithfully.

Another challenge of the conservative direct Christian influence model is the loss of moral high ground caused by revelations of abuse in evangelical churches. In recent years, many evangelical churches, schools, and leaders have faced credible accusations of abuse and mishandling of abuse allegations. Since 2019, the *Houston Chronicle*, the *Fort Worth Star-Telegram*, and others have uncovered hundreds of credible abuse and sexual assault allegations against evangelical pastors, many of whom continued working in churches.[56] These revelations have led some evangelicals to a reckoning with theology and church structures that allow abuse, while other evangelicals have been defensive and self-protective. Rachael Denhollander, an attorney and advocate for victims of sexual abuse, herself a theologically and politically conservative Christian, has experienced evangelical church leaders' refusal to address institutional coverup of sexual abuse.[57] Sovereign Grace Ministries, Bill Hybels, Bill Gothard, Ravi Zacharias, Kanakuk Kamps, and others in the disturbing litany of abuse scandals are all within the evangelical fold.

Sexual abuse and coverup are by no means only conservative or evangelical problems, as the Roman Catholic Church's sexual abuse scandal makes clear. But conservative evangelical direct Christian influence often focuses on laws related to sexual behavior (abortion, same-sex marriage, and so on), so frequent news of sexual predation and immorality smacks of hypocrisy.

Public perception that direct Christian influence on politics is bland and uncritical poses a challenge to the mission and witness of the church.

---

[56]Robert Downen et al., "Abuse of Faith," *The Houston Chronicle*, February 2019; "Hundreds of Sex Abuse Allegations Found . . . ," *Fort Worth Star-Telegram*, December 9, 2018.

[57]Morgan Lee, interview with Rachael Denhollander, "My Larry Nassar Testimony Went Viral: But There's More to the Gospel Than Forgiveness," *Christianity Today*, January 13, 2021.

One frequent observation is that Christians are selective about which convictions have policy implications versus which are private and personal. On what basis are some biblical convictions applied legally, but not others? Or how are biblical convictions defined and into what policy areas do they extend? It seems to many Americans that conservative Christians align with the Republican Party because of a few issues, then adopt or excuse the rest of the party's positions. Pro-life policy advocacy is a ready example. Christians who defend the right to life of babies in the womb are frequently accused of hypocrisy for rejecting welfare programs or supporting capital punishment. *Christianity Today* acknowledged this problem in a 2017 article noting the accusation, "if you were *really* pro-life . . . there are other, outside-the-womb causes you would champion just as ardently."[58] While accusations of hypocrisy are not always made in good faith, Christians can examine whether the ways we apply our faith to public policy are inconsistent in ways that damage our public witness.

A final challenge to the direct Christian influence model is the perception that what politically engaged conservative Christians really want is political power at any cost. Culture war rhetoric invites this perception. "Culture War" for most Americans connotes battles over social issues that Christians are at the forefront of advocating for or rejecting. James Davison Hunter popularized the term "Culture Wars" in 1991, when he wrote "America is in the midst of a culture war that has had and will continue to have reverberations not only within public policy but within the lives of ordinary Americans everywhere. . . . The personal disagreements that fire the culture war are deep and perhaps unreconcilable. *But these differences are often intensified and aggravated by the way they are present in public.*"[59]

Christians did not invent the culture wars, nor are we the only ones fighting them or even the only ones using belligerent rhetoric and methods to win them. But public perception that Christians are aggressive and power-hungry damages the public witness of a faith that purports to follow the Prince of Peace. In philosopher Peter Kreeft's 1998 article "How to Win the Culture War," the author explained, "our entire

---

[58]Matt Reynolds, "In Defense of Pro-Life 'Hypocrisy,'" *Christianity Today*, November 27, 2017, www .christianitytoday.com/ct/2017/december/in-defense-of-pro-life-hypocrisy.html.

[59]James Davison Hunter, *Culture Wars: The Struggle to Define America* (New York: Basic Books, 1991), 34. Italics in original.

civilization is in crisis," but Christians won't win the war "if you use the wrong weapons."[60] To those who might argue that Christianity's victory in the culture wars is assured because the "church is big and rich and free in America," Kreeft responded, "Yes. Just like ancient Israel. And if God still loves his Church in America, he will soon make it small and poor and persecuted, as he did to ancient Israel, so that he can keep it alive. If he loves us, he will prune us, and we will bleed, and the blood of the martyrs will be the seed of the Church again, and a second spring will come—but not without blood."[61] As the body of Christ, the church's model is crucifixion and resurrection, a model that is difficult to emulate from a position of power.

In the wake of the 2016 election of Donald Trump, days after a video recording of him bragging about groping and kissing women without their consent became public, some evangelical leaders began to seriously examine the close alignment between the evangelical movement and the Republican Party. Peter Wehner, a conservative evangelical, stated bluntly, "support for Trump comes at a high cost for Christian witness."[62] Even more starkly, Randall Balmer asserted, "after a long and lingering illness, evangelicalism died on November 8, 2016. On that day, 81 percent of white American evangelicals who for decades claimed to be concerned about 'family values' registered their votes for a twice-divorced, thrice-married, self-confessed sexual predator whose understanding of the faith is so truncated that he can't even fake religious literacy."[63]

Sociologists are in the midst of examining the impact of the Trump presidency on Christianity in general and evangelicalism in particular. While we must be cautious not to confuse causation with correlation, recent Pew Research Center data on Christian beliefs and behavior demonstrates that "people are giving up on Christianity. They will continue to do so."[64] Among academics who study these trends, many posit that

---

[60]Peter Kreeft, "How to Win the Culture War," *Crisis* 16, no. 6 (June 1998): 12-15, www.crisis magazine.com/vault/how-to-win-the-culture-war-2.

[61]Kreeft, "How to Win the Culture War."

[62]Peter Wehner, "The Deepening Crisis in Evangelical Christianity," in *The Spiritual Danger of Donald Trump*, ed. Ronald J. Sider (Eugene, OR: Cascade, 2020), 73.

[63]Randall Balmer, "Donald Trump and the Death of Evangelicalism," in *The Spiritual Danger of Donald Trump*, ed. Ronald J. Sider (Eugene, OR: Cascade, 2020), 78.

[64]Daniel Silliman, "Decline of Christianity Shows No Signs of Stopping," *Christianity Today*, September 13, 2022, www.christianitytoday.com/news/2022/september/christian-decline-inexorable -nones-rise-pew-study.html.

at least part of the reason for Christianity's decline is the tight bond between White evangelicalism and the Republican Party.[65] According to Ryan Burge, a pastor and political scientist, "The rate of self-identified Democrats giving up on church in their 20s–50s doubled from the end of Barack Obama's presidency to the end of Trump's. . . . At the same time, more Republicans started identifying as evangelical but not attending any worship services."[66] When people perceive evangelical alignment with the Republican Party as uncritical and unconditional, then disaffiliate from the body of Christ rather than become associated with a political agenda, it is a serious problem. This does not mean evangelical Christians should not be Republican; however, evangelicals need to examine the potential cost of their political unanimity for Christian witness.

The primary strength of direct Christian influence is its insistence that conscience and politics should not be divided. If a Christian believes an action is immoral, it is consistent to also believe that action should be illegal. Separatists and separationists approach this differently, allowing for the state to go one way as Christian conviction goes another. Direct Christian influence presupposes that our faith ought to be integrated with every area of life, including our political positions and party affiliations. At its best, direct Christian influence seeks the common good, believing that God's design will promote the flourishing of all people.

FAITHFUL DIRECT CHRISTIAN INFLUENCE

Direct Christian influence is a viable approach to faithfully engaging with American politics, when practiced with the above challenges in mind. A Christian can hold strong convictions and believe that these convictions reflect God's best for society and can advocate for their convictions in the public square. Such advocacy can communicate love of neighbor, respect, and humility. Those who pursue direct Christian influence will need to be wary of those who attempt to co-opt their political support through stirring up fear, anger, or resentment. To engage in direct Christian influence faithfully, one's posture is as important as one's policy positions.

---

[65]Paul A. Djupe et al., "Are the Politics of the Christian Right Linked to State Rates of the Nonreligious? The Importance of Salient Controversy," *Political Research Quarterly* 71, no. 4 (December 2018): 910-22.

[66]Daniel Silliman, "Polarized Out of the Pews," *Christianity Today*, November 2023, 13.

Principled Pluralism

Principled pluralism also has a Calvinist root, but it grows in a different direction than direct Christian influence. Principled pluralism applies Calvin's political theology in support of religious and structural pluralism for the sake of human flourishing. Because the United States is home to dozens of religions and hundreds of Christian traditions, Calvin's Geneva or Puritan New England are impractical models for American society. Moreover, the United States is organized with structural pluralism, which means many different institutions and systems manage the various spheres of society, including the church, government, family, education, marketplace, the arts, and others (in contrast to theocracy or military dictatorship, for example). God's sovereignty and natural law are foundational for the principled pluralist, who views each sphere, including civil government, as part of God's gracious provision for humanity. One can affirm principled pluralism without being Reformed theologically, but principled pluralism is based on Reformed thought

Origins of principled pluralism: Abraham Kuyper and common grace. Abraham Kuyper (1837–1920), a Dutch theologian and prime minister of the Netherlands (1901–1905), adapted Calvin's theology for a religiously diverse country with a representative government. Kuyper's theology of "common grace" began with God's covenant with Noah, in which God promised "I will never again curse the ground . . . nor will I ever again destroy every living creature as I have done" (Genesis 8:21). Drawing on Calvin's doctrine of providence, Kuyper saw the Noahic covenant as God's promise of common grace, whereby "sin will be restrained with the bridle and rein, so that sin will never again before the end of the world develop into such gruesome, hellish outburst and tyranny. . . . The best within man remains just as evil and wild, but the bars around its cage were fortified, so that it cannot again escape like it used to."[67] Common grace is the means by which God prevents humanity from destroying itself after the fall. Because of common grace, human society does not descend into chaos, and we are capable of morality and wisdom, which we can apply to government and other spheres of society.

Common grace enables humans to "fill the earth and subdue it" (Genesis 1:28) for the sake of human flourishing, without sin rendering

---

[67] Abraham Kuyper, *Common Grace: Noah-Abraham*, volume 1, part 1 (Grand Rapids, MI: CLP Academic, 2013), 32.

human efforts fruitless. Kuyper interpreted this first instruction to humanity as a cultural mandate, through which God blesses human cultural formation, including the societal structures we create.[68] Theologian Richard Mouw explains, when humanity lives in accordance with the cultural mandate, we "bring out creation's rich cultural potential, thus displaying God's multifaceted design—aesthetic, familial, economic, political, and so on—for the created order."[69] After the fall, God calls humanity to participate in the restoration of "patterns of obedient cultural formation for which we were created" through "the discovery and implementation of God's complex ordering design, both among and within the spheres," Mouw writes.[70] We can contrast this with an interpretation of Genesis 1:28 that justifies Christian efforts to bend creation to our will, or a worldview that puts sacred and secular at odds with each other. Principled pluralism's emphasis on the common good and human flourishing gives Christians the opportunity to creatively participate in God's restorative project through our work in the world.

Where government is concerned, common grace is evident in God's provision of natural law, which serves as a basis for civil law. John Calvin described natural law as innate knowledge of God's existence and a universal moral code, consistent with Paul's warning in Romans that immoral people are "without excuse" because of the evidence of creation itself (Romans 1:18-23). Thus, civil authorities need not base civil law on the Bible or Christian doctrine per se, because natural law is universally applicable and will not contradict Christian beliefs. In the principled pluralist approach it would be inappropriate to govern a diverse society according to explicitly Christian beliefs, yet natural law, which is an element of common grace, is understood as a universal foundation for legislation that people of different religious backgrounds can agree with. For example, murder, theft, or child neglect can be illegal on the basis of natural law, even though Christians also oppose these behaviors for specifically Christian reasons.

Applying principled pluralism: Sphere sovereignty. Common grace is evident in the plurality of spheres that order society, such as family, church, school, marketplace, and government. Kuyper called this "sphere

---

[68]Richard J. Mouw, "Some Reflections on Sphere Sovereignty," in *Religion, Pluralism, and Public Life,* ed. Luis E. Lugo (Grand Rapids, MI: Eerdmans, 2000), 94-95.

[69]Mouw, "Reflections," 94-95.

[70]Mouw, "Reflections," 95.

sovereignty," because God mediates his sovereignty through each sphere, granting each authority to manage the affairs that are proper to that sphere. Part of the civil government's role, as political scientist Corwin Smidt explains, is to "ensure that the various spheres of authority do not encroach on each other's domain and that the relationships between authorities (whether within one sphere or across different spheres) conform to a just order."[71] One sphere is not inherently more powerful or important than the others, and none should have total control of society. Thus, sphere sovereignty prevents tyranny by state or church. Government's role is to be an agent of common grace by enforcing justice, but it should not encroach on the church's sphere by demanding particular beliefs or moral convictions from citizens.[72]

Structural pluralism avoids the destructiveness of political ideologies that "ascribe ultimacy to some political ideal, thereby making it an idol," and "offer to 'save' society by eradicating the 'evils' that threaten their idol," Bruce Ashford and Dennis Greeson explain.[73] It avoids idolatry by limiting the role of each sphere. This limit prevents Christians from attempting to claim authority over the state or any other sphere, becoming worshipers of our own power, and taking salvation into our own hands. At the same time, structural pluralism is a check on the risks inherent to liberalism and democracy. Political scientist David Koyzis explains that liberalism pursues "progressive emancipation of the individual and the achievement thereby of liberty or freedom," which fails when "it offers a false salvation rooted in a fundamentally religious assertion of human autonomy against external authority," and when it fails to "distinguish adequately the state as an authoritative community irreducible to the voluntary consent of its constituent individuals."[74] Structural pluralism checks these possible failures by emphasizing the common good and conceptualizing the spheres of society as constituted by God instead of by human will alone.

Regarding democracy, Koyzis distinguishes between democracy as a political system and democracy as a creed that "can take on ideological

---

[71]Corwin Smidt, "The Principled Pluralist Perspective," in *Church, State, and Public Justice: Five Views*, ed. P. C. Kemeny (Downers Grove, IL: IVP Academic, 2007), 144.

[72]Smidt, "Principled Pluralist Perspective," 145.

[73]Bruce Riley Ashford and Dennis Greeson, "Modern Political Ideologies," in *Reformed Public Theology: A Global Vision for Life in the World*, ed. Matthew Kaemingk (Grand Rapids, MI: Baker Academic, 2021), 127.

[74]David T. Koyzis, *Political Visions and Illusions* (Downers Grove, IL: IVP Academic, 2019), 33, 62.

dimensions insofar as it embodies a belief in the near infallibility of the vox populi—the voice of the people. Where it is claimed that a policy is right simply because the majority wishes it," which can lead to majoritarian tyranny.[75] Again, principled pluralism guards against this distortion by locating the standard of right and wrong with God, instead of with human ideals or desires. Unflinching certainty in God's sovereignty prevents Christians from attempting to become our own political saviors by baptizing political ideologies then creating religious tyranny; it also allows Christians to recognize the proper limits of the plural spheres of society so that we can speak prophetic truth when the state or any other sphere transgresses its limits.

Sphere sovereignty differentiates the institutional roles of the church, the state, and other spheres of society, but it emphatically does not restrict Christians from being agents of God's grace and redemption in all spheres. Principled pluralism is not separatism; rather, as Smidt notes, "because Christians are called to seek justice (Amos 5:15, 24), Christians are called to political engagement; they are not to refrain from politics because it is deemed to be a sphere of activity outside the domain of God's sovereignty. God instituted government for the welfare of humankind. It makes no sense then that God would not want his children to be involved in politics."[76] The purpose of Christian political involvement is primarily to ensure that the government exercises its God-ordained authority by administering justice without overstepping its boundaries.

The limits sphere sovereignty places on government prevent the state from oppressing its subjects. Reformed theologian Gordon Spykman (1923–1996) explains that Christians are called into government, in part, to ensure that government honors and protects every person's "divinely ordained right to a just and equitable share in the rich resources of God's creation—the right to life, liberty, and a responsible exercise of their offices in the family circle, in the workplace, in community associations, and in society at large."[77] In principled pluralism, Christians are called to act within our spheres of influence in ways that will cause each sphere to operate consistently with God's design as revealed in the common grace of natural law.

---

[75] Koyzis, *Political Visions and Illusions*, 120.
[76] Smidt, "Principled Pluralist Perspective," 146.
[77] Gordon J. Spykman, "The Principled Pluralist Position," in *God and Politics*, 88.

EVALUATION OF PRINCIPLED PLURALISM

Abraham Kuyper said, "There is not a square inch in the whole domain of our human existence over which Christ, who is Sovereign over all, does not cry: 'Mine!'"[78] The certainty of God's sovereignty frees Christians from the need to assert God's power on God's behalf. It releases us from the pressure to Christianize society by force or to add God's name to laws or customs or institutions, because they already belong to God. Christians are free from concern about political victory because, as Ashford and Gleeson put it, "God has called us neither to victory nor to defeat, but to obedience. In the end, Christ will sit on the throne. His political vision will win the day."[79] When we are confident in God's sovereignty, when we know that God's power is not dependent upon human action, then we can relieve ourselves (and our laws) of the anxious notion that if Christians are not in power, then neither is God.

Recognizing God's sovereignty also rightly identifies God as the source of our inalienable rights. It is significant that the Declaration of Independence acknowledges the Creator, not the state, as the source of rights to life, liberty, and the pursuit of happiness. Kevin Hasson, founder of the Becket Fund for Religious Liberty, explains, "as the Declaration puts it, our rights are 'endowed' by no one less than the creator himself, so no merely human power may legitimately deprive us of them. . . . They didn't come from the state in the first place, so the state can't take them away."[80] The state acknowledges and protects these rights, but it does not create them and therefore cannot deny them. This distinction matters for people of all faiths and no faith. Principled pluralism provides a basis for understanding and applying God-given rights in a religiously diverse society.

Principled pluralism also provides a framework for Christian engagement in a religiously and philosophically diverse country. Because God's common grace extends to all people, Christians need not regard other religions or philosophies as inherently godless or as a threat. We can appreciate truth and beauty wherever it is found, because God is its author. Christians can cooperate with our Muslim, Hindu, Sikh, and nonreligious neighbors to promote the common good of our communities. Christians

---

[78] Abraham Kuyper, "Inaugural Address at the Dedication of the Free University," in *Abraham Kuyper: A Centennial Reader*, ed. James D. Bratt (Grand Rapids, MI: Eerdmans, 1998), 488.

[79] Ashford and Greeson, "Modern Political Ideologies," 134.

[80] Kevin Seamas Hasson, *Believers, Thinkers, and Founders* (New York: Random House, 2016), chapter 1, Kindle ed.

can participate in interreligious dialogue without fear that such participation compromises Christian convictions.

Principled pluralism is subject to critiques of natural law, since it regards
natural law as foundational, universal, and consistent with God's sovereignty. In a world that is increasingly scientific or naturalist, natural law is
largely reduced to the laws of the physical world without implications for a
universally shared morality. C. S. Lewis's suggestion that "human beings, all
over the earth, have this curious idea that they ought to behave in a certain
way" seems to fall flat in the twenty-first century.[81] While many natural law
proponents see it as a sure foundation for protecting unborn life or defining
marriage as heterosexual and monogamous, others reference natural law as
evidence for the opposite in each case. Who is ultimately the arbiter of what
is consistent with natural, or divine, law? This challenge runs much deeper
than a critique of Reformed political theology, but it applies here in particular since principled pluralism relies so heavily on natural law.

Another challenge comes from Reformed theologian Karl Barth, who I
introduced in chapter five. Barth argued that reliance upon natural law
replaced God's particular command with the interpretations of a "moralist,"
a mere human who makes decisions on the basis of conscience, which is
fallible. It makes human will, instead of God's revelation, the primary arbiter of morality.[82] For Barth, any elevation of human will or knowledge
above God's direct and special revelation is not only inherently unchristian,
but it is also potentially disastrous. He developed this critique while observing the uses and abuses of natural law by so-called Christians who
enthusiastically supported Adolf Hitler "in the honest belief that they have
finally received a positively messianic message."[83] Barth reflected in a 1941
letter to Great Britain, "it is impossible to make an impression on the evil
genius of the new Germany by seeking to refute it on the ground of Natural
Law" because it "can be interpreted in a pagan sense and thence, by a very
short cut, in a Hitlerian sense. . . . All arguments based on Natural Law are
Janus-headed. They do not lead to the light of clear decisions, but to the
misty twilight in which all cats become grey."[84] While principled pluralism

---

[81]C. S. Lewis, *Mere Christianity* (New York: Touchstone, 1996), 21.

[82]Karl Barth, *Church Dogmatics*, III.4.XII.52, ed. G. W. Bromiley and T. F. Torrance, trans.
A. T. MacKay et al. (Peabody, MA: Hendrickson Publishers, 2010), 5-6.

[83]Karl Barth, "Theological Existence Today," in *A Church Undone: Documents from the German
Christian Faith Movement, 1932-1940*, ed. Mary M. Solberg (Minneapolis: Fortress, 2015), 93.

[84]Karl Barth, *Letter to Great Britain from Switzerland* (London: Sheldon Press, 1941), 17.

does not rest entirely upon natural law, it does rely on a universal foundation for moral life that is difficult to apply in a world where citizens disagree about whether such a foundation even exists, let alone its moral or legal implication. Christians are left to argue that we should be the arbiters of natural law, without a compelling basis for such a claim in a religiously pluralist society.

Another challenge of Kuyper's sphere sovereignty approach is a lack of clarity about what ought to be done when one sphere of society fails to fulfill its vital function and thereby harms the common good. It is also not clear into which sphere certain functions like poverty alleviation or medical care ought to fall. For example, Christians debate whether it is the role of the church or the government to provide a safety net for the poor through food programs, housing assistance, or low-cost childcare. Some argue that feeding the hungry should be within the sphere of the church and other religious organizations, not the government. But if the church's resources fall short of meeting the needs of all Americans living in poverty, is it, then, appropriate for the government or another sovereign sphere to step in and fill the gap in care? Or does that violate sphere sovereignty in a way that actually prevents the church from fulfilling its social care role?

FAITHFUL PRINCIPLED PLURALISM

Principled pluralism is another approach to Christian political engagement that can be a faithful option. Christians in the United States can vote, hold public office, or advocate for policies that promote the common good and human flourishing. Faithful principled pluralism frees us from anxiety about Christian dominance, turning us toward love of neighbor and participation in God's work of restoration in the world. The pursuit of human flourishing and fulfilling the cultural mandate will lead some Christians to lean liberal and others to lean conservative economically and socially. Principled pluralists can be found in both the Republican and the Democratic Party, and ought to be salty promoters of the common good in any party. The common good is not a crude utilitarian calculus of the greatest benefit to the most people; rather, the common good is that which draws the world closer to God's justice and abundance. Our work in politics should promote human flourishing and offer our neighbors a foretaste of the coming Kingdom of God.

8

INVADING THE COUNTRY TO ESTABLISH THE KINGDOM

DOMINIONIST APPROACHES

SOMETHING REMARKABLE HAPPENED at Asbury University in February 2023. The small Christian college in Wilmore, Kentucky experienced what Asbury theology professors Jason Vickers and Thomas McCall have called the Outpouring. Vickers and McCall describe outpourings as occasions when "God makes God's presence and power manifest in a manner that is readily discernible, that leads to repentance and deep joy, and that conveys life-changing forgiveness and grace."[1]

On a seemingly normal Wednesday, an otherwise unremarkable chapel service transitioned into an extended time of prayer and worship, which turned into multiple days then weeks of students seeking the Spirit's presence in the chapel. Within hours, word was spreading on social media, and within days it became a nationwide and even global event. I followed daily updates from Indiana Wesleyan University, where many of my colleagues have close ties to Asbury. Some of my students traveled the several hours to Asbury, and their descriptions of the outpouring were consistent with others: an overwhelming sense of peace, comfort, stillness,

---

[1]Jason E. Vickers and Thomas H. McCall, *Outpouring: A Theological Witness* (Eugene, OR: Cascade Books, 2023), 6.

and joy. Music, prayer, and testimony filled the small space, but it was not raucous or ostentatious.

Amid this movement of the Holy Spirit, some Christian preachers who had no association with Asbury began to interpret the outpouring through a political lens, connecting spiritual revival to political rebirth. Many of the people and organizations who made these political connections are associated with a theological and political movement called dominionism or the closely related New Apostolic Reformation (NAR). Charisma News, a NAR organization, suggested, "Washington and the other Founders were prepared for their historic role in the founding of America by the First Great Awakening. Since the current revival is occurring on college and university campuses, is it possible that God is sending another Great Awakening to prepare a new generation of leaders for a rebirthing of America?"[2]

Preachers in the dominionist theological stream look for political and cultural revival, the fruit of which will be Christians gaining power over the spheres of society. As the dominionist statement "Watchman Decree" says, "we the church are God's governing body on the earth . . . we have been given legal power from heaven and now exercise our authority."[3] Thus, they interpreted the Spirit's movement at Asbury as a revival that would solidify Christians' legal authority over the United States, empowering them to bring about God's Kingdom reign on the earth.

Previous chapters have each explored ways Christians can bring our faith to bear on our political engagement. While based on different foundational theologies and visions of the Christian's relationship with society, each can be a valid approach to faithful citizenship, with some caveats. We now turn to two models of the relationship between kingdom and country that I believe are incompatible with faithfulness to Jesus Christ and harmful to the church's mission and witness in the world. This chapter examines dominionism, along with its theological forerunner, Christian reconstructionism, and its Pentecostal expression, the NAR.

---

[2]Eddie Hyatt, "Is the Next Great Awakening Launching from Asbury Revival?," Charisma News, February 16, 2023, www.charismanews.com/politics/opinion/91516-raising-a-new-generation-of -leaders-to-rebirth-america. Historian John Fea cataloged additional examples of responses to the Asbury revival at https://currentpub.com/2023/02/17/the-maga-evangelical-revivalists-are-no -longer-silent-about-asbury/.

[3]"Watchman Decree," Victory Channel, Kenneth Copeland Ministries, https://flashpoint.govictory .com/wp-content/uploads/sites/7/2022/06/WatchmanDecree.pdf.

DOMINIONISM

Dominionism, also known as the Seven Mountains Mandate or Kingdom Now theology, espouses the idea that Christians need to gain dominion over the spheres of society, including the sphere of government, to establish the Kingdom of God on earth. The theological precursor of dominionism was Christian reconstructionism, which teaches that America needs to be reconstructed as a theonomy in which biblical law is the template for civil law. One of the influential movements to grow out of dominionism is the NAR. These three movements—dominionism, reconstructionism, and the NAR—are not identical, but are so closely related that we can examine them together. These movements have exerted a great deal of political and cultural influence since the 1960s. In my analysis, I conclude that dominionism is a theological error and is harmful to the mission and witness of the church.

Origins of dominionism: Christian reconstructionism. Christian reconstructionism is the theological forerunner to dominionism, and its ideas and impact warrant careful analysis so we can recognize its far-reaching influence on faith and politics. Christian reconstructionism originated with the writings of Rousas John Rushdoony (1916–2001) in the 1960s. The social upheavals of the sixties and seventies are critical context for Rushdoony's ideas, as his writing shows strong reactions to declining church attendance, Supreme Court decisions against prayer and Bible reading in public schools, and the civil rights, gay rights, and women's rights movements.[4] Rushdoony's Christian reconstructionist ideas gained prominence through the activism of writers and preachers like Gary North (1942–2022) and Pat Robertson (1930–2023). It continues to influence politicians and policies today through networks of Christian churches and political action groups.

Rushdoony developed a reconstructionist interpretation of John Calvin's political thought that yielded a presuppositionalist and postmillennial theology. Presuppositionalism asserts that reasoning begins with presuppositions, most importantly presuppositions about the existence of God.

---

[4]Robert D. Putnam and David E. Campbell, *American Grace* (New York: Simon & Schuster, 2010), 83. In *Engel v. Vitale* (1962) the Supreme Court ruled that school-sponsored nondenominational prayer violated the Establishment Clause. In *School District of Abington Township, Pennsylvania v. Schempp* (1963) the Supreme Court ruled that requiring students to participate in classroom religious exercise, in this case Bible reading, violated the Free Exercise Clause. For Reconstructionist reactions to these movements, see especially Rousas John Rushdoony, *The Institutes of Biblical Law* (Phillipsburg, NJ: Presbyterian and Reformed, 1973), 294 and 425.

Christians presuppose God's existence, while secular society presupposes God's nonexistence. Christians should disregard conclusions that are based on secular presuppositions as inherently incompatible with a Christian worldview. Starting with Calvinist theology, Rushdoony concluded that "no fact is a fact apart from God nor has a full and valid interpretation apart *from Him*. Every fact is a God-created and God-interpreted fact, and this world exists only as a God-created and God-interpreted world."[5] This starting point led Rushdoony to insist that God is the only possible source of factual knowledge. God-given facts must be wholly accepted, since "to reject it in one area is to reject it in all," while information from any other source must be wholly rejected.[6] Information based solely on logic or natural sciences is suspect until confirmed by God's revelation in Scripture.

For Rushdoony, modern political philosophy "excludes God as the ultimate fact and limits Him to the possibility of being a fact among facts," and this leveling of fields of knowledge violates the sovereignty of God, compromises Christian conviction, and must be rejected in favor of God's revealed law.[7] The American ideal of individual human autonomy is based on rationalism, not revelation; therefore, any political system, including America's, that is founded on belief in human autonomy is doomed.

Since humanity's own "religious expression and consciousness cannot be trusted," God's revelation is the only standard for morality; thus, pluralism, secularism, and multiculturalism are unacceptable and even dangerous.[8] When we set aside divine revelation for the sake of tolerating diverse beliefs, Rushdoony argues we create "man-centered standards of morality," whereby "man insists on establishing his own way of salvation by means of works of morality and requires that God ratify man's values by making them His own."[9]

For Rushdoony, the goal of morality was not the common good or human flourishing. Those are human aims that relegate God to one possible foundation among many. Rather, the purpose of human morality is the "glory of God," and Christians advance this purpose, "first, by seeking

---

[5] Rousas John Rushdoony, *By What Standard?* (Fairfax, VA: Thorburn Press, 1974), 23. Originally published in 1958. Italics in original.
[6] Rushdoony, *By What Standard?*, 24.
[7] Rushdoony, *By What Standard?*, 61.
[8] Rushdoony, *By What Standard?*, 77.
[9] Rushdoony, *By What Standard?*, 81.

to establish the kingdom of God, second, by relying, not on his own will in this task, but on the revealed will of God in Scripture as his criterion, and third by recognizing that of himself he has no power to work towards the kingdom of God but must rely on the Holy Spirit."[10] Tolerating an array of perspectives forces the believer "to associate on a common level of total acceptance with the atheist, the pervert, the criminal, and the adherents of other religions as though no differences existed. . . . In the name of toleration, the believer is asked to tolerate all things because the unbeliever will tolerate nothing; it means life on the unbeliever's terms."[11]

In this view, Christianity is incompatible with America's constitutional form and values. Rushdoony puts it bluntly: "Christianity is completely and radically anti-democratic," and is "committed to a spiritual aristocracy."[12]

The second core aspect of Christian reconstructionist theology is postmillennialism. We encountered postmillennial eschatology through the social gospel, but Christian reconstructionist postmillennialism diverges from the social gospel in its goals, methods, and motives. While postmillennialists hold that the Kingdom of God progresses in time and will be fully established when Christ returns, for Rushdoony this progress must occur as Christians "exercise dominion and seek to bring all aspects of life under the authority of biblical law."[13] Christians reconstruct America as a Christian nation through gaining dominion over every area of society, starting with the godly (that is, patriarchal, nuclear) family, which "moves outward by marriage, and the interlocking network of law units is thereby spread further. The family governs itself, and, in so doing, its government covers many spheres of life and its future orientation means that its functions are not present-bound. Over the centuries, families have most tenaciously preserved past and present while working to govern the future."[14] As families come under God's dominion, God's dominion will then spread into all societal spheres through the influence of godly family members.

---

[10]Rushdoony, *By What Standard?*, 88.

[11]Rushdoony, *Institutes*, 294-95.

[12]Quoted in Randall Balmer, ed., "Rushdoony, Rousas John (1916–2001)," in *Encyclopedia of Evangelicalism* (Waco, TX: Baylor University Press, 2004), 594.

[13]Julie J. Ingersoll, *Building God's Kingdom: Inside the World of Christian Reconstruction* (Oxford: Oxford University Press, 2015), 9.

[14]Rushdoony, *Institutes*, quoted in Michael J. McVicar, *Christian Reconstruction: R. J. Rushdoony and American Religious Conservatism* (Chapel Hill: University of North Carolina Press, 2015), 137-38.

Rushdoony's vision for America requires Mosaic law to become the foundation for civil law. In his book *The Institutes of Biblical Law* (1973) Rushdoony argued that Christ did not fulfill or replace Old Testament law, but rather, Christ restored "man to a position of covenant-keeping instead of covenant-breaking, to enable man to keep the law by freeing man 'from the law of sin and death' (Rom. 8:2)."[15] Biblical law is not only for Christians: "civil law cannot be separated from Biblical law, for the Biblical doctrine of law includes all law, civil, ecclesiastical, societal, familial, and all other forms of law. The social order which despises God's law places itself on death row: it is marked for judgment."[16] Rushdoony's Christian reconstruction requires revolution, a radical reordering of society that is not merely an application of Christian beliefs or values to the Constitution, but a rewriting of the Constitution itself to codify biblical law.

Gary North, Rushdoony's son-in-law, explained the results of reconstruction in his book *Healer of the Nations* (1987). In the reconstructed Christian nation, all citizens "would acknowledge the sovereignty of the Trinitarian God of the Bible," and the Bible "would be acknowledged as the source of the nation's law-order." Exodus 18 would function as the blueprint for a court system, and people "would be free to do as they please unless they violated a specific piece of Bible-based legislation or a specific Biblical injunction that the Bible says must be enforced by the civil government," and "Covenanted [Christian] citizens alone may serve as judges." It follows naturally that the Bible "as the Word of God would be the final standard of justice" and the Constitution "(written or unwritten) would be officially subordinate to the Bible."[17] Based on Rushdoony's and North's presuppositionalism, only God's revelation can be a sure foundation for human law, even if the details of the law run counter to conscience (such as slavery or stoning people to death). Reconstruction will not happen organically, but through a "working activist movement."[18]

Contemporary influence of Christian reconstructionism. Christian reconstructionism's core tenets have been adopted and adapted by a wide range of theological and political figures who may or may not formally associate themselves with Christian reconstructionism. *Christianity Today*

---

[15] Rushdoony, *Institutes*, 3.

[16] Rushdoony, *Institutes*, 4.

[17] Gary North, *Healer of the Nations* (Fort Worth, TX: Dominion Press, 1987), 34-36.

[18] Gary North, *Backward, Christian Soldiers? An Action Manual for Christian Reconstruction* (Tyler, TX: Institute for Christian Economics, 1984), 150.

introduced many American Christians to reconstructionism when it
praised *The Institutes of Biblical Law* as "the most impressive theological
work of 1973," and described it as "a compendious treatment of a whole
gamut of questions in governmental, social, and personal ethics from the
perspective of the principle of law and the purpose of restoration of divine
order in a fallen world."[19] Even with popular exposure from *Christianity
Today*, reconstructionism's political influence was mostly under the radar
in the seventies and eighties. An account of a conversation between Gary
North and Christian education activist Robert Billings illustrates the
breadth of Rushdoony's influence. During a religious roundtable gathering
of national evangelical leaders in 1980, North expressed disappointment
to Billings that Rushdoony was not among the speakers, to which Billings
replied, "If it weren't for his books, none of us would be here."[20]

North, an economic historian, applied reconstructionist theology to
economic theory and policy. The author of over fifty books and hundreds
of articles and blog posts, North was considered a fringe figure by mainstream religious and political conservatives, who didn't take his ideas seriously.[21] However, his principles for biblical economics, explicated in the
ten-volume *Biblical Blueprint Series* (1986–1987, edited by North with six
contributing authors), found a ready audience in some politically conservative Christian circles. North detailed principles of banking, debt, the
gold standard, interest rates, and other details of micro- and macroeconomics. He forecasted catastrophic economic collapse, "inflation, then
mass inflation, then price controls, then tyranny, and finally a worldwide
deflationary depression."[22] The collapse wouldn't be limited to the economy,
North warned: "There will be terror and consternation when economic
disruptions, Communist terrorism, AIDS, and political extremism hit the
United States and other Western nations. People will not know where
to turn."[23]

Once this happens, North explained, "Christians had better be ready
with answers, both theoretical and practical. If they are unprepared, as
they are today, then those who take responsibility will inherit the power,

[19]Quoted in McVicar, *Christian Reconstruction*, 142.
[20]McVicar, *Christian Reconstruction*, 145.
[21]Sam Roberts, "Gary North, Apostle of Bible-Based Economics, Dies at 80," *New York Times*,
   March 4, 2022, www.nytimes.com/2022/03/04/us/gary-north-dead.html.
[22]Gary North, *Honest Money*, quoted in Ingersoll, *Building God's Kingdom*, 59.
[23]North, *Healer of the Nations*, 284.

and they will not be Christians."[24] North's economic ideas and crisis rhetoric were influential within the Tea Party (founded in 2009), for which he wrote a daily newsletter called *The Tea Party Economist*, and among some Libertarians, most notably former Texas congressman Ron Paul (b. 1935, in office 1976–1977, 1979–1985, 1997–2013), for whom North was a staffer in the 1970s.[25] Much of North's reconstructionism was filtered through his economic ideology and what he saw as its biblical basis.

While reconstructionism's economic inroads have largely been through libertarianism, its theological inroads were paved by Reformed theologian Greg Bahnsen (1948–1995), and its inroads to popular Christianity were Pat Robertson, the NAR, and the Christian homeschool movement. Greg Bahnsen's *Theonomy in Christian Ethics* (1977) stands alongside Rushdoony's and North's writings as a foundational text for Christian reconstructionism. The central point in Bahnsen's argument for Christian reconstructionist theonomy, a political structure in which God's law is also civil law, is his interpretation of Jesus' instructions regarding the law in the Sermon on the Mount.

For example, Bahnsen's translation of Matthew 5:17 reads, "'Do not (begin to) think that I came in order to abrogate the law or the prophets; I did not come to abrogate *but* to confirm.'"[26] He rejected the widely accepted interpretation that Jesus came to fulfill the law, and argued instead that "'fulfill' in Matthew 5:17 does not mean to abolish or replace the Mosaic law, but to make plain its full demand, true content, and purpose."[27] He translated Matthew 5:19, "'Therefore, whoever shall loosen one of these least commandments and shall teach men so shall be called least in the kingdom of heaven, but whoever shall do and teach them shall be called great in the kingdom of heaven.'" Bahnsen interpreted the passage as a warning "that a person's relation to the kingdom of God is determined by meticulous observance of the least details of the law. . . . The breaking of the very least stipulation of the law generates God's displeasure."[28]

Theonomy in Christian Ethics, and Bahnsen's interpretation of Matthew 5 in particular, proved controversial among his students and

---

[24]North, *Healer of the Nations*, 284.

[25]Ingersoll, *Building God's Kingdom*, 56.

[26]Greg L. Bahnsen, *Theonomy in Christian Ethics*, 25th anniversary ed. (Nacogdoches, TX: Covenant Media Press, 2002), 73.

[27]Bahnsen, *Theonomy in Christian Ethics*, 74.

[28]Bahnsen, *Theonomy in Christian Ethics*, 87.

colleagues at Reformed Theological Seminary, where many saw his insistence that biblical law was still binding for Christians as a fundamental misapplication of Jesus' teaching. Several of Bahnsen's students, however, went on to write dozens of books and became leaders of or contributors to political organizations and think tanks that continue to promote Christian reconstructionism today.[29]

The rise of televangelism in the 1980s brought Christian reconstructionism into Americans' living rooms. Rushdoony and other reconstructionists made guest appearances on Pat Robertson's Christian Broadcasting Network and his flagship program, *The 700 Club*. Through the new medium of televangelism, charismatic preachers fused the prosperity gospel with reconstructionist theology.[30] Robertson integrated reconstructionism into his own thinking, explaining to his television audience that God's plan "is for his people to take dominion. . . . What is dominion? Dominion is lordship. He wants his people to reign and rule with him."[31]

Although Robertson rejected the reconstructionist idea that "man, through his own efforts, is going to reconstruct the fallen earth and bring the millennial kingdom," he espoused other reconstructionist ideas refracted through a prosperity gospel lens.[32] He wrote in *The Secret Kingdom*, "Almighty God wants us to recapture the dominion man held in the beginning," which entails "the authority to govern all that is willing to be governed" as well as "authority over the untamed and rebellious. In both instances, God gave man a sweeping and total mandate of dominion over this planet and everything in it."[33] When Robertson ran for the Republican presidential nomination in 1987, he explained to a reporter, "the Lord intends his people to exercise dominion in his name," and expressed admiration for reconstructionist teachings "because they are in line with Scripture."[34] Robertson's media empire brought key aspects of reconstructionist ideas into the conservative evangelical mainstream, with lasting political implications.

Dominionist origins and beliefs. The Christian reconstructionist emphasis on dominion developed into a movement called dominionism.

---

[29]McVicar, *Christian Reconstruction*, 160.

[30]McVicar, *Christian Reconstruction*, 198.

[31]McVicar, *Christian Reconstruction*, 198.

[32]Pat Robertson, *The Secret Kingdom: Your Path to Peace, Love, and Financial Security*, rev. ed. (Dallas: Word Publishing, 1992), 243.

[33]Robertson, *Secret Kingdom*, 238, 239.

[34]McVicar, *Christian Reconstruction*, 198.

Dominionists do not have precisely the same goals as reconstructionists; in particular, they tend to place less emphasis on theonomy, but they align in the goal of gaining political power in order to exert biblical rule. Many dominionists also have a weaker connection to Calvinist theology than reconstructionists do, and instead have strong charismatic and Pentecostal influences. The foundational concept of dominionism is that "Christian believers are called to not only preach the gospel and win converts to Christ but also to establish the Kingdom of God on earth," according to Lance Wallnau (b. 1954) and Bill Johnson (b. 1951), two of the movement's leading figures.[35] The idea originated in 1975 with Loren Cunningham (1935–2023) and Bill Bright (1921–2003), founders of Youth With a Mission (YWAM, founded 1960) and Campus Crusade for Christ (now Cru, founded 1951), respectively. Each had a vision or revelation that identified seven areas (hence, Seven Mountains Mandate) that needed to be brought into conformity with a Christian worldview: education, religion, family, business, government, entertainment, and media.[36]

Dominionism has gained influence through evangelical and Pentecostal popular culture, with one major influencer being Bethel Church in Redding, California. Bethel is best known for its worship music production, but the church's lead pastor, Bill Johnson (b. 1951), is a leading expositor of dominionism. Johnson describes dominionism this way in *Invading Babylon* (2013): "There are seven realms of society that must come under the influence of the King and His Kingdom. For that to happen, we, as citizens of the Kingdom, must invade. The dominion of the Lord Jesus is manifest whenever the people of God go forth to serve by bringing the order of blessing of His world into this one."[37] This seems similar to the role of Christians in Kuyper's sphere sovereignty; however, one major difference is dominionism's view of the world as a spiritual battleground.

For dominionists, the conflict between society's laws and values and those of the Kingdom is the result of demonic influence that only Christians can recognize and cast out. Dominionist leader Alan Vincent explains, "spiritual powers control many of the pillars of our society and

---

[35]Lance Wallnau and Bill Johnson, eds., "Introduction," in *Invading Babylon: The 7 Mountain Mandate* (Shippensburg, PA: Destiny Image, 2013), 10.

[36]Matt Slick, "What Are the Origins of the Seven Mountains Mandate?," Christian Apologetics and Research Ministry, May 5, 2022, https://carm.org/carm/origins-of-the-seven-mountain-mandate/.

[37]Bill Johnson, "Invading Babylon," in *Invading Babylon*, 22-23.

our secular laws to such a degree that these spirits now rule the lives of the people in our cities. As I write, most of the spiritual gates over our cities are occupied by demonic powers working through their human agencies and not by God's people."[38] According to Vincent, Christians must "cleanse the geographical regions that have been used for demonic worship and overthrow the spiritual powers that have hindered the growth and fullness of the Kingdom of God on earth." He specifically names as demonic enemies, "ardent anti-Christian secularists, sexually perverse activists, militant atheists, witches and warlocks, the passionate promoters of New Age, the devotees of Mother Earth," and "activists who are demonically empowered to passionately promote political causes like abortion, homosexuality, . . . and militant atheism."[39] Dominionists cast the world in a Manichaean conflict between light and darkness, good and evil, angels and demons.

A dominionist movement: The New Apostolic Reformation. The NAR has further developed dominionist theology in a Pentecostal direction, emphasizing the authoritative role of prophets and apostles along with dominionism's view of spiritual warfare. The NAR began as an approach to global evangelization, but it has come to include domestic political action. C. Peter Wagner (1930–2016), a founder of the NAR movement and former professor at Fuller Seminary, took the Genesis 1:28 dominion mandate as the foundation for an aggressive approach to evangelization that included asserting Christians' authority over the seven spheres of society.[40] Wagner adopted these seven areas from Lance Wallnau, who identified them as "seven mountains or seven molders of culture" that constitute "the major battlefields for taking dominion over society."[41]

Wagner's teaching shows the influence of Kuyper's sphere sovereignty, Rushdoony's mandate to Christianize the world, and the Pentecostal understanding of spiritual warfare, and it has gained traction among evangelical and fundamentalist Christians in the United States.[42] In a 2011 interview, Wagner explained that Christians gain dominion in the political sphere by

---

[38]Alan Vincent, "Occupying the Gates of the Heavenly City," in *Invading Babylon*, 78.

[39]Vincent, "Occupying the Gates," 95, 94.

[40]McVicar, *Christian Reconstruction*, 200.

[41]C. Peter Wagner, *Wrestling with Alligators, Prophets and Theologians* (Ventura, CA: Regal, 2010), 262-63.

[42]McVicar, *Christian Reconstruction*, 200.

having "as many kingdom-minded people in influence in each one of these branches of government as possible so that the blessings of the kingdom will come."[43] Wagner understood dominion in spiritual terms, with a strong emphasis on demonic power and influence, and the need for Christians to gain influence in the spheres of society in order to hold back demonic forces. The demonic emphasis is clear in Wagner's explanation that "we now believe that God is mandating us to be involved in aggressive social transformation," and "we will only take dominion if the body of Christ becomes [spiritually] violent and declares war on the enemy!"[44] The NAR emphasizes the role of apostles who have been "raised up by God who have a tremendous authority in the churches of the New Apostolic Reformation," and of prophets, to whom God reveals his secrets before taking action in the world.[45]

NAR eschatology brings together reconstructionist postmillennialism with the premillennialist pessimism common in Pentecostalism. Religion scholar Daniel Wojcik describes the result as "avertive millennialism," in which "the Kingdom of God may come if the apocalyptic destruction is averted and the requirements for the collective salvation are met."[46] The world is headed toward catastrophe, but God has appointed prophets who can receive God's special revelation in order to avert the apocalypse and bring about the Kingdom of God through dominionist means. Thus, the authority of apostles and prophets in the NAR has soteriological and eschatological significance. For Christians who place themselves under the authority of NAR leadership, the temporal and eternal future of the world depends upon Christians adhering to the instructions of the apostles and prophets of the movement.

Dominionism in American politics. Christian reconstructionist, dominionist, and NAR political engagement takes a variety of forms, from direct influence on public policy and candidates, to declaring elections won or lost based on a cosmic battle between angels and demons. These movements overlap so significantly in their influence on contemporary American politics that their ideas and goals cannot be easily differentiated. While reconstructionism places more emphasis on the Mosaic law

[43]C. Peter Wagner, interview by Terri Gross, *Fresh Air*, NPR, March 10, 2011.
[44]C. Peter Wagner, *Dominion! Your Role in Bringing Heaven to Earth* (Shippensburg, PA: Destiny Image Publishers, 2022), 60, 118.
[45]C. Peter Wagner, interview by Terri Gross.
[46]Damon Berry, "Voting in the Kingdom: Prophecy Voters, the New Apostolic Reformation, and Christian Support for Trump," *Nova Religio* 23, no. 4 (2020): 76.

specifically and the dominionist and NAR movements emphasize God's miraculous intervention, they intersect at the point of intentionally engaging with the political sphere for the purpose of making the Kingdom of God a present reality.

Dominionism's political influence is most evident in education policy. Dominionists' core goal, explains religious studies scholar Julie Ingersoll, is "to produce generations of Christians who have been protected from the influences of humanists and who are thoroughly imbued with a biblical worldview."[47] Homeschooling is the front line of turning society's ship. Rushdoony laid the foundation for part of the Christian homeschooling movement when he warned parents against giving over childrearing to the government.[48] He wrote, "there can be no neutrality in education. Education by the state will have statist ends. [Therefore,] the best and truest educators are parents under God. The greatest school is the family."[49]

This emphasis on family-based education is influential in the Christian homeschool movement, where some of Rushdoony's lectures are widely circulated alongside other texts and curricula from a reconstructionist perspective. Because of this, historian Milton Gaither notes, "[Rushdoony's] writings have bequeathed to the conservative wing of the homeschooling movement both a strong sense of opposition between God's law and human laws and a tendency to think of itself as a divinely guided instrument in restoring a Christian America."[50] Rushdoony understood Christian homeschool as the means through which God would enact Christian reconstruction of America.[51] Of course, not all Christians who choose to homeschool are connected to Christian reconstructionism or use curricula that encourage this worldview, but some homeschool families may not be aware of reconstructionism's possible influence on their curriculum.

Another aspect of dominionism in the Christian homeschool movement is organizations and curricula designed to prepare Christian homeschoolers to enter politics as a career. A few examples give a sense of the dominionist influence. Christian Liberty Academy Satellite Schools (CLASS), founded by reconstructionist pastor Paul Lindstrom

---

[47]Ingersoll, *Building God's Kingdom*, 79.
[48]McVicar, *Christian Reconstruction*, 165.
[49]Rushdoony, *Institutes*, 182, 185.
[50]Milton Gaither, *Homeschool: An American History* (New York: Palgrave MacMillan, 2008), 137.
[51]Gaither, *Homeschool*, 137.

in 1967, was explicitly reconstructionist. A CLASS leader described the purpose of the program as providing "quality education to those who desire to prepare themselves and their children for their part in taking godly dominion in every aspect of life and thought."[52] The CLASS philosophy of education states,

> Christian education is engaged in spiritual and intellectual warfare with the kingdom of darkness. . . . Well-trained Christian students must be prepared to battle intellectually against the spirit of this age with an aggressive yet humble manner. CLASS desires to train Christian warriors and leaders who will go forth in the power of the Holy Spirit to win decisive victories for the honor, glory, and kingdom of Christ.[53]

In this statement, we recognize the goal of political dominion and the language of spiritual warfare.

Similarly, Bill Gothard (b. 1934) founded the Institute in Basic Life Principles (IBLP) in 1961, and he added a correspondence homeschooling program named the Advanced Training Institute (ATI) in 1984. Over decades, IBLP and ATI created a wide-ranging political network that includes former governors and presidential candidates Rick Perry of Texas and Mike Huckabee of Arkansas.[54] Gothard believes America's problems are the result of rejecting God's laws, and therefore the solution is for Christians to enter government to make laws that are in harmony with the Bible.[55] IBLP and ATI participants are instructed toward political activism for conservative causes. CLASS's Lindstrom and IBLP's Gothard were both removed from their organizations due to sex scandals, but their influence extends through hundreds of thousands of participants in their programs, including the Duggar family of reality TV fame.

In recent decades, many Christian homeschoolers have been influenced by Generation Joshua, whose vision is "to assist parents to raise up the next generation of Christian leaders and citizens, equipped to positively influence the political processes of today and tomorrow."[56] An explicitly

---

[52]Gaither, *Homeschool*, Kindle location 3464.

[53]"Philosophy of Christian Education," Christian Liberty Homeschools, accessed June 7, 2023, www.homeschools.org/philosophy-of-christian-education.

[54]Sarah Posner, "'Taliban Dan's' Teacher: Inside Bill Gothard's Authoritarian Subculture," Religion Dispatches, February 9, 2011, https://religiondispatches.org/taliban-dans-teacher-inside-bill -gothards-authoritarian-subculture/.

[55]Posner, "'Taliban Dan's' Teacher."

[56]"What Do We Believe?," Generation Joshua, accessed June 7, 2023, https://generationjoshua.org /about/what-we-believe.

political organization, Generation Joshua is a program of the Home School Legal Defense Association (HSLDA) and describes itself as "an active force in the political arena."[57] This branch of the Christian homeschool movement does not necessarily associate with the dominionist movement explicitly, but dominionist alignment is clear in their political focus.

Recognizing that homeschool is not an option for every family, dominionists also promote access to Christian private education, often through school choice or tuition voucher programs. For example, Betsy DeVos, secretary of education during the Trump administration, while not a self-identified dominionist, has promoted an education agenda consistent with dominionist aims. DeVos sees education as a biblical battleground and advocates school choice and voucher programs that allow Christian parents to send their children to schools that reinforce their biblical worldview.[58]

DeVos and her husband, a former candidate for governor of Michigan, have explained their engagement with education policy as a way "to confront the culture in which we all live today in ways which will continue to help advance God's kingdom."[59] Regardless of one's policy beliefs regarding school choice or tuition vouchers, a complex topic about which Christians express a wide range of opinions, we can recognize the parallels with dominionist ideas in DeVos's approach to education policy. Dominionists are interested in having people in the halls of power whose goals are in concert with theirs, and DeVos and others with similar education reform goals are contributing to dominionist aims, whether they intend to or not. To be clear, the problem is with the underlying dominionist theology, not with homeschool or parochial schools as educational options.

In 2016, many dominionist and NAR leaders saw divine intervention in the election of Donald Trump, and they compared Trump to biblical King Cyrus (Isaiah 45, Ezra 1). Six weeks after Trump announced his candidacy, NAR pastor Jeremiah Johnson published a prophecy claiming, "Just as I [God] raised up Cyrus to fulfill my purposes and plans, so I have raised up Trump to fulfill my purposes and plans prior to the 2016 election. You must listen to the trumpet very closely for he will sound the alarm and many

[57]"History," Generation Joshua, accessed June 7, 2023, https://generationjoshua.org/about/history.
[58]"Transcript of Interview at The Gathering 2001," The Center for Media and Democracy, accessed April 3, 2023, www.exposedbycmd.org/2017/01/23/betsy-devos-biblical-capitalism-transcript-interview-gathering-2001/.
[59]"Transcript of Interview at The Gathering 2001."

will be blessed because of his compassion and mercy."[60] Similarly, the month before the 2016 election, Lance Wallnau wrote, "I believe the 45th president is meant to be an Isaiah 45 Cyrus."[61] After Trump's 2020 election loss, Johnny Enlow prophesied that Donald Trump would be restored to office.[62] These kinds of prophetic pronouncements have fueled conspiracy theories and been cited as justification for violence, including the January 6, 2021 attack on the US Capitol.[63]

EVALUATION OF DOMINIONISM

Unlike the models of political engagement we have examined in previous chapters, I believe dominionism and its related approaches are so theologically problematic and so damaging to Christian mission and witness that they are incompatible with faithfulness to Jesus Christ and submission to his lordship. Christians have multiple faithful models for Christian political engagement. For biblical, theological, and missional reasons, Christian reconstructionism, dominionism, and the NAR are not among them.

In 1987, fourteen years after *Christianity Today* introduced the world to Rushdoony, it published a critique of Christian reconstructionism that "deftly translated Reconstructionism's theological implications into the idiom of political dystopia."[64] Rodney Clapp explained the basics of Christian reconstructionism, then pointed out that "Reconstruction does not actually provide the clear, simple, uncontestably 'biblical' solution to ethical questions that it pretends to, and that are so attractive to many conservative Christians."[65]

Christianity Today had brought Christian reconstructionism into the mainstream conversation regarding the relationship between religion and democracy, even as the religious right, some of whose leaders had strong

---

[60]Quoted in Hanna Amanda Trangerud, "The American Cyrus: How an Ancient King Became a Political Tool for Voter Mobilization," *Religions* 12:354 (2021): 14-15.

[61]Quoted in Morgan Lee, "The King Cyrus 'Anointing' of Trump," Eternity News, May 21, 2019, www.eternitynews.com.au/opinion/the-king-cyrus-anointing-of-trump/.

[62]Julia Duin, "The Christian Prophets Who Say Trump Is Coming Again," Politico, February 18, 2021, www.politico.com/news/magazine/2021/02/18/how-christian-prophets-give-credence-to-trumps-election-fantasies-469598.

[63]Miles T. Armaly, David T. Buckley, and Adam M. Enders, "Christian Nationalism and Political Violence: Victimhood, Racial Identity, Conspiracy, and Support for the Capitol Attacks," *Political Behavior* 44 (2022): 937-60.

[64]McVicar, *Christian Reconstruction*, 202.

[65]Rodney Clapp, "Democracy as Heresy," *Christianity Today*, February 20, 1987.

reconstructionist influences, was ascendant in American politics. But this new article opened the movement to widespread evangelical critique. Hal Lindsey, most famous for his mainstreaming of premillennial dispensationalism through his book *The Late Great Planet Earth* (1970), wrote, "No matter how appealing the idea of the Church taking over the world and establishing the Kingdom of God is, it is not what the Bible teaches."[66]

Christian reconstructionism's approach to biblical interpretation lays a shaky foundation for the whole reconstructionist and dominionist project. While some praised Rushdoony and others for their strict adherence to biblical inerrancy, their approach crosses from inerrancy to biblicism as it takes the Old Testament as a model for all time without regard for the historical, cultural, and even covenantal differences between biblical Israel and the contemporary United States. As Rodney Clapp described it to readers of *Christianity Today*, "the Reconstructionists are frequently criticized for not adequately appreciating the historical and cultural distance between nomadic, agricultural Israel and modern technological America. Most biblical interpreters would compare this hermeneutical gap to the Grand Canyon; the Reconstructionists treat it like a crack in the sidewalk."[67] The Hebrew Bible is not a set of timeless principles to be abstracted and applied without regard for context.

In contrast to Rushdoony's insistence that Jesus confirmed and reinforced the Mosaic law, Paul Schrotenboer, who holds a principled pluralist position (see chapter seven), says, "Christ fulfilled (*Pleerosai*) the law. He is the end (*telos*) of the law to all who believe (Rom. 10:4). Therefore Christ's function was more than simply to confirm the law."[68] Christians should thoughtfully consider what force the Old Testament legal codes hold for Christians or for civil society today, and the answer requires greater nuance than either simple rejection or complete continuity. To reject the idea that Mosaic law is binding for all times and places is not to reject biblical authority; rather, it is imperative that Christians understand the Mosaic law within its context in the history of Israel and within the arc of the biblical narrative. Christians across the hermeneutical spectrum recognize the details of Mosaic law as specific to a time, place, and people,

---

[66]Hal Lindsey, *The Road to Holocaust,* quoted in McVicar, *Christian Reconstruction*, 205.

[67]Clapp, "Democracy as Heresy."

[68]Paul G. Schrotenboer, "The Principled Pluralist Response to Theonomy," in *God and Politics: Four Views on the Reformation of Civil Government*, ed. Gary Scott Smith (Phillipsburg, NJ: Presbyterian and Reformed, 1989), 57.

and therefore not wholly applicable today in the way that reconstructionists attempt to apply it.

The NAR has different hermeneutical problems, as the movement's understanding of biblical authority has distinctly Montanist and gnostic tendencies. The Montanist sect in Christianity's first centuries, also known as New Prophecy, believed the Holy Spirit delivered new revelations that were equal or superior to biblical revelation.[69] Nearly two thousand years later, NAR leader Bill Johnson writes of ongoing revelation, by which the Holy Spirit reveals secrets hidden in Scripture, "new things God is opening up in his word."[70] Johnson advocates for coming to Scripture in a way that sets aside the author's intent and the historical context so the Holy Spirit can reveal new meaning. This view is also similar to Gnosticism, an ancient idea that proposed a secret knowledge, access to which was reserved for those to whom God reveals it. In Montanism and Gnosticism, Scripture is only a starting point for further revelation. These Montanist and gnostic ideals have influenced some NAR leaders' approaches to politics in ways that have done harm to liberal democracy and civil society in recent years.

Reconstructionist, dominionist, and NAR leaders and laity have frequently applied messianic language to politicians who they believe will enact their political agenda. Some described Donald Trump in messianic terms, as one anointed by God. Pat Robertson said on *The 700 Club*,

> I think, somehow, the Lord's plan is being put in place for America and these people are not only revolting against Trump, they're revolting against what God's plan is for America. These other people have been trying to destroy America. . . . They want to fight as much as they can but I think the good news is the Bible says, "He that sits in the heavens will laugh them to scorn," and I think that Trump's got something on his side that's a lot more powerful than the media.[71]

The movie *The Trump Prophecy* (2018), based on the prophetic visions of firefighter Mark Taylor, declared Trump's unlikely 2016 electoral victory had been a miracle of God, marking Trump as God's chosen man. The film

---

[69]S. L. Greenslade, *Early Latin Theology* (Louisville, KY: Westminster John Knox, 2006), 29.

[70]Bill Johnson, *Dreaming with God* (Shippensburg, PA: Destiny Image, 2006), chapter 8 audiobook.

[71]Pat Roberston, *The 700 Club*, February 15, 2017, www2.cbn.com/video/700-club/700-club-february-15-2017.

includes interviews with NAR leaders. The belief that God has a hand in choosing the president can be consistent with Christian beliefs about God's sovereignty and providence, but the NAR goes beyond a trust in God's sovereignty by encouraging people to believe that Trump was uniquely anointed.[72] In the same vein, NAR leader Dutch Sheets said of the October 2023 election of Michael Johnson (R-Louisiana) as Speaker of the House of Representatives, "God has given us a miracle in the election of Congressman Michael Johnson to this position. He's a godly man, raised up for such a time as this."[73]

A final reason for rejecting the dominionist approach to politics is the evidence of its unhealthy fruit. Dominionism has provided theological justification for religiously motivated violence and domestic terrorism. Catherine Wessinger, a scholar of religion and violence, explains,

> The world is seen as a battleground between good and evil, God and Satan, us and them. This radical dualism expects, and often produces conflict. It identifies particular groups and individuals as enemies. It is the embattled worldview of people engaging in warfare. Many religious people hold this dualistic worldview and wage their warfare spiritually with prayers, faith, and worship as their weapons. But if the warfare becomes physical, people are killed, they kill others, people are martyred and die for a cause.[74]

While Rushdoony, North, and Bahnsen did not directly promote violence, some of their successors embraced vigilantism. Michael Bray was convicted of destroying seven abortion facilities in Delaware, Virginia, Maryland, and the District of Columbia in 1985. By Bray's account, "the only abortion chamber in Dover was gutted by fire," burned to the ground in a conflagration he started with gasoline and matches. Mark Juergensmeyer, an expert in religiously motivated violence who interviewed Bray, explains, "Bray found intellectual company in a group of writers associated with the more conservative Dominion theology, the position that Christianity must reassert the dominion of God over all things, including secular

[72]Ryan Burge, "How Many Americans Believe Trump Is Anointed by God?," *Religion News Service*, November 25, 2019, https://religionnews.com/2019/11/25/how-many-americans-believe-trump-is-anointed-by-god/.

[73]Susan Davis, "Speaker Johnson's Close Ties to Christian Right—Both Mainstream and Fringe," *Morning Edition*, NPR, November 15, 2023, www.npr.org/2023/11/15/1211536399/speaker-johnson-christian-nationalism-evangelical.

[74]Catherine Wessinger, *How the Millennium Comes Violently* (New York: Seven Bridges Press, 2000), 17.

politics and society."[75] Dominionism directly influenced Bray and anti-abortion activist Paul Hill, who murdered Dr. John Britton in 1994.[76]

The violence endemic to the dominionist worldview was apparent in the language and actions of dominionist and NAR leaders during the 2016 and 2020 elections and the January 6, 2021 attack on the US Capitol. In 2016, dominionist leader Lance Wallnau wrote *God's Chaos Candidate*, in which he warned, "we are up against a malevolent and demonic agenda aimed to destroy the global force for kingdom expansion that is America."[77] Prophetic assertions fueled conspiratorial narratives that framed "opposition to President Trump as a satanic assault on God's prophetic plan."[78] When one candidate is equated with the divine will and all who oppose him are called demonic, we can hardly be surprised when spiritual warfare becomes physical warfare. Battleground rhetoric heated up in the weeks after the November 2020 election. Self-described apostle Don Lynch told his congregation on December 31, "buckle up your seatbelts on your horse you're riding and get ready to gallop and get your sword bloody in the spirit of God."[79]

Pat Robertson assured his *700 Club* audience on January 4, 2021, "Something very dramatic that will change the outcome of that vote. . . . The Holy Spirit of God will enter into this situation."[80] On January 5, dominionist speakers exhorted rally attendees, "pick up that weapon and find you are strong enough to wield it. Finish this! Finish this! I say, finish this!" and "Expose the neck, swing the sword, finish the job."[81] The rhetorical call to violence cannot be decoupled from the assaults and deaths that followed. As Matthew Rowley notes, "Miracles, visions and prophecies hardened opposition to Biden's victory—they erected alternative silos of knowledge wherein defeat could only stem from nefarious causes. On 6 January 2021,

[75]Mark Juergensmeyer, *Terror in the Mind of God: The Global Rise of Religious Violence*, 4th ed. (Oakland, CA: University of California Press, 2017), 29, 36.

[76]Kathy Sawyer, "Turning from 'Weapon of the Spirit' to the Shotgun," *Washington Post*, August 7, 1994, www.washingtonpost.com/wp-srv/national/longterm/abortviolence/stories/hill.htm.

[77]Lance Wallnau, *God's Chaos Candidate: Donald J. Trump and the American Unraveling* (Keller, TX: Killer Sheep Media, 2016), 144.

[78]Berry, "Voting in the Kingdom," 84.

[79]Rick Pidcock, "The New Apostolic Reformation Drove the January 6 Riots," *Baptist News Global*, January 10, 2023, https://baptistnews.com/article/the-new-apostolic-reformation-drove-the-january-6-riots-so-why-was-it-overlooked-by-the-house-select-committee/.

[80]Matthew Rowley, "Prophetic Populism and the Violent Rejection of Joe Biden's Election," *International Journal of Religion* 2, no. 2 (2021): 153.

[81]Pidcock, "The New Apostolic Reformation."

lethal violence followed in the wake of miraculous discourse employed in the service of seizing political authority for Trump."[82] Violence is not a perversion or misapplication of dominionism; it is the logical result of its foundational beliefs.

The propensity toward violence not only reveals a deeply flawed theology, but damages Christian witness. For these hermeneutical, theological, and missional reasons I conclude that Christian reconstructionism, dominionism, and the NAR are incompatible with faithful citizenship in the Kingdom of God.

FAITHFUL REJECTION OF DOMINIONISM

At its best, dominionism is a desire for Christians to influence politics in a direction consistent with godliness. However, the movement's error is in its belief that Christians can cause the Kingdom of God to be realized through Christians gaining political power. The public presence and influence of this movement has harmed Christian mission and witness by contributing to the impression that Christians are more committed to gaining political power than we are to loving our neighbors. For Christians who are drawn to dominionism, the two Calvinist approaches we considered in chapter seven can be faithful alternatives.

Similarly, Christians who are charismatic or Pentecostal need not embrace the NAR, but can examine biblical foundations of prophecy and charismatic gifting to ensure charisms are practiced consistent with Scripture. As Christians, we should be open and attentive to what the Holy Spirit is doing in the world; at the same time, we should be cautious about people and movements that claim unique insight into God's work, especially when their rhetoric fuels division and violence. Dominionism promises the whole world; all it will cost is our souls.

---

[82]Rowley, "Prophetic Populism," 155.

9

ERODING THE DISTINCTION BETWEEN KINGDOM AND COUNTRY

CHRISTIAN NATIONALISM

"IT DISTURBS ME TO SEE churches in America filled with American flags and singing patriotic songs."

This statement surprised me as a college sophomore on a study course in Germany. At the monastery in Erfurt where Martin Luther himself had been a monk, Rev. Heino Falcke (b. 1929), one of the most influential pastor-theologians of twentieth-century East Germany, was telling our class about his ministry behind the Iron Curtain and making connections to current events. I didn't understand Falcke's significance in German church history then, but his words carried a weight that has now burdened me for over half my life.

It was less than two years after 9/11, and the patriotism that characterized Americans' response to the attacks was still in full force. Images of flag-adorned churches had made their way around the world, and for Falcke they looked eerily similar to what he had witnessed as a young boy in Hitler's Germany. He assured us that he did not equate President Bush with Adolph Hitler or the United States with Nazi Germany. Nevertheless, the sight of national symbols in sacred spaces sparked concern about whether some Christians might be subsuming the Christian faith into political allegiance, as so many German Christians had done in the 1930s, and had continued to do in communist East Germany.

In 1972, Falcke argued that the church "should offer neither all-out opposition, nor total and uncritical support" to the political regime of the day, nor should it "seek merely a form of pragmatic accommodation with the authorities in an attempt to guarantee a limited role for church life."[1] Church leaders bringing national symbols into the sacred spaces signaled to Falcke "pragmatic accommodation" at best, and political complicity at worst. In 2004, Falcke wrote, "If we believe that our freedom can be guaranteed through particular language, institutions and behavior then we have become the victims of fear for our own freedom and identity. Our main concern becomes the church itself and this introversion becomes its 'Babylonian Captivity.'"[2] Falcke exhorted churches not to focus so much on maintaining legal or cultural favor that they lose sight of the church's missionary identity. His warning should give us pause as we consider the ways Christians can lose sight of our Kingdom citizenship in favor of our citizenship in the country.

The previous chapter examined dominionism, concluding that it is incompatible with Christian faithfulness in politics. We now turn to Christian nationalism, which overlaps significantly with dominionism, but has more broad and sometimes subtle influence in the United States. Christian nationalism is wholly incompatible with faithfulness to Jesus Christ and counterproductive to the church's mission and witness in the world.

Christian Nationalism

Christian nationalism is a political ideology first and foremost. Instead of being a Christian approach to politics, it is a political approach to Christianity. Christian nationalism subordinates the Kingdom to the country such that commitment to Jesus Christ and his church dissolves under its corrosive influence. Christian nationalism is incompatible with faithful citizenship in the Kingdom of God.

Definition and origins of Christian nationalism. Nationalism is an ideology that defines group membership based on real or perceived shared

---

[1]Stephen Brown, "Introduction to Heino Falcke," *Ecumenical Review* 56, no. 2 (April 2004): 160-65, 162.
[2]Heino Falcke, "Christ Liberates—Therefore, the Church for Others," *Ecumenical Review* 56, no. 2 (April 2004): 166-83, 174.

cultural, historical, or kinship traits. A nation forms as people become aware that they share language, national myths, ethnicity, religion, or other traits; excluded from the nation are people who lack those salient traits. Benedict Anderson calls nations "imagined communities" because "the members of even the smallest nation will never know most of their fellow-members, meet them, or even hear of them, yet in the minds of each lives the image of their communion."[3] Thus, a nation is a community of shared identity, not a geopolitical entity. The United States, as a so-called nation of immigrants, has always struggled with national self-definition because it lacks a single shared culture, language, ethnicity, or religion. Much of our cultural unrest throughout history has come down to competing definitions of American national identity.

Christian nationalism regards Christianity as the trait that ought to unite a nation. Sociologists Andrew Whitehead and Samuel Perry define Christian nationalism in the United States as "a cultural framework—a collection of myths, traditions, symbols, narratives, and value systems—that idealizes and advocates a fusion of Christianity with American civic life."[4] Philip Gorski and Samuel Perry explain Christian nationalism as a "deep story," in which,

> America was founded as a Christian nation by (white) men who were "traditional" Christians, who based the nation's founding documents on "Christian principles." The United States is blessed by God, which is why it has been so successful; and the nation has a special role to play in God's plan for humanity. But these blessings are threatened by cultural degradation from "un-American" influences both inside and outside our borders.[5]

Moreover, according to Whitehead and Perry, "the 'Christianity' of Christian nationalism . . . includes assumptions of nativism, White supremacy, patriarchy, and heteronormativity, along with divine sanction for authoritarian control and militarism. It is as ethnic and political as it is religious."[6] Significantly, the "Christianity" in Christian nationalism refers to culture, history, and morality, not necessarily the theological tenets of Christian orthodoxy. Because this version of "Christianity" is malformed

---

[3]Benedict Anderson, *Imagined Communities* (New York: Verso, 2006), 6.

[4]Andrew Whitehead and Samuel L. Perry, *Taking America Back for God* (Oxford: Oxford University Press, 2020), 10.

[5]Philip Gorski and Samuel L. Perry, *The Flag and the Cross* (Oxford: Oxford University Press, 2022), 4.

[6]Whitehead and Perry, *Taking America,* 10.

and misappropriated, it is not an option for faithful Christian political engagement. Christian nationalism is not a version of Christianity with which we can simply agree to disagree; rather, it is a political ideology that sacrifices core Christian convictions on the altar of power. Christian nationalist ideology is, therefore, not compatible with Christian orthodoxy.[7]

Christian nationalism is not merely patriotism. Historian and theologian John Wilsey makes the distinction clear: "Nationalism is tribalistic, triumphalist, idolatrous, exclusivist, and violates justice. But patriotism is an expression of devotion to country that is defined by justice."[8] Christian nationalists sacralize the nation by fusing Christian heritage with national identity, then insist the sacred country can do no wrong. Patriots, by contrast, are not willfully blind to the country's flaws, but instead, "seek to rectify those flaws, and learn from the failures so as not to repeat them," writes Wilsey.[9] Nationalism is exclusionary by nature, while patriotism welcomes all who share a commitment to the country's ideals. Patriotism appreciates the bonds of what theologian Richard Mouw calls "civic kinship," a connection by which we "acknowledge our shared peoplehood with those who are different from us."[10] Christian nationalism is not merely a Christian expression of patriotism. A Christian can be patriotic without adopting a Christian nationalist ideology that is at odds with both Christianity and patriotism.

In the early American colonies, *European* and *Christian* were practically interchangeable, which shaped the way colonists imagined themselves. Theologian Willie Jennings explains, "there is within Christianity a breathtakingly powerful way to imagine the social, to imagine and enact connection and belonging," and for many White American Christians that imagination was racialized in the colonies, leading to centuries of race-based exclusion.[11] *Christian* and *European* became interlocking identities, and the assumed superiority of Christianity and Europeanness became

---

[7]On the incompatibility of Christian nationalism with Christian orthodoxy, see Whitehead and Perry, *Taking America*; Gorski and Perry, *Flag and the Cross*; Paul D. Miller, *The Religion of American Greatness: What's Wrong with Christian Nationalism* (Downers Grove, IL: InterVarsity Press, 2022).

[8]John D. Wilsey, *American Exceptionalism and Civil Religion: Reassessing the History of an Idea* (Downers Grove, IL: IVP Academic, 2015), 116.

[9]Wilsey, *American Exceptionalism and Civil Religion*, 116.

[10]Richard Mouw, *How to Be a Patriotic Christian: Love of Country as Love of Neighbor* (Downers Grove, IL: InterVarsity Press, 2022), 35.

[11]Willie James Jennings, *The Christian Imagination: Theology and the Origins of Race* (New Haven, CT: Yale University Press, 2010), 4.

justification for enslaving, killing, and forcibly removing those who were not Christian or European. Because the version of Christianity that formed early American national identity was synonymous with European descent, American national identity has frequently excluded those who are not European-descended and (Protestant) Christians.

Because of the fusion of Christianity and Europeanness, Christian nationalist rhetoric and violence spiked with each historical wave of non-Protestant and non-European immigration. The late nineteenth and early twentieth centuries saw fierce anti-Catholic rhetoric and violence. As the Catholic population increased in the early nineteenth century, evangelical Protestants worried that "Catholics represented a theological, moral, and political threat to the American way of life."[12] A burgeoning genre of anti-Catholic literature depicted Catholicism as a political threat, inherently undemocratic, and laboring under "Romish tyranny."[13] The anti-Catholic hysteria led to rioting and death in the mid-nineteenth century, and suspicion about whether a Catholic could be a true American reemerged during John F. Kennedy's presidential campaign.

Chinese, Japanese, and Muslim immigrants have faced similar threats and violence because they were not European Christians. When the Fourteenth Amendment (1868) granted citizenship to all people born in the United States, regardless of "previous condition of servitude," it was met with violent opposition in the form of Jim Crow laws, lynch mobs, and voter intimidation. The Ku Klux Klan became the archetypical representative of Christian nationalism, with its "America for Americans" rallying cry, and its definition of "a 100% American" as native-born, English-speaking, Protestant, and White.[14] Klan leaders insisted "the United States is a white Protestant country," and urged construction of "a wall of steel, a wall as high as heaven" to keep immigrants out.[15] Anxiety about shifting and expanding definitions of Americanness underlies each wave of Christian nationalism, animating much religious-political rancor into the present.

---

[12]Stephen Prothero, *Why Liberals Win the Culture Wars (Even When They Lose Elections)* (New York: HarperOne, 2016), 61.

[13]Prothero, *Why Liberals Win*, 77.

[14]Jordan Fischer, "The History of Hate in Indiana: How the Ku Klux Klan Took Over Indiana's Halls of Power," *WRTV Indianapolis*, December 8, 2016, www.wrtv.com/longform/the-ku-klux -klan-ran-indiana-once-could-it-happen-again.

[15]Timothy Egan, *A Fever in the Heartland: The Ku Klux Klan's Plot to Take Over America, and the Woman Who Stopped Them* (New York: Viking, 2023), xviii.

Christian nationalism also entails what John Wilsey calls "closed American exceptionalism," which is the belief that America is a chosen nation with a divine commission, that its chosen status makes it innocent of historical wrongdoing, and that its history and ideals are glorious. According to Wilsey, closed American exceptionalism "potentially makes America an object of worship, bestowing a transcendent status upon it. And it sets America up as a necessary player in redemption history. From a biblical standpoint, this soteriological form of American exceptionalism paves the way toward heterodoxy at best, heresy and idolatry at worst."[16] American exceptionalism is evident in *The American Patriot's Bible*, which includes the biblical text punctuated by commentary about "the word of God and the shaping of America." A prefatory "Call to Action" tells readers, "to be born in a land of freedom, to live in a nation founded as 'One Nation, Under God' by those who served the one true God of the Bible, is both a tremendous privilege and a great responsibility." It goes on to warn readers, "our nation is rapidly drifting from its biblical foundations. . . . We are engaged in a great spiritual battle that threatens our country, our families, and our lives. Only God's intervention will return America to solid footing and restore a moral nation that righteousness will exalt."[17] For Christian nationalists, America's uniquely chosen status is central to individual and collective identity.

Christian nationalist organizations have periodically attempted to have Congress declare the United States a Christian country. The National Association to Secure the Religious Amendment of the Constitution, founded in 1864, proposed a constitutional amendment "to acknowledge God, submit to the authority of his Son, embrace Christianity, and secure universal liberty."[18] The Presbyterian-led organization made some headway in Congress, but it largely faded in the early twentieth century. A similar organization, the Christian Amendment Movement, took this draft constitutional amendment to Congress in 1947: "This nation devoutly recognizes the authority of the law of Jesus Christ, Saviour and Ruler of Nations, through whom are bestowed the blessings of Almighty God."[19] The

---

[16]Wilsey, *American Exceptionalism and Civil Religion*, 18-19.

[17]Richard G. Lee, "A Call to Action," in *The American Patriot's Bible* (Nashville: Thomas Nelson, 2009).

[18]Andrew Myers, "The National Reform Association," *Log College Press*, January 27, 2018, www .logcollegepress.com/blog/2018/1/26/the-national-reform-association.

[19]The Christian Amendment Movement, "The Christian Amendment Movement: What it Is, Why America Needs It" (pamphlet), 1960–1969, Baylor Church-State Archives, accessed April 26, 2023, https://digitalcollections-baylor.quartexcollections.com/Documents/Detail/the-christian -amendment-movement-what-it-is-why-america-needs-it/816085.

Christian Amendment Movement believed the amendment was necessary because "we cannot preserve our cherished national heritage unless Jesus Christ himself is at the center of our national life. . . . The best defense against tyranny is the commitment of the nation to Jesus Christ and to Christian principles of civil government."[20]

Here again, Christianity refers to tradition and morality in service to the country, not necessarily confessional convictions. Congress held a hearing on a Christian amendment in 1954, but nothing came of it.[21] Similar Christian amendment attempts continued for the next several decades but never gained much traction because the religious diversity of the country makes official recognition of the Christian religion untenable.[22] Today, the National Reform Association hopes to secure a Christian amendment, but it has made no meaningful progress toward that goal.[23]

Christian nationalists believe the United States was founded as a Christian nation, and therefore Christianity ought to have a privileged status. Academic and amateur historians have analyzed Christianity's influence on America's founding, parsed the meaning of words, detailed the historical context, examined the lives of the Founders, and arrived at a range of conclusions about America's Christian founding. Those who argue that America was founded as a Christian nation generally believe the United States ought to promote Christian heritage and values as essential to American identity and codify America's "deep story" in culture and curriculum.[24]

Some Christian nationalists go as far as saying the founding documents were inspired by God, a status Christian orthodoxy reserves for Scripture alone. For example, WallBuilders, an organization that describes itself as

---

[20]Christian Amendment Movement, "Christian Amendment Movement."

[21]Katharine Batlan, "One Nation Under Christ: US Christian Amendment Attempts and Competing Visions for America in the 1940s and 1950s," *Journal of Church and State* 61, no. 4 (June 2019): 658-79.

[22]Batlan, "One Nation Under Christ," 679.

[23]The National Reform Association's mission is to amend the preamble of the Constitution to read: "WE, THE PEOPLE OF THE UNITED STATES, recognizing the being and attributes of Almighty God, the Divine Authority of the Holy Scriptures, the law of God as the paramount rule, and Jesus Christ, the Messiah, the Savior and Lord of all, in order to form a more perfect union, establish justice, insure domestic tranquility, provide for the common defense, promote the general welfare, and secure the blessing of liberty to ourselves and to our posterity, do ordain and establish this Constitution for the United States of America." National Reform Association, "Mission Statement," National Reform Association (NRA), accessed April 26, 2023, https:// nationalreformassociation.weebly.com/.

[24]See Mark David Hall, *Did America Have a Christian Founding? Separating Modern Myth from Historical Truth* (Nashville: Thomas Nelson, 2019).

"dedicated to presenting America's forgotten history and heroes, with an emphasis on the moral, religious, and constitutional foundation on which America was built," has produced a curriculum called "Biblical Citizenship."[25] This curriculum "emphasizes the idea that the Founding Fathers, as well as the Declaration of Independence and Constitution, were divinely inspired and that religious liberty is an important value to protect."[26]

Note how religion functions as a foundation for the country's history and moral values, and that the founding documents are on par with Christian Scripture in this description. A 2021 poll found that a sizable minority of Americans believe the "US Constitution was inspired by God, reflects God's vision for America" (18 percent) and the "federal government should advocate Christian values" (13 percent).[27] What precisely these values are is unclear. The insistence that the United States was founded by Christians to be a Christian nation reduces Christianity to moral values and cultural heritage, rendering core doctrinal convictions obsolete.

Christian nationalism in America today. Sociologists who follow Christian nationalism have raised alarms about the destructive power of this ideology. In their landmark study of the movement, Andrew Whitehead and Samuel Perry classified survey respondent as "*Rejectors, Resisters, Accommodators,* or *Ambassadors*" of Christian nationalism, based on their responses to a series of questions.[28] Rejectors keep Christianity and politics separate; Resisters lean away from Christian nationalism; Accommodators lean toward Christian nationalism; and Ambassadors support Christian nationalism.[29] Whitehead and Perry found that about

---

[25]"About Us," WallBuilders, accessed April 27, 2023, https://wallbuilders.com/about-us/. The founder of WallBuilders, David Barton, who holds a degree in religious education but has no academic training in history, has written extensively on the Christian origins of America's founding. At least one of his books, *The Jefferson Lies*, was found to be so full of factual errors that the publisher withdrew it from publication.

[26]Mya Jaradat, "What Is Biblical Citizenship?," *Deseret News*, November 1, 2021, www.deseret .com/faith/2021/10/31/22740655/what-is-biblical-citizenship-rick-green-religion-politics -churches-christian-nationalism.

[27]Gregory A. Smith, "In U.S., Far More Support Than Oppose Separation of Church and State," Pew Research Center, October 28, 2021, www.pewresearch.org/religion/2021/10/28/in-u-s-far -more-support-than-oppose-separation-of-church-and-state/.

[28]Whitehead and Perry, *Taking America*, 10. The six statements on the survey, with which respondents expressed their level of agreement or disagreement: 1. The federal government should declare the United States a Christian nation; 2. The federal government should advocate Christian values; 3. The federal government should enforce strict separation of church and state; 4. The federal government should allow the display of religious symbols in public spaces; 5. The success of the United States is part of God's plan; 6. The federal government should allow prayer in public schools.

[29]Whitehead and Perry, *Taking America*, 26, 31, 33, 35.

21 percent of Americans are Rejectors, 26 percent are Resisters, 32 percent are Accommodators, and 20 percent are Ambassadors.[30] Whitehead and Perry also found that "Christian nationalism isn't localized primarily within particular religious traditions but is undergirded by a combination of conservative political ideology, belief in the Bible, apocalyptic visions of societal decline, and divine militarism."[31]

The single strongest predictor of Christian nationalism is not orthodox Christian theology or regular church attendance; instead, "the strongest predictor of Christian nationalism is identifying oneself with political conservatism."[32] As previous chapters have demonstrated, a Christian can be politically conservative without being a Christian nationalist, but Christian nationalism is a distinctly conservative movement. Moreover, Whitehead and Perry's research showed sincere religious commitment and Christian nationalism lead people to opposite moral worldviews.[33] For example, survey data showed Christian nationalists are significantly less likely than committed Christians to believe seeking justice and caring for the vulnerable are part of what it means to be a good person.[34] On the basis of these and other findings, Whitehead and Perry conclude, "Christian nationalism is not 'Christianity' or even 'religion.'"[35] In other words, Christian nationalism is a political ideology that deforms faith commitments, not a Christian approach to political engagement.

The data on Christian Nationalism do not allow us to relegate it to an inconsequential minority. A 2023 Public Religion Research Institute/ Brookings survey found that 35 percent of White evangelical Protestants are sympathizers and 29 percent are adherents of Christian nationalism, compared to 19 percent and 10 percent of all Americans. White evangelical Protestants showed the highest levels of support for Christian nationalism, but a slim majority of "other Protestant of color" and about one-third of White mainline Protestants also showed support for Christian nationalist ideology.[36]

---

[30]Whitehead and Perry, *Taking America*, 25.

[31]Whitehead and Perry, *Taking America*, 13.

[32]Whitehead and Perry, *Taking America*, 13.

[33]Whitehead and Perry, *Taking America*, 13.

[34]Whitehead and Perry, *Taking America*, 14-15.

[35]Whitehead and Perry, *Taking America*, 20.

[36]PRRI/Brookings, "A Christian Nation? Understanding the Threat of Christian Nationalism to American Democracy and Culture," accessed May 3, 2023, www.prri.org/wp-content

Is it possible people view Christian nationalism unfavorably but do not realize some of their views align with it? The PRRI/Brookings survey found that 54 percent of adherents to Christian nationalism have a very favorable or somewhat favorable view of the term "Christian nationalism" itself.[37] Illustrating the inherent danger of this ideology, 40 percent of adherents to Christian nationalism believe, "true American patriots may have to resort to violence in order to save our country," compared to only 16 percent of all American who agree. Similarly, about 17 percent of Americans agree with the statement, "The United States is a white Christian nation, and I am willing to fight to keep it that way," which reinforces the ethnic element of Christian nationalism.[38] Christian nationalist ideology is common among American Christians today, and the correlation between this ideology and violence should raise alarms for all of us.

In recent years, some pastors and politicians have embraced Christian nationalism or dismissed the term as a liberal smear against conservative Christians. Dinesh D'Souza, a conservative political author, said in a post on Truth Social, "Christian nationalism is good and healthy because Christianity redeems nationalism and gives it a gentler, more humane and more universal thrust."[39] Robert Jeffress, senior pastor of the sixteen-thousand-member First Baptist Church in Dallas, Texas, said in an interview, "[the left] say they are opposed to people who say America was founded as a Christian nation, Americans who believe not only in the spiritual heritage of our nation, but believe that we ought to use elections to help return our country to its Christian foundation. If that's Christian nationalism, count me in. Because that's what we have to do."[40] Jeffress's

---

/uploads/2023/02/PRRI-Jan-2023-Christian-Nationalism-Final.pdf, 5-6. The Christian nationalism definitions were based on respondents' level of agreement with the following statements: 1. The U.S. government should declare America a Christian nation; 2. U.S. laws should be based on Christian values; 3. If the U.S. moves away from our Christian foundations, we will not have a country anymore; 4. Being Christian is an important part of being truly American; 5. God has called Christians to exercise dominion over all areas of American society.

[37] PRRI/Brookings, "Christian Nation?," 12.

[38] PRRI/Brookings, "Christian Nation?," 27, 30.

[39] Dinesh D'Souza, Truth Social post, July 27, 2022, https://truthsocial.com/@DineshDSouza/posts/108719525751357299.

[40] Quoted in Stephanie Martin, "Pastor Robert Jeffress: If Voting One's Values Is Christian Nationalism, 'Count Me In,'" *Church Leaders*, October 31, 2022, https://churchleaders.com/news/437559-pastor-robert-jeffress-voting-values-christian-nationalism.html.

church is well-known for his outspoken support for Donald Trump and its God-and-country worship services.[41]

As for politicians, Rep. Marjorie Taylor Greene (R-Georgia) said in an interview, "We need to be the party of nationalism and I'm a Christian, and I say it proudly, we should be Christian nationalists."[42] Her fundraising website sells "Proud Christian Nationalist" T-shirts. Michael Flynn, former national security adviser to Donald Trump, called for, "One nation under God, and one religion under God."[43] He urges attendees at his ReAwaken America rallies to get involved in the spiritual and political battle.[44] Turning Point USA Faith holds events such as "Freedom Night in America" and the "Free America Tour" that fuse Christianity with nationalism. We should not reject all examples of patriotism or Christian conservatism as nationalistic; however, we need to be aware that the union of God and country can introduce Christians to nationalistic silos, culminating in eroded faith and possible political radicalization.[45]

EVALUATION OF CHRISTIAN NATIONALISM

We began this chapter with Rev. Heino Falcke's concern about the fusion of patriotic and religious symbols in the United States after the 9/11 attack. We look to Germans who preceded Falcke to explain why Christians must reject Christian nationalism. Dr. Reinhold Krause proclaimed at the Berlin Sports Palace in 1933, "the pure teaching of Jesus must again become the foundation of the church. . . . If we take from the gospels what speaks to our German hearts, then what is at the heart of Jesus' teaching comes clearly and brilliantly to light and coincides—and we can take pride in

---

[41]Diana Chandler, "Vice President Speaks During First Baptist Dallas' Annual Patriotic 'Celebrate Freedom Sunday' Service," *Baptist Press*, June 29, 2020, www.baptistpress.com/resource-library /news/vice-president-speaks-during-first-baptist-dallas-annual-patriotic-celebrate-freedom -sunday-service/.

[42]Marjorie Taylor Green, interview with Next News Network, July 24, 2022, video posted on Twitter, https://twitter.com/NextNewsNetwork/status/1551204108471861248.

[43]Quoted in Rachel Scully, "Michael Flynn Says of the US: 'We have to Have to Have One Religion,'" *The Hill*, November 13, 2021, https://thehill.com/homenews/media/581443-michael-flynn -says-of-the-us-we-have-to-have-one-religion/.

[44]Michelle R. Smith and Richard Lardner, "Michael Flynn Is Recruiting an 'Army of God' in Growing Christian Nationalist Movement," *PBS Newshour*, October 7, 2022, www.pbs.org/newshour/politics /michael-flynn-is-recruiting-an-army-of-god-in-growing-christian-nationalist-movement.

[45]Jack Jenkins, "How the Capitol Attacks Helped Spread Christian Nationalism in the Extreme Right," *Washington Post*, January 26, 2022, www.washingtonpost.com/religion/2022/01/26 /christian-nationalism-jan-6-extreme-right/.

this—completely with the demands of National Socialism."[46] Krause portrayed Martin Luther as a German folk hero who "was always on the side
of the values of German ethno-national identity," and called Adolf Hitler
"the liberator and savior whom God has sent."[47]

While this speech fractured the German Christian movement of which
Krause was a member, the statement also represented a significant faction
of Germans who welcomed Hitler and the Nazi Party as catalysts for cultural and religious renewal.[48] The German Christian movement intentionally removed Christian doctrine from Christian identity, reducing
Christianity to a cultural heritage and traditional value system.[49] The Nazis'
promise of spiritual renewal appealed to the German people, but the renewal the Nazi Party offered was a revived spirit of ethnonationalism
under a thin veneer of Christian rhetoric. German Christian nationalists
reduced Christianity to cultural heritage and morals, made that heritage
essential to German identity, then justified the eradication of anyone labeled a threat to that identity. We might protest, *But that clearly wasn't
Christian!* Of course it wasn't! It was Christian nationalism.

One cannot be a faithful citizen of the Kingdom of God while adhering
to Christian nationalist ideology. From the outset, we should reject Christian
nationalism because it is not compatible with orthodox Christian beliefs.
Political theorist Paul D. Miller explains the contradiction between the
ideals of Christian nationalism and biblical Christianity: "Americans are
not God's chosen people; those who trust in Jesus from every tribe, tongue,
people and nation are. The divine mission of God's chosen people is not to
spread political liberty, national sovereignty, or capitalism; it is to spread
the gospel of Jesus Christ. (They are not the same thing.)"[50] The coming of
the Holy Spirit at Pentecost defined the church in a way that excludes the
possibility of nationalism. The Holy Spirit erased ethnic and national definitions of religion and removed the boundaries that divided people based on

---

[46]Reinhold Krause, "Speech at the Sports Palace in Berlin," in *A Church Undone: Documents from
the German Christian Faith Movement, 1932–1940*, ed. Mary M. Solberg (Minneapolis: Fortress
Press, 2015), 259. National Socialism is Nazism.

[47]Krause, "Speech," in *Church Undone*, 252, 253-54.

[48]Doris Bergen, *Twisted Cross: The German Christian Movement in the Third Reich* (Chapel Hill:
University of North Carolina Press, 1996), 17. The German Christian Movement refers to a
specific faction within the German Protestant Church that aligned itself with Naziism. It does
not refer to all Christians in Germany or all Christians who are German. The movement's name
was intentionally inclusive and ambiguous.

[49]Bergen, *Twisted Cross*, 44.

[50]Miller, *Religion of American Greatness*, 130.

language, culture, geography, or bloodlines. The Holy Spirit forged a movement that has no ethnic, national, or linguistic boundaries, precisely the opposite of Christian nationalism's exclusionary ideology.[51]

If the abrogation of Christian orthodoxy isn't reason enough to reject it, Christian nationalism also promotes White supremacy, xenophobia, conspiracy theories, and violence. Christian nationalist ideology is deeply rooted in White supremacy, whether that be an avowed nativist belief in the superiority of European-descended people, or the more subtle and insidious assumption that White people, culture, and institutions are superior to non-White people, culture, and institutions. Today, that White supremacy often manifests as insistence that people of color do not experience interpersonal or systemic discrimination. Those who hold Christian nationalist views tend to believe that White people experience as much discrimination as Black and other minority Americans do.[52]

Race-based discrimination against White people does happen, but the perception that it is on par with discrimination against people of color is difficult to square with data about the criminal justice system or school discipline, for example.[53] Supporters of Christian nationalism do not believe a Black person is more likely than a White person to receive the death penalty for the same crime.[54] In fact, a Black person is statistically more likely than a White person to receive the death penalty for the same crime.[55] Eighty-three percent of White adherents of Christian nationalism reject the idea that "generations of slavery and discrimination have created conditions that make it difficult for many Black Americans to work their way out of the lower class."[56] The evidence that discriminatory home mortgage lending practices have hindered the accumulation of generational wealth contradicts that belief.[57]

---

[51]Miranda Zapor Cruz, "Burning Away Barriers and Blowing Down Walls," Missio Alliance, June 1, 2022, www.missioalliance.org/burning-away-barriers-and-blowing-down-walls/.

[52]PRRI/Brookings, "Christian Nation?," 17.

[53]Keith Payne, "The Truth about Anti-White Discrimination," *Scientific American*, July 18, 2019, www.scientificamerican.com/article/the-truth-about-anti-white-discrimination/.

[54]PRRI/Brookings, "Christian Nation?," 7.

[55]Colleen Long, "Report: Death Penalty Cases Show History of Racial Disparity," Associated Press, September 15, 2020, https://apnews.com/article/united-states-lifestyle-race-and-ethnicity-discrimination-racial-injustice-ded1f517a0fd64bf1d55c448a06acccc.

[56]PRRI/Brookings, "Christian Nation?," 17-18.

[57]See Richard Rothstein, *The Color of Law: A Forgotten History of How Our Government Segregated America* (New York: Liveright Publishing, 2017).

White supremacy is evident when people insist the racial economic disparity in the United States is only the result of lack of education or effort among Black Americans, despite evidence to the contrary.[58] While White supremacy is not unique to Christian nationalism, it is an inseparable part of its ideology and it damages the body of Christ. In recent years, an as-yet-difficult-to-quantify number of Black Christians have left predominantly White churches, citing the "absence of a church-wide stand against police brutality" and "rhetoric from church leaders that ignores how health inequities and racism are affecting the Black community right now."[59] Christian nationalism corresponds with an active rejection of working for racial justice and active acceptance of White supremacy, which makes it incompatible with a biblical vision of the Kingdom of God.

Christian nationalism embraces and normalizes xenophobia. PRRI/ Brookings found that 82 percent of adherents to Christian nationalism agree that "the American way of life needs to be protected from foreign influence," and 71 percent agree that "immigrants are invading our country and replacing our cultural and ethnic background."[60] Stephen Wolfe, an apologist for Christian nationalism, defends racial and ethnic prejudice when he claims, "choosing similar people over dissimilar people is not a result of fallenness, but is natural to man as man . . . Indeed, one *ought* to prefer and to love more those who are more similar to him, and much good would result in the world if we all preferred our own and minded our own business."[61]

Xenophobia is readily apparent in the relationship between Christian nationalism and anti-immigrant sentiment. Christian nationalism is associated with "greater endorsement of negative immigrant stereotypes" and with "dehumanization attitudes toward immigrants."[62] Christians can come to a range of conclusions about immigration policy, but Christians'

---

[58]See William Darrity Jr., et al., "What We Get Wrong About Closing the Racial Wealth Gap," Samuel DuBois Cook Center on Social Equity, April 2018, https://insightcced.org/wp-content /uploads/2018/07/Where-We-Went-Wrong-COMPLETE-REPORT-July-2018.pdf.

[59]Dara T. Mathis, "The Church's Black Exodus," *The Atlantic*, October 11, 2020, www.theatlantic .com/politics/archive/2020/10/why-black-parishioners-are-leaving-churches/616588/.

[60]PRRI/Brookings, "Christian Nation?," 19.

[61]Stephen Wolfe, *The Case for Christian Nationalism* (Moscow, ID: Canon Press, 2022), 24-25.

[62]Rosemary Al-Kire et al., "Protecting America's Borders: Christian Nationalism, Threat, and Attitudes Toward Immigrants in the United States," *Group Processes and Intergroup Relations* 25, no. 2 (November 2020), www.researchgate.net/publication/345703082_Protecting_America's _borders_Christian_nationalism_threat_and_attitudes_toward_immigrants_in_the _United_States.

attitudes toward human beings should not include stereotypes or dehumanization. Christians ought to be known for our love of neighbor; therefore, xenophobia and the Christian nationalism that engenders it are incompatible with Christian faith.

Christian nationalists are more likely than other Americans to believe conspiracy theories, which damages Christian witness when Christianity is associated with gullibility or ignorance and when conspiracy theories turn violent. A 2020 survey found that 73 percent of Christian nationalist ambassadors, using Whitehead and Perry's terminology, also believed the core tenets of the QAnon conspiracy theories.[63] The 2023 PRRI/Brookings Christian nationalism survey found that 58 percent of believers in the QAnon conspiracy theories are Christian nationalist adherents or sympathizers, which represents about 14 percent of the total US population.

QAnon includes the belief that "the government, media, and financial worlds in the United States are controlled by a group of satan-worshipping pedophiles who run a global child sex-trafficking operation." This belief could be harmless lunacy except that believers in QAnon also affirm, "American patriots may have to resort to violence in order to save our country."[64] The significant overlap between Christian nationalism and belief in conspiracy theories has led some observers to conclude that Christian faith makes people susceptible to conspiratorial thinking.[65] This may contribute to the impression that Christianity is anti-intellectual, reinforcing the long-simmering stereotypes the Scopes Trial popularized in the 1920s (see chapter four).

Finally, physical and rhetorical violence are endemic to Christian nationalism, which is part of what makes it incompatible with Christian faithfulness. Christian nationalism motivates some of its adherents to engage in violent actions to advance their cause, costing lives and damaging Christian witness. In a recent example, Christian nationalism was central to the January 6, 2021 attack on the US Capitol. On the morning of January 6, conspiracy theorist and radio host Alex Jones screamed from a stage, "God is on our side. . . . The state has no jurisdiction over any of us," and

---

[63] Gorski and Perry, *Flag and the Cross*, 107-8.

[64] PRRI/Brookings, "Christian Nation?," 31.

[65] Aden Cotterill, "When It Comes to Conspiracy Theories, Is Christianity Part of the Problem or Part of the Solution?," *Australian Broadcasting Corporation*, December 20, 2020, www.abc.net.au/religion/why-are-christians-susceptible-to-conspiracy-theories/13003550.

urged the crowd to "keep our eyes on Christ and never back down and never surrender."[66]

Eric Metaxas, a conservative talk radio personality and author, said, "We are here today to cry out to the God of heaven to ask him to have mercy on the greatest nation in the history of the world. . . . We are what God is doing in the United States today . . . and today, we're going to see heaven move."[67] Michael Flynn urged the crowd, "We're going to knock those walls down. So be proud. Be proud as Christians. Be proud as patriots. And what we . . . do is we give witness today to our faith in God, our love of country, the United States of America, for our Constitution, and for our President Donald J. Trump. God bless America."[68]

After the Capitol was violently breached, Christian nationalist language came from many directions. Jacob Anthony Chasley, who became known as the QAnon Shaman and was convicted on federal charges related to his role in the attack, prayed in the Senate chamber: "Thank you for filling this chamber with patriots that you love and that love Christ. Thank you divine, omniscient, omnipotent, and omnipresent creator God for blessing each and every one of us here and now . . . Thank you for allowing the United States of America to be reborn."[69] Another man exhorted from a bullhorn, "Let us pray Second Chronicles, chapter 7, verse 14, over our nation. Let us pray."[70] From the rally stage to the Senate dais, people evoked Christian nationalist ideas about America's divine purpose and defended their actions based on reclaiming America for God. Flags and posters also signaled Christian nationalism, with words and images including, "Jesus Saves," a Jesus fish symbol, "Jesus is My Savior, Trump is My President," Jesus Christ wearing a red "Make America Great Again" cap, and a banner with an icon of Jesus Christ and the words "Trump is President, Christ is King," among many others.[71]

---

[66]Quoted in Bradley Onishi, *Preparing for War* (Minneapolis: Broadleaf, 2023), 163-64.

[67]Quoted in Andrew L. Seidel, "Events, People, and Networks Leading up to January 6," in *Christian Nationalism and the January 6th 2021 Insurrection*, ed. Baptist Joint Committee for Religious Liberty et al., February 9, 2022, https://bjconline.org/wp-content/uploads/2022/02/Christian_Nationalism_and_the_Jan6_Insurrection-2-9-22.pdf. Metaxas is perhaps best known for his bestselling biography of Dietrich Bonhoeffer, which is widely rejected among Bonhoeffer scholars for its factual errors and ideological bias.

[68]Quoted in Seidel, "Events, People, and Networks," 18.

[69]Quoted in Seidel, "Events, People, and Networks," 35.

[70]Quoted in Seidel, "Events, People, and Networks," 20.

[71]See examples in Andrew Seidel, "Attack on the Capitol: Evidence of the Role of White Christian Nationalism," in Baptist Joint Committee on Religious Liberty et al., *Christian Nationalism*; at

The undeniable connection between the violence of January 6 and Christianity has done real damage to Christian witness in the United States. If this is the fruit of Christian nationalism, then the tree is dead and incompatible with abundant life in Christ. And even if Christian nationalist ideology never led to violence, it would still be incompatible with Christianity for its embrace of White supremacy and xenophobia, and its reduction of Christianity to a mere code of heritage and morals.

FAITHFUL REJECTION OF CHRISTIAN NATIONALISM

Christian nationalism is not a viable option for faithful Christian citizenship in the Kingdom of God, and it is detrimental to faithful citizenship in the country. Christians across the political and theological spectrum have raised alarms about the damage Christian nationalism causes as a theological error and a political danger. The Baptist Joint Committee for Religious Liberty (BJC) launched Christians Against Christian Nationalism in 2019 with the support of a broad cross-section of Christians—Catholic and Protestant, progressive and conservative, denominational leaders, academics, and lay people. Over 30,000 people, including myself, have signed their online statement, which reads in part:

> Christian nationalism seeks to merge Christian and American identities, distorting both the Christian faith and America's constitutional democracy. Christian nationalism demands Christianity be privileged by the State and implies that to be a good American, one must be Christian. It often overlaps with and provides cover for white supremacy and racial subjugation. We reject this damaging political ideology and invite our Christian brothers and sisters to join us in opposing this threat to our faith and to our nation.[72]

Christians Against Christian Nationalism continues to produce and compile resources to educate people and combat Christian nationalism. David French, a conservative evangelical Christian and *New York Times* columnist, has consistently written against Christian nationalism, calling it "a blueprint for corruption, brutality, and oppression."[73] Michael Horton,

---

the #CapitolSiegeReligion hashtag on X (Twitter); accessed May 16, 2023, https://uncivilreligion
.org.

[72]"Christians Against Christian Nationalism Statement," BJC, accessed May 4, 2023, www.christians
againstchristiannationalism.org/statement.

[73]David French, "The Spiritual Lessons of a Christian Nationalist Military Defeat," *The Dispatch*,
October 9, 2022, https://thedispatch.com/newsletter/frenchpress/the-spiritual-lessons-of
-a-christian/.

a conservative Calvinist theologian, has rejected Christian nationalism because "*Jesus* is the fulfillment of that story, not America. He is the true Israel. The United States is not God's chosen people. . . . To identify Christ's kingdom with any kingdom of this age is to reject 'one holy, catholic [worldwide] and apostolic church.'"[74]

Where we recognize tendencies toward Christian nationalism within ourselves or those who influence us, we must discern the work of the Spirit to turn us toward a more faithful way of living in the world. We can be patriotic, but we cannot allow love of country to fuse with love of God and erode the distinction between the Kingdom of God and the country. Christian nationalism is a theological error and a political ideology that distorts our faith and damages our witness.

---

[74]Michael Horton, "Q&A with Michael Horton on Recovering Our Sanity," *Challies.com* (blog), February 14, 2022, www.challies.com/sponsored/qa-with-michael-horton-on-his-new -book-recovering-our-sanity-how-the-fear-of-god-conquers-the-fears-that-divide-us/. Italics in original.

KINGDOM CITIZENSHIP

THE WAY OF KINGDOM CITIZENSHIP leads us into tension, because tension is where the Holy Spirit transforms us. We are citizens of a Kingdom that is eternal, universal, and abundant, dwelling in a country defined by temporality, boundaries, and scarcity. Christians have the opportunity to participate in the country's government, even as we acknowledge the United States is not, has never been, and will not become the Kingdom of God.

Different theological traditions and historical contexts have led Christians to develop a variety of approaches to faithfully living as citizens in the Kingdom and the country. We have considered a range of separatist, separationist, social gospel, and Calvinist approaches as viable options for Christians who want to be faithful to Christ in our political lives. We have also considered reasons dominionism and Christian nationalism are incompatible with Christian faithfulness. We have faithful alternatives to passive disengagement or partisan division.

As we thoughtfully form and evaluate our own political views, we can consider a variety of approaches and resist the temptation to resolve the tension with uncritical partisan alignment. We can also understand and respect our sisters and brothers in Christ who come to different political conclusions. Since Christian convictions do not fully align with party platforms, we should expect party affiliations and policy preferences to differ among Christians. As we grow in grace, we add salt to a political world in desperate need of flavor. We can follow Christ into the tension.

KINGDOM CITIZENSHIP IS . . .

While Christian faithfulness can lead to a range of political approaches, underlying any approach should be a discernible *Christianness*. We should inhabit the political world in a way that marks us as citizens of the Kingdom of God first. The ten approaches I've examined are not completely separate. They overlap and diverge, so we likely will find ourselves identifying with aspects of several approaches. Instead of choosing only one approach and adhering to it dogmatically, I suggest we can be most faithful in politics if we bring together aspects of each faithful approach. Based on my assessment of the approaches, my Christian convictions, and my own political engagement, I suggest that Kingdom citizens are most faithful when we are salty, prophetic, separationist, social, and pluralist.

Salty. Being salty requires us to be clear about the demands of our Christian faith, and to communicate in a way that causes others to value the dimension of flavor we offer. If we are Kingdom citizens first, we will recognize when the demands of faith diverge from the party line. If we agree with our parties about everything, we have lost our saltiness and allowed our Kingdom citizenship to be distorted by party allegiance. Salt, in the correct proportion, makes things taste better. Salt is also a preservative. It can slow the natural process of decay. Our salty participation in the political process should help ward off the self-destructive tendencies of political divisiveness and rancor.

Saltiness does not come naturally. As we saw in the research on social identity, social intuition, and partisan animosity in chapter three, our natural tendency is to allow our worst instincts free rein, thereby living into the effects of sin instead of embodying redemption. Redeemed people are called to be salt, which requires us to stir up the grace that is in us that we may be in and for the world according to Christ's command. Christians should be gracious and humble, yet clear, as we communicate our positions and points of deviation from the party line. Partisan politics has trained us to dehumanize those across the partisan divide. As French philosopher Emmanuel Levinas wrote, "to be in relation with the other face to face—is to be unable to kill."[1] When we hurl epithets and accusations at enemies, we dehumanize them and ourselves. When we recognize God in the face of other people, we are disarmed and can add salt where savory flavor is desperately needed.

Prophetic. Being prophetic requires us to see reality clearly, then bear witness to truth through words and actions. It does not mean claiming to have special authority or secret revelations about the future. We look to

---

[1]Emmanuel Levinas, "Is Ontology Fundamental?," in *Entre Nous: Thinking-of-the-Other*, trans. Michael B. Smith and Barbara Harshav (New York: Columbia University Press, 1998), 10.

the biblical prophets as models for our call to prophetic truth-telling. The Hebrew prophets had one job: speak the truth as God reveals it. Prophetic truth-telling reveals God's purposes, lifting the veil that separates the sin-sick world from its healer. The Hebrew prophets spoke truth to those in power, particularly when the powerful worshiped idols, amassed wealth through unjust means, oppressed the poor, or disregarded the Sabbath. Thomas Gillespie explains, in the New Testament, "authentic prophecy bears witness to the reality and meaning of the Lordship of Jesus in accordance with the salvation event that effected his exaltation."[2]

Prophets reveal the truth about the suffering we cause and the ripples of suffering across history. Prophetic truth-telling also reveals the hope and promise of God's final victory, inviting people to participate in the already-but-not-yet Kingdom of God. Kingdom citizens are prophetic when our speech or action reveals God's divine will, bears witness to Jesus Christ, and discloses the implications of Christ's lordship for our political contexts. Thus, the call to prophetic truth-telling requires attentiveness to the Spirit of God, so we can discern truth and proclaim it courageously.

Separationist. Separation allows us to clearly differentiate the Kingdom from the country, even as our Kingdom citizenship informs and relativizes our civic engagement. Separation does not, however, require us to privatize our Christian beliefs and remove our convictions from public discourse. Instead, separation allows us to bring our convictions into our civic engagement in a way that invites people to consider their veracity, instead of a way that demands others submit to them. History indicates the separation of church and state has allowed Christianity to flourish in the United States in a way it has not in Europe.[3] In short, separation has helped, not hindered, the mission and witness of the church.

Separation gives Christians the opportunity to show love and hospitality by safeguarding our neighbors' religious liberties. Russell Moore, former head of the Ethics and Religious Liberty Council of the Southern Baptist Convention, wrote of separation,

> A government that can tell you a mosque or synagogue cannot be built because it is a mosque or a synagogue is a government that, in the fullness of time, will tell an evangelical church it cannot be constructed because of our

---

[2]Thomas W. Gillespie, *The First Theologians* (Grand Rapids, MI: Eerdmans, 1994), 89.
[3]Peter Berger, Grace Davie, and Effie Fokas, *Religious America, Secular Europe? A Theme and Variations* (New York: Routledge, 2008), 23-46.

claims to the exclusivity of Christ. Those voices (though a distinct minority, to be sure) that claim to be Christian but seek to restrict religious freedom for others are perhaps unknowingly on a campaign to destroy religious liberty. They would set the precedents that will be used to destroy churches, and they will give the opponents of religious liberty the charge that the issue isn't about freedom at all but about seeking government approval of one's religion.[4]

Christian defense of religious liberty is an act of love and hospitality toward our religiously diverse neighbors, and a downpayment on our own future religious liberty in a country with a declining Christian majority. Religious liberty for Christians is only as safe as religious liberty for practitioners of other religions.

Social. Kingdom citizens ought to retain, and in some cases reclaim, a social understanding of Christianity and consider the political implications of the commandment to love our neighbors. A social approach to faith in public life often runs counter to the American spirit of individualism and self-sufficiency that many Christians have embraced.[5] Kingdom citizens recognize that humans bear the image of God in our social nature, not only in our individuality. Our understanding of the image of God begins with our Creator, who is one God and three persons. The three persons eternally indwell such that one person of God cannot be conceived of apart from the others. A trinitarian concept of humanity in the image of God means we are inseparable from each other. This truth has serious political implications, because our political engagement can be either an expression of American individualism or Christian mutuality.

The social focus of Kingdom citizens moves us away from a dehumanizing utility calculus or a self-seeking hedonism, and moves us toward evaluating our political actions according to their impact on those whom society deems less valuable. In recent years "social justice" has acquired a negative connotation for some Christians, who associate justice with secular political movements so strongly that they reject justice itself along with these movements.[6] Christians disagree about the proper role of the

---

[4]Quoted in Tom Strode, "Moore: Religious Liberty for non-Christians as Well," *Baptist Press*, June 9, 2016, www.baptistpress.com/resource-library/news/moore-religious-liberty-for-non-christians-as-well/.

[5]See chapters one and two of Soong-Chan Rah, *The Next Evangelicalism: Freeing the Church of Western Cultural Captivity* (Downers Grove, IL: InterVarsity Press, 2009).

[6]Ryan Burge, "Even Christians Who Are Democrats Are Abandoning the Social Gospel," *Religion News Service*, October 6, 2022, https://religionnews.com/2022/10/06/even-christians-who-are-democrats-are-abandoning-the-social-gospel/.

government in rendering aid to the poor or intervening in private business to advance equity. We have different philosophies about what approaches to charity are most effective in the short and long terms. But the command to care for widows and orphans or to love our neighbors as ourselves is not as hard as we sometimes make it out to be.

Pluralist. Pluralism, following Abraham Kuyper's theology of sphere sovereignty, is a helpful framework for Christians in a country that is religiously diverse and institutionally complex. Pluralism means Christians are secure in God's sovereign authority over all creation, which frees us from grasping for political control. Christians can promote human flourishing within a diverse and complex society, including through influencing government, motivated by the common good instead of fear of losing power. Pluralism sets limits around the roles of different spheres of society, which guards against tyranny, including religious tyranny.

Further, pluralism allows Christians to work alongside diverse neighbors for the common good. Makoto Fujimura, a Christian artist who is Japanese American, writes that "a 'non-Christian' culture like Japan, unaware of the Holy Spirit's work within it, contains cultural works that bear witness to the invisible work and wisdom of God. By the grace of God, the diverse cultural works of Japan bless the nations and glorify God."[7] Kingdom citizens need not fear displacement by or cooperation with people of diverse religions, because God is sovereign. Through common grace God instills humanity with a capacity to promote human flourishing for the sake of the common good, even if Christians do not dominate politics or culture.

Kingdom Citizens Are ...

Living as Kingdom citizens in the political world calls us to apply the characteristics above in concrete ways. As we develop and reconsider our opinions about public policy and decide which candidates to vote for in local, state, and national elections, we will be tempted to outsource our critical thinking to politicians, family, online influencers, or pastors. We should resist that easy release from political tension, and instead make the effort to be engaged, informed, and conflicted.

---

[7]Makoto Fujimura, "Japanese Aesthetics and Reformed Theology," in *Reformed Public Theology: A Global Vision for Life in the World*, ed. Matthew Kaemingk (Grand Rapids, MI: Baker, 2021), 167.

Engaged. "Decisions are made by those who show up," said *The West Wing*'s fictional president Josiah Bartlett.[8] It is a maxim worth remembering in a country where we have the right to vote, to petition the government, to speak in public forums regarding legislation, and even to protest. I did much of my dissertation research digging through an archive filled with the writings of Soviet religious dissidents. These newspapers, speeches, and sermons by people who had no civil liberties, many of whom were deported or murdered for criticizing the Soviet government, gave me a new appreciation for rights we take for granted in the United States, including free speech, free press, and free assembly. It can be easy to become cynical about the government. And yet, showing up is an act of faithful citizenship. We need to love our neighbors enough to pay attention to what is happening in our communities, the country, and around the world, and to be faithfully engaged for the sake of the common good and Christian witness.

Engagement means more than watching cable news, listening to talk radio, and absorbing the views of our favorite political entertainers. In fact, these behaviors are more likely to make us bland. A first step to engagement can be to follow the proceedings of your state legislature. Pay attention to local newspapers, radio stations, or television shows that report on local government in a nonpartisan way. As we learn more about local and national policy issues, we may discover a passion for a few key issues that inspire us to show up. We can contact our representatives, participate in town hall meetings, attend public demonstrations, join local advocacy groups, or even run for office. Not everyone has the same time and resources to show up in the same ways, but we all have some capacity to engage with government.

Informed. Kingdom citizens should make an effort to be well informed and should also have the humility to admit when we lack information. Confidence in our opinions should be proportional to how informed we are about an issue, policy, or candidate. Ironically, more information will often lead to less political certainty. We should seek out the most accurate information available and intentionally counteract confirmation bias.

Several years ago, I agreed to participate in a research study about the impact of news sources on political opinions. Participants in the study were asked to follow several news organizations with different partisan leanings, such as the center-right *Wall Street Journal* and the center-left

---

[8] Aaron Sorkin, "What Kind of Day Has It Been?," *The West Wing*, season 1, episode 22.

New York Times. It was fascinating to see how different news organizations covered different issues and to read erudite editorials written through different policy lenses. I continue to follow a wide range of news sources, being aware of their political and ideological tendencies so I can seek a balanced information diet. The "Media Bias Chart," though not perfect, is a good place to start to identify the partisan leanings of news sources and to cultivate a healthy field of fact-based information.[9] Christians should avoid sources that do not subscribe to standards of journalistic ethics or that use incendiary or dehumanizing rhetoric to fire up their audience. Anger and fear are not fruit of the Spirit, so information sources that intentionally foster anger and fear are not trustworthy guides for Kingdom citizens.

Conflicted. Kingdom citizens should be conflicted about our policy opinions and partisan leanings. Most policy decisions benefit some people and cost others. We should not delude ourselves into thinking that making the "right" policy decision will only have positive consequences, even when we believe the costs are justified. For that reason, Kingdom citizens should not be single-issue voters. It is easy to choose one or two topics, form a settled opinion about them, and then allow those opinions to steer all other political behavior. When we feel very strongly about an issue, it can be difficult to take opposing viewpoints seriously or listen when people tell us a policy we support is causing harm. Love of neighbor compels us to good faith consideration of opposing perspectives. Even if our position does not change, we should feel conflicted about real or potential harm and address the consequences of policies we endorse. Being conflicted does not mean never making up our minds or being neutral, but it can mean writing our positions in pencil instead of blood and being prepared to change our minds. When we refuse to be conflicted, settling instead for a false simplicity, we are inclined to become bland partisans.

Kingdom Citizens Can . . .

Kingdom citizens can embody the fruit of the Spirit in the political world in a way that lowers the temperature of divisive rhetoric and replaces it with fruitful civil discourse. We are empowered to dispel the fear and anger that lead to physical and verbal assaults by seeking shalom. The world will

---

[9] "Interactive Media Bias Chart," *Ad Fontes Media*, accessed May 26, 2023, https://adfontesmedia.com/interactive-media-bias-chart.

know we are Christians by our love, which is on display in the ways we bridge political divides.

Contribute to civil discourse. Our social media feeds, churches, friends, and even our neighborhoods tend to echo our own perspectives back to us. When we do encounter disagreement, we perceive it as a threat and either recoil or lash out. Many Christians struggle to have constructive conversations across political disagreement because we believe our view is the Christian one, so the other's view must be unchristian. When the person with whom we disagree is also a Christian, we might deem them not only wrong, but heretical. In our zeal to be right and righteous, we make enemies and exacerbate division.

In his book *All About the Bass*, philosophy professor Scott Burson suggests "exorcising demonization" as a tactic for engaging across difference. Burson encourages readers to "revalue" the other by recognizing "when the cognitive distortion of viewing your other as disgusting and subhuman surfaces," actively discarding these distortions as "trash," and replacing these thoughts with truth about the value of the other person.[10] Burson urges Christians to reject the fallacy that "righteous indignation excuses rude rhetoric," and embrace the call to "model unity, kindness, and love within the Christian fold."[11] He points out that "mean-spirited Christians do more damage to the cause of Christ than any attack leveled by non-believers."[12] Evangelical Christians, who are more uniformly partisan than White mainline Christians, are perceived as narrow-minded and uptight, among other negative adjectives.[13] Our ability to deviate from partisan blandness and add just the right amount of salt can shift negative stereotypes about Christians. The people with whom we disagree should nevertheless be able to describe our discourse as loving, joyful, peaceful, patient, good, kind, generous, faithful, gentle, and self-controlled (Galatians 5:22-23).

Seek shalom. Seeking shalom means participating in God's redeeming work in the world. In our political engagement this can mean many things, from advocating for policies that promote human flourishing, to engaging

---

[10]Scott Burson, *All About the Bass: Searching for Treble in the Midst of a Pounding Culture War* (Eugene, OR: Cascade, 2021), 128-29.

[11]Burson, *All About the Bass*, 7, 9.

[12]Burson, *All About the Bass*, 12.

[13]"U.S. Adults See Evangelicals Through a Political Lens," Barna, November 21, 2019, accessed May 18, 2023, www.barna.com/research/evangelicals-political-lens/.

in civil discourse in a way that gives life and wisdom to all who participate, to electing and holding accountable civil servants who promote the common good. Seeking shalom begins in the small moments of our daily lives. As Anglican priest Tish Harrison Warren reminds us, "I cannot seek God's peace and mission in the world without beginning right where I am, in my home, in my neighborhood, in my church, with the real people right around me."[14] When political disagreements arise, we can ask questions, motivated by a genuine desire to build bridges instead of burning them down. *Why is that topic important to you? Where can I learn more? Can you help me understand?* If the person seems receptive to conversation, we may have the opportunity to share how their views or their manner of expressing them affect us and people we care about. But we may also simply have a chance to spend time with someone, to hear them, to be formed by the practice of seeking shalom with them, even if it is not reciprocated.

Seeking shalom should also be a communal practice of the church. Sadly, our congregations too often imitate the country's political strife. The liturgical life of the church can be an antidote to political rancor. As Kaitlyn Schiess writes, "corporate worship is the center of our political engagement because it is in this context that we learn how to live the lives that God asks of us. Corporate worship teaches us to focus our ethical judgments on God's moral framework. It teaches us what rhythms of life God has created for us, and it teaches us how to treat our neighbors."[15]

Seeking shalom is difficult work. It may even come at a personal cost. But the alternative is more costly. If indeed God's plan for humanity is to heal the brokenness and alienation that sin brought into the world, then refusal to participate in God's restorative work is sin. Our choice in each political conversation, with each policy we prefer or candidate we endorse, is between seeking or breaking shalom. This is the holy work of redeemed Kingdom citizens bearing the fruit of our redemption in a broken world.

KINGDOM CITIZENS IN CHURCH LEADERSHIP

Christians who are in positions of authority in churches or Christian institutions have a unique role in living out Kingdom citizenship. I include

---

[14]Tish Harrison Warren, *Liturgy of the Ordinary: Sacred Practices in Everyday Life* (Downers Grove, IL: InterVarsity Press, 2016), 77.

[15]Kaitlyn Schiess, *The Liturgy of Politics: Spiritual Formation for the Sake of Our Neighbor* (Downers Grove, IL: InterVarsity Press, 2020), 101.

myself in this category, as a preacher and a professor at a Christian university. We must steward our pastoral calling faithfully, including in the ways we engage with politics. As we embrace the characteristics and behaviors of Kingdom citizenship, we remember that we are pastors, not politicians, and therefore we should be nonpartisan, but not neutral.

A pastor, not a politician. Vocational ministry comes with a warning: "Not many of you should become teachers, my brothers and sisters, for you know that we who teach will face stricter judgment" (James 3:1). Our role is to "equip the saints for the work of ministry, for building up the body of Christ" (Ephesians 4:12). When a church leader publicly aligns with or endorses a specific party or candidate, we are building up a political party instead of building up the body of Christ. Our role is to model and lead people to "unity of the faith and of the knowledge of the Son of God" (Ephesians 4:13). When we tell the people in our care which candidate to choose or what policy position to hold, we reinforce political division and claim Jesus for one side. When church leaders conflate faithfulness to Christ with support for a party, policy, or politician, we model bland partisanship or even Christian nationalism. If we use political buzzwords that reinforce partisan biases, dehumanize opponents, or stoke fear and anger, we are out of step with Kingdom citizenship. But when we model Kingdom citizenship, the people in our care learn to do the same and our fellowship can bear witness to the unity of the body of Christ.

Some church leaders may feel called to pursue public office, which almost always requires partisan affiliation. As we saw in chapter three, affiliating with a party can lead to uncritical partisan alignment. Before running for office, church leaders should examine their motives and discern whether they have the Christian maturity to resist becoming a bland partisan. Clergy who seek public office should have a reputation for modeling civil discourse and seeking shalom, making space for honest discussion in their faith communities and fostering a spirit of unity in Christ that is not threatened by political partisanship. They should not lose sight of their pastoral role, being mindful that their campaign ads, debate tactics, and policy initiatives reflect on the church and continue to disciple people toward the Kingdom or toward the country.

Nonpartisan, not neutral. Church leaders need to be nonpartisan; however, that does not mean being neutral about matters of Kingdom significance that also connect to partisan politics. If we are faithful to teach "the whole purpose of God" (Acts 20:27), we will necessarily address topics that impact public life and which people will perceive as political. Indeed, anything that relates to life in the *polis*, the city, is political by definition. If we are modeling Kingdom citizenship, our congregations will have a hard time pinning us down politically. Our gospel proclamation should reveal the Kingdom, not reinforce the country.

Christian leaders need not be silent about Kingdom convictions and should take clear positions on issues when Scripture compels us to do so. But we should not teach or even give the impression that the cause of Christ or the mission of the church is aligned with or obeisant to the Democratic or Republican parties or any candidate for public office. It is one thing to preach about sexual ethics or care for refugees, and another to instruct people to vote for the Democratic or Republican ticket. It is one thing to host a forum for local candidates or a town hall for an elected official; it is another to turn the sermon over to a stump speech or host a candidate's rally. These lines are not always clear, so we must seek guidance and wisdom and continually examine our own political positions for alignment with the Kingdom. We can and should teach what it means to follow Christ even into the political fray and address specific issues with which the gospel is concerned, but we should do so in a way that helps people approach politics with critical thought and room for disagreement. Ultimately, our own lives will be our most powerful sermon. What do our political lives preach?

GENERAL INDEX

SCRIPTURE INDEX

Missio Alliance

Missio Alliance has arisen in response to the shared voice of pastors and ministry leaders from across the landscape of North American Christianity for a new "space" of togetherness and reflection amid the issues and challenges facing the church in our day. We are united by a desire for a fresh expression of evangelical faith, one significantly informed by the global evangelical family. Lausanne's Cape Town Commitment, "A Confession of Faith and a Call to Action," provides an excellent guidepost for our ethos and aims.

Through partnerships with schools, denominational bodies, ministry organizations, and networks of churches and leaders, Missio Alliance addresses the most vital theological and cultural issues facing the North American church in God's mission today. We do this primarily by convening gatherings, curating resources, and catalyzing innovation in leadership formation.

Rooted in the core convictions of evangelical orthodoxy, the ministry of Missio Alliance is animated by a strong and distinctive theological identity that emphasizes

Comprehensive Mutuality: Advancing the partnered voice and leadership of women and men among the beautiful diversity of the body of Christ across the lines of race, culture, and theological heritage.

Hopeful Witness: Advancing a way of being the people of God in the world that reflects an unwavering and joyful hope in the lordship of Christ in the church and over all things.

Church in Mission: Advancing a vision of the local church in which our identity and the power of our testimony is found and expressed through our active participation in God's mission in the world.

In partnership with InterVarsity Press, we are pleased to offer a line of resources authored by a diverse range of theological practitioners. The resources in this series are selected based on the important way in which they address and embody these values, and thus, the unique contribution they offer in equipping Christian leaders for fuller and more faithful participation in God's mission.

missioalliance.org | twitter.com/missioalliance | facebook.com/missioalliance